Contents

Preface

Becoming a partner in a close relationship is a central part of life. However, few of us have received much direct training in how to make a success of this role. I want this book to help you as prospective and existing partners to create and cultivate happiness in your couple relationships.

What you inwardly think provides the major influence on how you outwardly communicate. I aim to show you how you can develop the power of your mind so that you can communicate more effectively and lovingly. By using insights from the new cognitive therapies, I provide you with the exciting prospect that increasingly you can gain strength and skills to build and deepen your relationships.

I intend this book not only for those of you who stand on the threshold of your relationship journeys, but for those who have already gone some distance. Some of you may be taking part in human communication and relationship education courses run by colleges and universities and by voluntary agencies. Others may be training to become counsellors and helpers. Some readers may be counselling clients and desiring to support your counselling work with reading. Still other readers may be members of the general public wishing to become happier and more fulfilled in your relationships.

Despite their importance, I have deliberately excluded cross-cultural and parenting aspects of partner skills. My main reason for this is that I wanted to avoid creating confusion rather than clarity by having too many agendas.

In the first two chapters I show how you can create your mind, your way of communicating, and much of what you feel. I emphasize that how you think and how you communicate can each be broken down into a set of skills: namely, mind skills and communication skills. Then in Chapter 3, I briefly review how influences from your past may have hindered as well as helped you to acquire and maintain good mind and communication skills.

Part Two of the book, on empowering your mind, focuses on six central skills for developing and using your mind to create happy relationships. There is a chapter on each of the skills of creating self-talk, visual images, rules, perceptions, explanations and expectations.

Part Three of the book, on developing your communication, focuses on how you can develop your skills in each of seven important areas: becoming more outgoing,

LEEDS METROPOLITAN UNIVERSITY

City Campus Learning Centre
Leeds LS1 3HE

Items should be returned on or before the last date shown below
All items are subject to recall if required by another reader.

Charges are levied for the late return of items.

Renewal may be made by personal application, in writing or by telephoning
(0113) 283 3106 and quoting the barcode number below.

Date Due	Date Due	Date Due	Date Due
31 OCT 2002			
10. DEC			
24 DEC 2008			

3308a

Other books by Richard Nelson-Jones also published by Cassell:

Practical Counselling and Helping Skills: Text and Exercises for the Lifeskills Counselling Model, 4th edition
Relating Skills: A Practical Guide to Effective Personal Relationships
The Theory and Practice of Counselling, 2nd edition
Using Your Mind: Creative Thinking Skills for Work and Business Success

Cassell
Wellington House
125 Strand
London WC2R 0BB

Cassell & Continuum
370 Lexington Avenue
New York
NY 10017-6550

www.cassell.co.uk

First published 1999

British Library Cataloguing-in-Publication Data
A catalogue record for this book is available from the British Library.

ISBN   0-304-70505-5 (hardback)
        0-304-70506-3 (paperback)

Typeset by BookEns Ltd, Royston, Herts
Printed and bound in Great Britain by TJ International Ltd, Padstow, Cornwall

listening better, showing you care, sharing intimacy, enjoying sex together, managing anger and communicating assertively, and managing relationship problems.

An important feature of the book is that the chapters in Parts Two and Three end with Activities that prospective or actual partners can perform to improve their skills. Though some of these require you to be in a relationship, you can still gain benefit from many of them by doing them on your own. In addition, the Activities can be performed as part of counselling or relationship training. I encourage you to work through the Activities to develop your ability to apply the skills. However, it is one thing to 'talk the talk' and another to 'walk the walk'. Therefore, wherever possible, also practice the skills diligently in the crucible of your daily life.

This is an optimistic book that assumes that humans are capable of altruism and compassion, but require knowledge, skills and discipline to bring out the best in themselves and in others. I sincerely hope that you, the readers of this book, can create and cultivate much happiness, contentment and joy through applying the partner skills I describe here. May your use of these skills make your relationships a celebration of life as well as of your love and commitment to one another.

Acknowledgements

I thank the following people for their participation in developing this book: Naomi Roth, my previous Cassell editor, for helping me to articulate the book's central ideas and framework; Ruth McCurry, my current Cassell editor, for proofing and editing the manuscript to increase its readability; Marita McCabe, Professor of Clinical Psychology at Deakin University in Melbourne, Australia, for reviewing and commenting on the chapter on 'Enjoying sex together'; the numerous people, both friends and clients, who have provided me with insights on how to create happy relationships; and lastly, Helena Power and the production staff at Cassell for their work on presenting this book so nicely.

PART ONE
INTRODUCTION

1

Creating and Developing Your Mind

*Something we were withholding made us weak
until we found it was ourselves.*

Robert Frost

Nearly all humans become partners, and frequently fall out of becoming partners, in close relationships. When asked what makes for happy relationships, often partners answer 'good communication'. This answer is certainly correct. However, a further question is 'What makes for good communication?' The main assumption of this book is that your mind influences and creates your communication. Put another way, how you create your mind, your internal communication, influences how you create your actions, your external communication. Your mind is a powerful tool that you always have at your disposal to use for good or ill. A simple analogy is that of driving a car: barring unforeseen circumstances, how skilfully you think determines how well you drive. The expression 'As goes the horse, so goes the cart' provides a more old-fashioned analogy.

Relationships are processes that take place both within and between partners' minds. In any relationship, you develop and react to your thoughts and pictures about one another. Furthermore, since relationships are two-way processes, how you think and communicate influences how your partner thinks and communicates towards you. However, you need not stay stuck in repetitive patterns of communication that do not work for you. You can empower yourself and your relationships by developing your mind. The good news is that each of you is capable of bringing out the best in yourself and in one another by training yourself to think effectively. By thinking skilfully, you are more likely to engage in the kind of communication that brings love, joy, happiness and contentment into your lives.

CREATING YOUR MIND

The greatest discovery of my generation is that human beings can alter their lives by altering their attitude of mind.

William James

What is mind?

Let's start our task of helping you become mentally tougher and more loving by exploring how you create your mind. The word mind has many meanings. The word brain is a possible synonym for mind. One way to view your mind is that it is the psychological component of your brain. An important meaning of mind is that of intellectual capacities or powers. The noun intellect refers to the faculty of reasoning, knowing and understanding. An intelligent person is quick of mind. However, people with high IQs do not always fare well in the practicalities of life. As anyone who has spent time in universities knows, high intellectual intelligence is no guarantee of communicating well to others. Also, such people can use their quickness of mind against themselves: for instance, avoiding personal responsibility by being facile at making excuses.

A debate exists as to whether there are other types of intelligence than quickness of mind. For example, Gardner has proposed six types of intelligence: linguistic, musical, logical-mathematical, spatial, bodily-kinaesthetic, and personal. The personal 'intelligences' consist of two aspects: access to one's own feeling life and *'the ability to notice and make distinctions among other individuals* and, in particular, among their moods, temperaments, motivations, and intentions' (Gardner, 1993, p. 240)

Similarly the concept of emotional intelligence has been proposed by Salovey and Mayer (1990). Emotional intelligence can be broken down into five domains: knowing one's emotions; managing emotions; motivating oneself; recognizing emotions in others; and handling relationships. Goleman (1995) proposes that in a sense people have two minds and two different, yet overlapping, kinds of intelligence: rational and emotional. Carl Rogers, the founder of the Person-Centred school of counselling and psychotherapy, adopted a similar position on the role of emotions in being rational. The more you are open to your significant feelings and experiences, the more likely you are to be rational. Rogers' ideal was that of wholeness rather than living in a compartmentalized world of body and mind (Rogers, 1980).

Biological contexts for creating your mind

You create your mind and thoughts within three important contexts: biological, social and cultural, and from the learning influences of your past. How you as an individual learned, maintained in the past and currently maintain strengths and deficits in creating your thoughts is the subject of Chapter 3. In this section I focus on some biological considerations that can provide limitations or boundaries to the notion that you are totally responsible for creating your thoughts.

The human brain weighs about three pounds and is composed of cells and neural juices. Human brains are about three times the size of those of non-human primates, our closest relatives in evolution. The brainstem, beginning at the top of the spinal chord, was the earliest part of the brain to evolve. Goleman writes: 'From the most primitive root, the brainstem, emerged the emotional centers. Millions of years later in evolution, from these emotional areas evolved the thinking brain or "neocortex", the great bulb of convoluted tissues that make up the top layers' (Goleman, 1995, p. 10). The size of the neocortex or cerebral hemispheres increases up the phylogenetic scale from reptile to non-human primate to human. Goleman argues that the underlying emotional brain has both positive and negative repercussions for rational thinking. On the one hand, humans as animals have the propensity to react emotionally to situations without the cortical centres fully understanding what is happening. There can be a failure to activate the neocortical processes that lead to balance and impulse control. Colloquially, if you are in the grip of strong emotions like anger and anxiety, you can fail to think straight. Indeed, your thinking may be positively dangerous. The emotional brain can also be a force for rationality and work in cooperation with the thinking mind to guide decisions – what Rogers might call being open to your experience and inner valuing process (Rogers, 1980).

The instincts provide another biological context for how you think. You are subject to instincts of varying degrees of strength, such as survival, shelter, sex, belonging and aggression. Other instincts may operate less strongly and be what Maslow (1970) refers to as instinct remnants. The human capacity for altruism may be one such instinct remnant.

Humans seem biologically programmed to search for meaning. Your brain instantly attempts to pattern or organize random stimuli into figure and ground – foreground and background. When situations or sets of stimuli defy patterning, you experience an uneasiness that persists until you fit the situation into some recognizable pattern. Your search for a meaning to your life represents this need to fit situations into a pattern. This search is your response to being acutely unsettled in a chaotic, unpatterned world (May and Yalom, 1995).

Humans may be subject to evolutionary templates, though their existence is more speculative than that of the instincts. In Jung's notion of the collective unconscious evolutionary history feeds forward into present thinking. The collective unconscious represents memory traces from humans' ancestral past, including when humans were not a separate species. All humans have roughly the same collective unconscious (Jung, 1939).

Your capacity for thinking is influenced by individual differences: for instance, humans can be grouped according to biologically influenced personality types, such as introversion and extroversion. For the purposes of this book, the degree to which people differ in their biological propensities to irrational as well as to rational thinking is a very important consideration. For most people, biological propensities to irrationality fall well short of recognized psychiatric disorders (American Psychiatric Association, 1994).

Sexual and affectionate orientation – whether you are gay, heterosexual or bisexual – represents another important area of individual difference that influences how you think. The fact that homosexuality has existed in all known cultures across all periods of time suggests that it contains a large biological element.

Social and cultural contexts for creating your mind

Throughout history, people's minds have been influenced by contextual considerations such as the time in history in which they live, technological change, culture, race, and social class, amongst others.

First, let me illustrate this point by briefly examining differing views of the concept of love. There are huge variations in how love is defined across the ages and across cultures. For example, in some periods and cultures, love has been viewed as a lofty asexual experience, whereas other cultures and periods have included a sexual component. Also, how people view the beloved is shaped by culturally defined patterns of acceptability. In addition, the function of love varies across cultures. For instance, love is the foundation for marriage in individualistic cultures; in collectivist cultures, kin networks and economic pressures loom larger (Beall and Sternberg, 1995).

Social and cultural considerations are also relevant to attitudes towards homosexuality. For instance, no longer do the psychiatric professions in America, Britain and Australasia categorize homosexuality as a mental disorder. Furthermore in these cultures, though still far short of universal acceptance, there is increasing tolerance of and understanding of gay and bisexual people. Thai culture is even more accepting of gay and lesbian people, though again there are limits to this tolerance. Also, engaging in homosexual behaviour does not automatically imply that you think of yourself as homosexual. For example, some Thai males manage to retain a heterosexual self-concept so long as they are the penetrators or 'kings' rather than the penetrated or 'queens' in sexual encounters.

The prevailing economic system is another social and cultural context that influences the content of your mind. Prominent among capitalist values are those of competition, consumerism, and accumulation of wealth. Arguably, such values permeate personal relationships. For example, people may judge themselves and one another by the size of their wallets rather than the size of their hearts (De Angelis, 1997). The purpose of life may be seen as acquiring and conspicuously consuming more possessions rather than developing what the Buddhists call the four Divine Abodes of Mind: loving kindness, compassion, sympathy and equanimity. Capitalism may also encourage virtues as well as vices in relationships: for instance, a sense of self-reliance and of responsibility for providing for dependents. The values of any prevailing economic system will influence how you think and hence how you relate.

MIND SKILLS

The happiness habit is developed simply by practising happy thinking.
Norman Vincent Peale

Inasmuch as mind 'drives' communication, relationships are mind games that partners can play with varying degrees of skill. How can you control your thoughts so that you can beneficially influence how you communicate? First, you can understand that you have a mind with a capacity for super-conscious thinking – or thinking about thinking – that you can develop. Second, you can become much more efficient in thinking about your thinking if you view your mental processes in terms of skills that you can train yourself to control. Third, in daily life, you can assiduously practise using your mind skills to influence your communication.

What are skills?

One meaning of the word skills pertains to *areas* of skill. For instance, albeit overlapping, broad areas of skills include: relating skills, study skills, leisure skills, health skills and work skills. A second meaning of the word skills refers to *level* of competence or expertise. For instance, in a specific skills area you can be skilled, unskilled or a mixture of the two.

The third meaning of the word skills is less common. This meaning relates to the knowledge and sequence of choices entailed in implementing a skill. The main way that I can help you to acquire, develop and maintain satisfactory levels of competence in specific skills areas is by training you in their required sequences of choices.

The concept of mind skills is not best viewed in either/or terms in which you either possess or do not possess a skill. Rather, in any skills area, it is preferable to think of yourself as possessing either good skills or poor skills, or a mixture of the two. If you make good choices in a skills area, for instance in the mind skill of perceiving accurately, this is a strength. If you make poor choices in a skills area, this is a deficit. In all mind skills areas, in varying degrees you are likely to possess elements of both good skills and poor skills. For instance, in the skills area of perceiving accurately, you may perceive moderately accurately, but still possess systematic errors or 'tricks of the mind' that distort information. The object of working on your mind skills is, in one or more areas, to help you shift the balance of your good and poor skills more in the direction of strengths. Put another way, the object is to help you affirm yourself and your partner by making better relationship choices.

Some central mind skills

Below are brief descriptions of the six central mind skills targeted in this book. These skills are derived from the work of leading cognitive therapists, such as Aaron Beck and Albert Ellis. Rather than describe the skills in detail here, I devote a separate chapter to each of them in the next part of the book.

- *Creating self-talk.* Instead of talking to yourself negatively before, during and after specific situations, you can acknowledge you have choices and make coping self-statements that assist you to stay calm and cool, establish your goals, coach you in what to do, and affirm the strengths, skills and support factors you possess.
- *Creating visual images.* You can use visual images in ways that calm you down, assist you in acting competently to attain your goals, and help you to resist giving in to bad habits.
- *Creating rules.* Your unrealistic rules make irrational demands on yourself, others, and the environment: for instance, 'I must always be approved of by my partner', 'My partner must not make mistakes', and 'Everything about our relationship

must be fair'. Instead you can develop realistic rules: for instance, 'I prefer to be approved of by my partner, but it's unrealistic to expect this all the time'.

- *Creating perceptions.* You can avoid perceiving yourself and your partner either too negatively or too positively. You distinguish between fact and inference and make your inferences as accurate as possible.
- *Creating explanations.* You can explain the causes of events accurately. You avoid assuming too much responsibility by internalizing, 'It's all my fault', or externalizing, 'It's all your fault'.
- *Creating expectations.* You are realistic about the risks and rewards of future actions. You assess threats and dangers accurately. You avoid distorting relevant evidence with unwarranted optimism or pessimism. Your expectations about how well you will relate are accurate.

In reality, some of the mind skills overlap. For instance, all of the skills, even visualizing, involve self-talk. To distinguish the skill of using self-talk I stipulate a definition by stating that mostly it refers to self-statements relevant to coping with specific situations. Interrelationships between skills can also be viewed on the dimension of depth. Arguably, people possessing the rule 'I must always be approved of by my partner' are more prone to perceiving cues of rejection from her or him than those not possessing such a rule.

Creative thinking − or creating your mind through how you think − can be defined in two main ways: neutral and positive. A neutral definition of creative thinking is that it constitutes the processes of using either good or poor mind skills, or a mixture of both. A positive definition is that creative thinking constitutes the processes of using good mind skills and managing to avoid using poor mind skills.

DEVELOPING YOUR MIND

The highest possible stage in moral culture is when we recognize we ought to control our thoughts.

Charles Darwin

What constitutes a well-developed mind?

To be effective as a partner in a close relationship, you require the mental toughness that comes from a well-developed mind. Life in any relationship is full of challenges, including the challenge of relating to one another 'full-on' on a daily basis. Though the cognitive therapies provide useful information about what constitutes a well-developed mind, a possible criticism is that they insufficiently emphasize partners' broader responsibilities towards one another rather than just the individual's pursuit of happiness and fun.

The literature of the world's great religions provides another valuable set of insights on mental maturity. The emphases on purifying your mind, self-transcendence and loving your neighbour are important characteristics which, if appropriately rather than rigidly applied, can add power to your mind.

Inner strength is another way to describe the well-developed mind. You have a sound sense of what values are important to you, yet are open to new experiences and information. You feel centred and yet allow yourself to be influenced by the experiencing and feedback of others. At the same time as having a mind of your own, your mind incorporates the emotions, preferences and needs of your partner. You are neither easily threatened nor psychologically self-protective when there is no realistic need for this. You are capable of relating to your partner on the basis of mutual respect rather than needing to control or be controlled by her or him.

In this book, I show how you can adapt concepts from the cognitive therapies to think more kindly and behave better in your everyday relationships. I adopt a humanistic and secular approach to mental development and maturity. Undoubtedly, some readers will wish to add a spiritual dimension: namely, that by purifying your mind you become more in touch with the underlying spiritual core of your nature. Christians might say 'The kingdom of God is within' as Jesus did (Luke 17: 21) and Buddhists would refer to one's innate Buddha nature.

Personal responsibility

When you are being personally responsible you are in the process of making the choices that maximize your happiness and fulfilment (Nelson-Jones, 1995). Personal responsibility is a positive concept whereby you are responsible for your well-being and making your own choices. It contrasts with a common meaning of responsibility, namely that of responsibility to others, including living up to their standards. Though the process of personal responsibility is difficult, it also liberates. It frees you to concentrate on how you can be most effective. It entails neither focusing on other people's faults nor feeling that you need say 'my fault' all the time. This book aims to help you adopt and implement a fundamental attitude of personal responsibility for becoming a better partner in your close relationships by developing and using your mind and communication skills.

Training and using your mind

Learning and implementing specific mind and communication skills can involve three steps:

- first, public or outer use of language between trainers and learners;
- second, aware private or inner use of self-talk on the part of learners;
- third, automatic use of inner self-talk as learners gain fluency in using the skill.

An analogy is that of learning to drive a car: first the instructor tells you what to do, then you are aware of instructing yourself, and lastly your self-instructions become automatic. During this process, your use of driving skills moves from feeling awkward to feeling natural. The same feelings can occur as you learn and then gain fluency in implementing specific mind and communication skills.

Motivation is essential if you are to train your mind – you have to see that it will bring benefits to yourself and those you care for. As with training in any area, for instance for a sport, you need to know what the requisite skills are. Also, you have to train and practise hard. Vague injunctions to develop your mind and vague intentions to train and practise are likely to do more harm than good.

In Part Two of this book, I adopt the approach of assisting you to train your mind by first focusing on mind skills in their own right. You can read the chapters and do the activities that accompany each chapter. My assumption is that you are using some, if not all, of these mind skills already, but you could be using them more often and better. In Part Three, I aim to help you integrate the different mind skills with the skills of communicating with your partner. Again, you can read the chapters and do the activities.

Transfer of training to real life is essential. It is one thing to do the activities either in the quiet of your room or in the relative safety of a training group and quite another to have the discipline to implement mind and communication skills in the crucible of real-life relationships. You can only improve if you practise, practise and practise both in your mind and in your daily communication.

WHAT ARE HAPPY RELATIONSHIPS?

If you contribute to other people's happiness, you will find the true good, the true meaning of life.

The Dalai Lama

Within any two-person relationship is each individual's relationship as well as their joint relationship. Happiness in a relationship is a matter of perception. Furthermore the criteria partners apply to it vary according to the nature of the relationship, such as being a couple or just friends, the stage of the relationship, such as dating or living together, and whether or not partners have children. In addition, because partners have a stable relationship, it does not necessarily follow that they have a good quality relationship (Fincham, 1997).

Virtually all humans seek happiness from close personal relationships, even though sometimes they may act in ways that sabotage it. Three important aspects of happiness are: positive emotions, satisfaction with your life, and absence of negative emotions and psychological distress (Argyle, 1987; Lu and Shih, 1997). Satisfaction with your life can be further broken down into satisfaction in various domains of living: for instance, home or work.

Presence of positive emotions

In successful relationships certain emotions predominate and are felt by both partners, though not always to the same degree or at the same time. The giving and receiving of love is the main positive emotion that characterizes happy relationships. Love entails the willingness to transcend yourself to nurture the happiness and growth of another human being. Such love is generous and giving rather than greedy and getting. It contains a large element of altruism and is not just based on the social exchange of favours. To be truly loving requires that you are comfortable with yourself and not motivated by deficiencies in your own emotional make-up. The mature person feels enhanced rather than impoverished by giving. Despite ups and downs, in a successful couple relationship both partners experience the joy of nurturing the happiness and growth of one another. Your love provides the foundation for all other emotions in your relationship.

What are some of the other feelings that characterize happy relationships? An important feeling is that of mutual respect. Partners are proud to be associated with one another and behave in ways that maintain one another's esteem and trust. Partners also feel understood by one another at a deep level which leads to pleasurable feelings of emotional freedom and spontaneity. Part of this feeling of freedom is that partners can enjoy experiencing themselves and one another as sensual and sexy beings. Furthermore partners are likely to stimulate one another, have fun together and enjoy each other's sense of humour. In addition, partners feel secure and emotionally supported as they experience one another's friendly affection and companionship.

Relationship satisfaction

In a couple relationship, partners may have differing levels of both overall satisfaction with their relationship and of satisfaction with the different components of it. Your expectations for the criteria for satisfaction will vary over time: for instance, concerning frequency of sexual intercourse. Also, both as individuals and as a couple, your interests and values may shift. Thus, part of relationship satisfaction relates to the ability to encourage one another to keep developing as separate individuals and yet accommodate these changes within the relationship.

What are some of the components of relationship satisfaction? Below is a list of 21 items that partners might use to gauge their degree of relationship satisfaction. For each item, the relevant question is 'In your relationship how satisfied (or how pleased) are you with ...?' If you wish, you may use the left-hand column to rate each item on a 1 to 10 scale, with 0 indicating 'not at all satisfied', 5 'half satisfied/ half dissatisfied', and 10, 'extremely satisfied'.

Rating	*Items*
_____	The extent of our common values
_____	How we demonstrate affection
_____	How intimately we talk to one another
_____	Our sex life
_____	How stimulated we are by one another
_____	How much we laugh together and have fun
_____	Our recreational activities
_____	The friends we share in common
_____	How we deal with our own and each other's parents
_____	Our level of commitment to the relationship
_____	How we address problems in our relationship
_____	How we make major decisions
_____	How we handle crises and unexpected negative events
_____	How we encourage one another's development
_____	How we handle our finances
_____	How we handle our jobs/careers

_____	How we divide and manage our household tasks
_____	The amount of time we spend at home
_____	The amount of personal space we have
_____	The kinds of parents we are (if relevant) or how we relate to children and young people (if not parents)
_____	Our involvement in the wider community

Many readers who decide to rate the items will give mostly positive ratings. However, any item you rated 0, 1, 2 or 3 is a cause for concern and requires addressing. You can also add up your ratings for each item to get a rough guide to your overall level of relationship satisfaction: the possible range of overall scores is from 0 to 210. Any overall score under 105 may indicate a poor level of satisfaction.

How satisfied do you think your partner is with your relationship? Either or both of you can rate the above list of items as though answering for your partner. Then, you can choose whether or not to check the accuracy of your ratings with her or him.

Absence of negative emotions and psychological distress

Partners come to relationships with numerous individual differences and expectations, are buffeted by constant changes within and outside the relationship, and each partner inevitably possesses some mind skills and communication skills deficits. Hence, relationships can be sources of meaninglessness, unhappiness, loneliness, psychological distance, physical and emotional violence, continued emotional scarring, and emotional and financial insecurity.

In close relationships, a total absence of negative emotions and psychological distress is an unrealistic goal. The concept of the perfect relationship is perfect nonsense. Indeed relationships can possess both high levels of conflict and satisfaction (Argyle and Henderson, 1985). Assuming a reasonable level of initial compatibility, how partners handle their negative emotions and differences is important in distinguishing successful from unsuccessful relationships. Much relationship distress can be prevented and ameliorated where partners are committed to developing and using good mind and communication skills.

Using mind and communication skills

I will act as if what I do makes a difference.

William James

Mind and communication skills are the component skills for creating and cultivating happy relationships. As a partner you can use all the skills covered in this book to affirm yourself through loving another. The use of each skill provides you with the opportunity to care for one another's growth and, in the process, to grow together.

Relationships constantly challenge partners to be active and vigilant in developing and maintaining their mind and communication skills. Rogers (1973) observes that 'the dream of a marriage "made in heaven" is totally unrealistic, and that every continuing man–woman relationship must be worked at, built, rebuilt, and continually refreshed by mutual personal growth' (p. 39). I extend Rogers' comments to gay and lesbian relationships and to all intimate friendships. Developing and maintaining your skills requires personal responsibility, courage and mental cultivation. As partners you show your love not just by disciplining yourself, but through supporting one another's growth in the interests of your joint relationship. Also, most partners are the ancestors of future generations. Whether you have children of your own or help nurture other people's children, how well you use your mind and communication skills can influence, for good or ill, how happy are their lives and close relationships.

2

Creating Your Communication and Feelings

As the shadow follows the body,
as we think, so we become.

Sayings of the Buddha

The last chapter emphasized how you can empower yourself by creating and developing your mind. However, relationships do not just take place in the head and the heart, but on the ground as well. The success of your close relationships comes not just from what you think and feel, but from how well you are able to communicate this to your partner and others. Human relationships exist by sending and receiving external messages. Skilled partners take pains to create and develop not only their minds, but their external communication as well. In this chapter I review aspects of verbal and nonverbal communication. Furthermore, I illustrate the relationships between how you feel, physically react, and communicate and how you think.

Repertoire of communication skills

You may already be a skilled communicator, but not think of yourself as using communication skills. However, if you want to improve and develop your external communication you are more likely to do so if you can identify the relevant skills. Successful partners require a *repertoire* of communication skills. Sometimes you may not have a particular skill in your repertoire: for instance, the ability to say no to an unreasonable request. Other times you may want to strengthen a particular skill: for instance, showing gratitude. With some skills, you may also want to strike a more appropriate balance: for example, giving feedback without either being too wishy-washy or coming on too strong. Some poor communication skills should be eliminated altogether: for instance, physical or sexual abuse.

Elsewhere, I have identified thirteen communication skills areas: disclosing, listening, showing understanding, managing shyness, choosing a partner, trust, caring, intimacy, companionship, sexual relating, assertion, managing anger and solving relationship problems (Nelson-Jones, 1996a). In Part Three of this book, I narrow this list down to focus on how you might communicate better in seven central areas: becoming more outgoing, listening better, showing you care, sharing intimacy, enjoying sex together, managing anger and asserting yourself, and managing relationship problems.

CREATING YOUR COMMUNICATION

All the time actors like Helena Bonham-Carter and Tom Cruise make choices about their verbal and nonverbal communication that create their roles. Similarly, a major function of movie directors like Stephen Spielberg is to help actors make skilled choices in how they come across on the screen. In the daily life of your relationships, you too can take care to choose how best to communicate.

Within each communication skills area, there are five main ways you can create your communications or send messages. *Verbal* communication consists of messages that you send with words: for example, saying 'I love you' or 'I hate you'. *Vocal* communication consists of messages that you send through your voice: for instance, through your volume, articulation, pitch, emphasis and speech rate. *Bodily* communication consists of messages that you send with your body: for instance, through your gaze, eye contact, facial expression, posture, gestures, physical proximity and clothes and grooming. *Touch* communication is a special category of bodily communication. Messages that you send with your touch include: what part of the body you use, what part of another's body you touch, and how gentle or firm you are. *Action-taking* communication consists of messages that you send when you are not face to face with others: for example, sending flowers or a legal writ.

All communication messages are encoded by senders and then decoded by receivers (Argyle, 1994). Mistakes can be made at both ends. Senders may not send the messages they wish to send. Much human communication is either poor or unintentional. Also, senders sometimes intentionally seek to deceive. At the receiving end people with poor listening skills may decode even the clearest of messages wrongly. However, you are much more likely to be misunderstood if you have poor skills in the area of creating communication.

Verbal communication

How skilled are you at creating verbal communication? Are you able to say what you mean and mean what you say? Are you able to find the right words for the right occasion or are you at a loss for words? Do you speak too much or too little or roughly the right amount? Below are some examples of people with *strengths* in how they create verbal communication.

On their second date, Lauren, 27, chose her words carefully to tell Darren, 25, who asked her to be his girlfriend: 'I like you a lot and want to get to know you better. However, for the time being at least, I want to keep seeing other guys as well.'

Ross, 21, had been sexually abused by a close family friend when he was a boy. He thinks that his relationship with Stephen, 20, will be deepened as a result of his sharing this 'secret' and says: 'I don't want to make you feel uncomfortable, but I want to share with you something unpleasant that happened when I was growing up.'

On their tenth wedding anniversary, Rick goes out of his way to plan an evening with activities that he knows his wife Emma will enjoy. Emma says: 'I'm having a wonderful time. Thank you so much for your thoughtfulness and consideration. I love you.'

One verbal communication skill is to take clear responsibility for speaking for yourself. Thomas Gordon, in his book *Parent Effectiveness Training* (1970), makes a useful distinction between 'You' messages and 'I' messages. 'You' messages focus on the other person and can be judgemental: for example, 'You don't love me' or 'You're selfish to ask me to play with you when I've only just got home'. 'I' messages use the word 'I' and are centred in the sender, as can be seen in all of the above examples. Other useful verbal communication skills include stating your feelings tactfully and honestly, as in the examples of Lauren and Emma, and appropriately disclosing personal information, as in the example of Ross.

Vocal communication

As the old saying goes, 'It ain't what you say, but how you say it'. When talking, your overall communication consists of voice and body *framing* communications which may or may not match your verbal communication, the *literal* content of what you say. These framing communications are extremely important. Your vocal and bodily communications can either correspond to, heighten, lessen or contradict the intention of your verbal communication. For instance, Pat may be saying 'Everything is all right in my relationship with Mike' at the same time as talking with a choked voice and frowning. Here, it does not take an expert decoder to surmise that everything is not all right. Before going on his first date with Rachel, Todd says 'I'm feeling pretty confident' in a quick, shallow voice and with a nervous smile. How both Pat and Todd frame their verbal communications speaks more loudly than what they actually say.

If you can create appropriate vocal communications, you have acquired a very useful skill in dealing with others. Your vocal messages can speak volumes about what you truly feel and how emotionally responsive you are to others' feelings. Often people out of touch with their feelings speak in flat and monotonous ways, even though using words expressing strong feelings. Others show their anxiety by coming on far too loud and strong.

Following are five dimensions of vocal messages. They form the acronym VAPER – volume, articulation, pitch, emphasis and rate. *Volume* refers to loudness or quietness. You need to disclose at a level of audibility that is comfortable and easy to hear. Some people let their voices trail away at the end of sentences. Some unnecessarily quieten their voices to match other people's voices. Though a booming voice overwhelms, speaking too quietly may communicate that you are a 'wimp'. A firm and confident voice is a good starting point from which you can make variations as appropriate, for instance by speaking more gently or more loudly.

Articulation refers to the clarity of your speech. You are easier to understand if you enunciate words well. *Pitch* refers to the height or depth of your voice. An optimum pitch range includes all the levels at which a pleasing voice can be produced without strain. Errors of pitch include either being too high pitched or too low pitched.

It is important that your voice uses *emphasis* when sharing your feelings and feelings nuances and also when responding to others' feelings. You may use too much emphasis and seem melodramatic, or you may use too little emphasis and come across as wooden. In addition, you may use emphasis in the wrong places.

Often speech *rate* is measured by words per minute. Your speech rate depends not only on how quickly you speak words, but on the frequency and duration of pauses between them. If you speak very quickly, you may appear anxious and others may have difficulty understanding you. On the other hand, too ponderous a speech rate can be boring. However, pausing and being silent at the right times is another important aspect of speech rate.

Bodily communication

Both when speaking and listening you disclose yourself through how you create your bodily communication. For instance, whether speaking or listening, if you continue looking out of the window without good reason, you send a negative message. Some of the main forms of bodily communication are listed below.

Facial expressions are perhaps the main vehicle for sending body messages. Ekman, Friesen and Ellsworth (1972) have found that there are seven main facial expressions of emotion: happiness, interest, surprise, fear, sadness, anger, and disgust or contempt. Your mouth and eyebrows can convey much information: for instance, 'down in the mouth' and 'raised eyebrows'. There are display rules which indicate which facial expressions can be shown when: for instance, at funerals, down-turned mouths are more appropriate than up-turned ones – even for people who are only at the funeral to make sure that the corpse is really dead!

Gaze and eye contact form an important area of bodily communication. *Gaze*, or looking at other people in the area of their faces, is both a way of showing interest and also a way of collecting facial information. Speakers look at listeners about 40 per cent of the time and listeners look at speakers about 70–75 per cent of the time. Gaze is useful for coordinating speech: for example speakers look just before the end of utterances to collect feedback about their listener's reactions (Argyle, 1992). Women are in general more visually attentive than men in all measures of gaze (Henley, 1977; Argyle, 1994). *Eye contact* is a more direct way of sending messages, be they of interest, anger or sexual attraction. Seeing 'eye to eye' is better than having 'shifty eyes'. The dilation of pupils is another source of eye messages: dilated pupils can indicate 'bedroom eyes' or sexual interest, while undilated pupils may get decoded as 'beady little eyes'.

Gestures are physical movements that can frame or illustrate words, coming before, during or after what is being said. An example of using a gesture to display and emphasize an emotion is clenching your fist to show aggression. Gestures may also illustrate shapes, sizes or movements, particularly when these are difficult to describe in words. How you gesture can vary according to your sex. Eakins and Eakins (1978) suggest that men's gestures are larger, more sweeping and forceful, while women's gestures are smaller and more inhibited.

Gestures can also take the place of words: for example, nodding your head either up-and-down or sideways for saying 'yes' or 'no', respectively. As a brief activity that highlights the power of your conditioning, alternate between shaking your head sideways as you say 'yes' and nodding your head up and down as you say 'no'. How did you feel and what did you think about doing that?

Your *posture* may convey various messages. If you are confident you may 'walk tall'. When feeling less confident you may not stand so erect, put your chest out, or square your shoulders. Height tends to be associated with status: for instance, you 'talk down to' or 'talk up to' someone. Short people may be at a disadvantage unless body posture is changed: for instance, by sitting down. Turning your body towards someone is more encouraging than turning away from them. Also, whether you lean forwards or backwards may indicate interest or disinterest.

Posture may also communicate how anxious you are: for instance, sitting with your arms and legs tightly crossed suggests that you are emotionally as well as literally uptight. However, especially for women, you may appear too relaxed: men may mistakenly perceive uncrossed and open legs as a sign of sexual availability whether you wear a skirt, trousers or jeans. Such perceptions manifest a double standard in how people decode body messages.

The degree of *physical proximity* that is comfortable for Britons, Australians and North Americans is generally the same (Hall, 1966). The zones vary according to the nature of the relationship. In the *intimate zone*, between 6 and 18 inches (15 and 45 cm), it is easy to touch and be touched. This zone is reserved for spouses, lovers, close friends and relatives. The *personal zone*, between 18 and 48 inches (45 and 120 cm) is appropriate for less close friends and for parties and other social gatherings. The *social zone*, between 4 and 12 feet (1.2 and 3.6 m), is comfortable for shop and business transactions and for people not known at all well. The *public zone*, over 12 feet, is the distance for addressing public gatherings.

People stand or sit closer to those whom they like. Men may be readier to enter a woman's space than the reverse and women more ready to move out of the way (Eakins and Eakins, 1978). Physical distance is used in starting and ending conversations: for instance, you go up to someone to start a conversation and edge away as a signal to finish one.

If *clothes* do not make the woman, man or child, they certainly send many messages. These messages include: social and occupational standing, sex-role identity, ethnicity, conformity to peer group norms, rebelliousness, how outgoing you are, and your sexuality. People dress for effect. You wish to influence others' impressions of you. A young man who goes to a party in a sober blue suit defines himself very differently to a young 'stud' in tight jeans that outline his genitals.

Your personal *grooming* also provides important information about how well you take care of yourself and how you wish others to see you. For instance, you may be clean or dirty, tidy or untidy, and smelly or fresh. Additionally, the length, styling and care of your hair sends messages about you.

Touch communication

Touch can be an extremely important way to create communication. In touching another you are in their close intimate zone. Touch connects humans in a most fundamental way. In parent-child relationships touch offers security, tenderness and affection. Touch is a major way in which adults can demonstrate protection, support and caring for one another. There are numerous social rules and taboos regarding who may touch, which parts of the body, when. Women may feel freer to touch other women than men to touch other men.

Touch messages can be positive or negative. Positive touch messages are those which the recipients appreciate. You can express affection and tenderness through a light touch on the hand, arm or shoulder; holding hands; walking arm in arm; an arm over the shoulders; a caress on the side of the face; a semi-embrace; a warm hug; and a kiss on the cheek or mouth – to mention but some ways.

Negative touch messages are those which, with varying degrees of severity, violate another's physical and psychological well-being. Women, men and children can each be the victims of negative touch messages. Though wives sometimes may punch, scratch and throw things at their husbands, serious acts of domestic physical violence are mainly committed by men.

Action-taking communication

Actions speak louder than words. In today's slang, your actions are 'the bottom line'. How you act is crucial in the development of trust. If you say you are going to do something, do you actually do it? People have differing skill levels at communicating through their actions. For instance, if you go overseas and want to maintain a close relationship with your partner while you are away, you can communicate through phone calls, letters and, possibly, through faxes and e-mail. If you fail to keep in touch, your relationship will suffer.

Promises, promises, promises. A good definition of a 'phoney' is someone whose actions fall far short of their verbal, vocal and bodily communications. The importance of sending good action-taking communications in initiating, developing and maintaining effective relationships cannot be overemphasized. Below are two examples in which the way each partner acts is inconsistent with their verbal communications.

> Pete, 24, has repeatedly told his partner Tessa, 26, that he is no longer prepared to wash the dishes all the time. Tessa says: 'I want to mend my lazy ways. I'll do my fair share.' Every time Tessa breaks her agreement to wash up on a specified day, Pete ends up washing the dishes himself.

Jack, 27, says: 'I believe in relationships that are fifty-fifty. There should be a level playing field and no double standards.' Jack's partner Sophie, 24, responds: 'That's just how I feel too.' However, Jack pays the rent, usually pays for their entertainment, and mostly takes the initiative in bed.

Genuineness: creating consistent communications

Since humans can create communications in so many different ways, genuineness becomes important. Above I gave illustrations of people with poor skills in having their actions match their words. When sending messages you can be deceiving others, yourself or both. However, human communication is often more complex than this and involves shades of grey. If you have good skills of sending messages 'loud and clear', your vocal, bodily, touch and action-taking communications match your verbal communication. If you fail to send consistent verbal, vocal, bodily, touch and action-taking communication you make it harder for listeners to decode your overall communication accurately. Also, you increase the chances of their perceiving you as insincere. In general, verbal communication is easier to control than nonverbal communication. Thus you can often pick up important messages about the real meaning of a communication by attending to how things are being said.

YOUR FEELINGS AND PHYSICAL REACTIONS

Seeing's believing, but feeling's the truth.

Thomas Fuller

Common feelings include happiness, sadness, anger, anxiety and sexual arousal. Feelings represent your animal nature and are not skills in themselves. Dictionary definitions of feelings tend to use words like 'physical sensation', 'emotions' and 'awareness'. All three of these words illustrate a dimension of feelings. Feelings as *physical sensations* or as *physical reactions* represent your underlying animal nature. People are animals first, persons second. As such you need to learn to value and live with your underlying animal nature. Also, to get it working for rather than against you. The word *emotions* implies movement. Feelings are processes. You are subject to a continuous flow of biological experiencing. *Awareness* implies that you can be conscious of your feelings. However, at varying levels and in different ways, you may also be out of touch with them.

Physical reactions both represent and accompany feelings and, in a sense, are indistinguishable. For example bodily changes associated with anxiety can include: galvanic skin response – detectable electrical changes taking place in the skin; heightened blood pressure; a pounding heart and a rapid pulse; shallow, rapid breathing; muscular tension; drying of the mouth; stomach problems, such as ulcers; speech difficulties, such as stammering, speaking rapidly and slurring words; sleep difficulties, including difficulty getting to sleep, disturbed sleep and early morning waking; and sex difficulties, for instance, complete or partial loss of desire. Other physical reactions include a slowing down of body movements when depressed and dilated eye pupils in moments of anger or sexual attraction. Sometimes you react to your physical reactions. For example, in anxiety and panic attacks, first you may feel tense and anxious and then become even more tense and anxious because of this initial feeling.

Experiencing, expressing and managing feelings

Your feelings and physical reactions are central to your close relationships. However, that does not mean that you can do nothing about them. 'Lose your mind and come to your senses' was a favourite saying of the late Fritz Perls, the founder of the Gestalt approach to counselling and psychotherapy. I would like to rephrase Perls' saying to become 'Use your mind and come to your senses'. Your feelings and physical reactions are extremely important in their own right, in their influence on your partner's feelings and physical reactions, and in the communication between you. Consequently, you should strive to use your feelings to the benefit rather than the detriment of the growth of yourself, your partner and your relationship.

Three areas in relationships, albeit overlapping, where feelings, and accompanying physical reactions, are important are experiencing feelings, expressing feelings and managing feelings. Below I illustrate each area with a brief example.

Experiencing feelings
Hannah, 19, puts on a brave face much of the time because she finds it very difficult to experience angry feelings in her relationship with her boyfriend Ryan. When Hannah starts acknowledging her anger, she gets very anxious about it.

Expressing feelings
Sandy and Amy, both in their late 30s, are going through a bad patch in their marriage. Underneath each thinks the other has many good points and would like to make their relationship work. However, Sandy in particular has difficulty openly expressing affection towards Amy. Amy experiences him as far too negative and critical and increasingly chooses emotional withdrawal as a way of handling her hurt.

Managing feelings
Liam, 28, is very jealous of his wife Charlotte, 24. He gets upset and angry when she talks to other men and afterwards picks fights with her. Liam has no evidence that Charlotte has ever been unfaithful.

Each of the above examples shows that experiencing existing feelings can be insufficient to help relationships progress. You can use your mind to feel and communicate more appropriately. Hannah's relationship with Ryan might be more honest if she could use her mind to overcome her anxiety and acknowledge rather than deny her anger. Then Hannah would be in a position to choose how to communicate her feelings. Sandy and Amy's relationship might be better if Sandy could use his mind to free him to develop his skills of expressing affection and Amy could use her mind to free her to develop her skills of assertively asking for affection rather than emotionally withdrawing. Also, Liam might stop driving Charlotte away with his unreasonable jealousy if he could use his mind to understand his insecurity and challenge the accuracy of his perceptions about Charlotte's interest in other men.

CREATING HOW YOU FEEL AND COMMUNICATE

A main theme of this book is that your mind significantly mediates or influences feelings and communication to the point where they become the consequences or results of what is going on in your mind. This is a simplification of the position advanced by writers such as Ellis (1995), Beck (Beck and Weishaar, 1995) and the cognitive-behavioural therapists. It is based on a simple ABC framework, where A stands for the activating event, B stands for beliefs, and C stands for consequences. Your consequences, what you feel, how you physically react and what you do at C, can be either helpful or harmful. These consequences are due not so much to what happened at A, as to your beliefs or how you think at B about what happened at A. In short, you heavily influence your feelings and communication by how you think about activating events.

The situation-thoughts-consequences (STC) framework

Above I referred to the ABC framework where your responses to activating events are influenced by your beliefs at B to provide consequences for how you feel, physically react and act at C. If you can alter your beliefs at B, you can alter how you feel and communicate at C.

Here I provide you with an STC framework for analysing the relationships between mind, feelings and communications or between how you think, feel and act (Nelson-Jones, 1996b). In this framework, STC stands for situation, thoughts, and consequences. Though the basic idea of the ABC and STC frameworks is the same, I have changed the letter A to S because ordinary people talk about situations rather than activating events. The reason T has been substituted for B is because thinking allows for many more aspects of mind than only beliefs. The use of C is the same and again consequences fall into three categories: feelings, physical reactions and actions or communication. In your relationships, more often than not, how you feel, physically react and communicate in specific situations is mediated by your thoughts at T rather than a direct response to the actual situation.

Let's take a before and after example of Megan, aged 35, who was divorced a year ago and now becomes shy on first dates with men whom she does not know well.

S1 – Situation: Megan is eating in a restaurant on her first date with Joe.

T1 – Thoughts: Megan's thoughts include 'I must make a good impression', 'I always get tense on first dates', and 'Joe is evaluating me all the time'.

> **C1 – Consequences**: In consequence, Megan feels timid and fearful. Her physical reactions include tension in her face and neck, and her mouth going dry. Megan's communication consequences include revealing little of herself and smiling nervously.

Now let's imagine that Megan has learned some more effective mind skills. She may also have learned some more effective communication skills that help her to think more confidently on first dates. Following is her revised STC, with the name of her date changed from Joe to James.

> **S2 – Situation**: Megan is eating in a restaurant on her first date with James.
>
> **T2 – Thoughts**: Megan thinks 'We're here to enjoy ourselves', 'Some tension is inevitable on first dates and I know I can handle it', and 'This date gives James and me the opportunity to know each other better. If we don't hit it off, James is not the only fish in the ocean.'
>
> **C2 – Consequences**: In consequence, Megan feels moderately relaxed and confident. She experiences no major physical discomfort. Megan's communication consequences include participating actively in the conversation and laughing with amusement.

If you can see the relationships between your mind, feelings, physical reactions and communication, you are in a better position to identify and develop appropriate skills to manage a range of situations in your relationships. When you detect self-defeating feelings, physical reactions and communications, you can look for thoughts that may contribute to them. Then, as in the example of Megan, you can create more skilful thoughts.

The STC framework can be used to analyse and alter your underlying mind skills as well as your various thoughts. For example, when Megan thought 'I must make a good impression' she was exhibiting the poor mind skill of choosing an unrealistic rule, namely, 'I must be liked by everyone'. Furthermore, when Megan thought 'Joe is evaluating me all the time' she was probably exhibiting the poor mind skill of perceiving inaccurately. Megan may have jumped to this conclusion about Joe without having any real evidence for it. Often people exhibit the same characteristic poor mind skills in many situations. Consequently, in this book I go beyond examining your thoughts to help you develop mind skills that should empower you to feel better and communicate more effectively in a variety of situations both inside and outside of your primary couple relationship.

3

Influences from Your Past

Yet each man kills the thing he loves,
By each let this be heard,
Some do it with a bitter look,
Some with a flattering word.

Oscar Wilde

As partners you bring to your relationship your past histories. One of these histories relates to what happened when you were growing up. Another history relates to your previous intimate relationships. In varying degrees, you are both the beneficiary and victim of your histories and of your own contribution to them. In this chapter I focus mainly on influences from your childhood and adolescence rather than on later influences.

When growing, you received numerous messages relevant to learning both skills and confidence. Sometimes openly, and often subtly, these messages contained information about how worthy of respect you were. Noted family therapist Virginia Satir used the analogy of the cooking pot to describe self-esteem – whether it was full or empty, dirty or possibly cracked. She wrote: 'I am convinced that the crucial factor in what happens both *inside* people and *between* people is the picture of individual worth that each person carries round with him – his *pot*' (Satir, 1972, p. 21). Some psychologically resilient people can weather early negative messages without great damage to their self-esteem. Others are more psychologically vulnerable. Even in relatively nurturing environments such people experience psychological pain which they then carry forward into their later lives. Probably most people lie somewhere in the middle. If the circumstances of your childhood and adolescence were mainly nurturing, probably you grew up with adequate self-esteem. If you grew up in a hostile, inconsistent and emotionally retarding environment, you risk carrying a big black ball of underconfidence into your future relationships.

In his funeral address for Princess Diana, her brother Earl Spencer observed that for all her outward status and glamour, his sister remained 'a very insecure person at heart, almost childlike in her desire to do good for others so she could release herself from deep feelings of unworthiness' (Spencer, 1997). In her public life, Princess Diana showed immense mind and communication skills gifts that she acquired, maintained and then allowed her public role to activate even further. However, partly due to painful childhood experiences, Princess Diana also possessed some poor mind and communication skills which she also acquired, maintained and then activated. In life, Princess Diana struggled to come to terms with the influences of her past so that she and others could have happier present and future lives. Like Princess Diana, to a greater or lesser degree everyone has to come to terms with past influences that interfere with possessing good mind and communication skills.

This chapter focuses on how you learned your mind and communication skills. In relation to any skill, your past consists of two parts: first, how you learned or acquired the skill initially, and then how you have maintained, developed, weakened or lost it once initially acquired. In reality, the division between acquiring skills and maintaining skills is not that clear cut. Nevertheless, the distinction is important because the influences from your past that you carry forward into your present and future relate more to how you are maintaining good and poor skills *now*, rather than to how you acquired them in the first place.

LEARNING MIND AND COMMUNICATION SKILLS

Learning mind and communication skills takes place within biological, social and cultural contexts, some of which I mentioned in Chapter 1. Here I focus on some central influences on the development of your skills. One of the strange things about learning mind and communication skills is that, despite their importance, they tend to be acquired indirectly rather than by direct instruction. Often I have asked workshop participants and college students whether they have attended courses on these topics. Invariably, very few have attended communication skills courses and even fewer have attended mind skills courses. In addition, though this pattern may be slowly changing, most people still do not use the term skills when talking about relationships.

Supportive relationships

Children require supportive relationships. Bowlby (1979) talked of the concept of a secure base, otherwise referred to as an attachment figure. He noted accumulating evidence that humans of all ages are happiest and most effective when they feel that standing behind them is a trusted person who would come to their aid should difficulties arise. Hazan and Shaver (1987) go further and suggest that styles of attachment between infants and their parents are reflected in three later styles of adult loving: secure, anxious/ambivalent, and avoidant. *Secure* attachment is based on a sense of confidence and security in intimacy. *Anxious/ambivalent* attachment is characterized by dependency, lack of confidence in attachment and feeling unappreciated by others. Lastly, *avoidant* attachment is characterized by lack of acceptance of others, avoidance of closeness, and anxiety in intimate situations.

Rogers has also stressed the need for supportive parent-child relationships characterized by high degrees of respect, genuineness and empathic understanding whereby children can feel sensitively and accurately understood (Rogers, 1951). Supportive relationships can be provided by many people other than parents; for instance, relatives and teachers. When growing up, most people seem to need at least one primary supportive relationship.

Learning from examples

Learning from observing significant others is one of the main methods of learning. You can learn how you think, feel and communicate from examples. Generally your parents provide the most important early influences on your mind and communication skills. Most of you carry your parents round in your heads long after leaving home.

Psychologists use the term 'modelling' to describe learning from observing others. You learn from listening to and watching people like your parents who demonstrate behaviour, including their mind skills. Demonstrating involves both an observer and a demonstrator. Demonstration is more likely to be effective if the observer attends well and retains the material efficiently, and if the demonstrated behaviour results in valued outcomes.

Observing behaviour does not automatically mean that this behaviour 'feeds forward' and is adopted in future relationships. Observers can consciously think about what they see. In extreme cases, children may be thoroughly put off by observing parental behaviour and think 'I want to avoid being like that at all costs!' Some parents may have similar thoughts after observing their children's behaviour. Perhaps, especially in societies undergoing rapid change, children also serve as examples for their parents.

Frequently learning from observing others differs when the focus is on mind rather than communication skills. With communication skills the old saying 'Monkey see, monkey do' is much more likely to apply. Mind skills are not visual in the sense that communication skills are. Also, it is rare for mind skills to be clearly verbalized. More often than not people talk and behave in ways that assume good or poor mind skills. For instance, some parents think in overgeneralized terms with a great emphasis on how their children and others 'should' be. To the extent that they demonstrate rigid and punitive standards, they also demonstrate poor rule-creating skills. Furthermore, children can absorb deficient mind skills and then in later life possess the added barrier of remaining unaware that this has happened.

In addition to observing examples of unskilled thinking and communicating, children may lack the benefit of watching good examples. Having insufficient opportunity to observe people who think and communicate skilfully about their problems means that they lose a valuable source of learning.

In the following examples of demonstrating mind and communication skills, the first illustrates good skills and the second shows poor skills.

Demonstrating good skills

On occasions when she was growing up, Chloe and her dad would have disagreements and argue. However, once tempers had cooled, Chloe's father would sit down with her, listen to her side of the story, state his own viewpoint calmly, and try to reach a mutually acceptable solution to their problems. In such discussions Chloe sensed that, even though he might not agree with it, her dad perceived her position reasonably accurately. Now Chloe is 32, married to Jason, 34, and they have three children. Whenever problems and conflicts occur in her marriage or family life, Chloe tries to stay calm, accurately perceive other people's positions as well as her own, and work towards constructive solutions that deal with the real issues, yet respect differences of opinion.

Demonstrating poor skills

The style of managing conflict in the Robinson family is one of competitive combat. Each parent has to be right, has 'legitimate' reasons for anger, and shouts and points fingers. They do not listen to each other. Blame is the name of the game. Their children, Katie, 10, Jenny, 8, and Jeff, 5, observe and learn poor skills from how their parents fight.

In the good skills example, Chloe's dad demonstrates the mind skill of perceiving accurately and the communication skills of listening well and solving relationship problems constructively. In the poor skills example, the Robinson children observe each parent demonstrate the mind skills deficiencies of perceiving inaccurately and of externalizing the cause of their conflict. In addition, the children observe the poor communication skills of not listening properly and of destructively solving relationship problems.

Think of the ways in which your parents, or substitute parents, handled problems, be they in their own lives, with you or with other members of the family. How do you consider the mind and communication skills you use now in dealing with relationship problems may have been influenced by each of their examples?

Learning from consequences

Frequently, learning from observing role models and learning from rewarding or unrewarding consequences intermingle. When growing up, many people provided positive and negative consequences for your thoughts and communications. Both good and poor skills may have been either rewarded, or discouraged and possibly punished, or ignored, or a mixture of these. The basic idea is that you have a higher probability of repeating thoughts and communications for which you received positive consequences than those resulting in negative consequences.

However, you do not just receive consequences, you think about past and present consequences, and then make rules and predictions to guide your future behaviour. Often how you think can strengthen, weaken or otherwise alter the impact of consequences you receive from how you communicate. In addition, your genetic

make-up influences your likelihood of being conditioned by rewarding consequences. If you are introverted you are more likely to be influenced than if you are
extroverted.

Rewarding consequences played a large part in helping or hindering you in
acquiring effective mind and communication skills. Virtually from birth, you received
messages about how 'good' or 'bad' your thoughts and communications were.
Usually, with the best of intentions, adults try to reward children for developing the
skills necessary to cope with the world. When rewarding children, many times adults
'get it right'. However, sometimes adults provide rewards in deficient ways. For
example, most people learn their mind and communication skills from a mixture of
observing others, unsystematic feedback and trial-and-error. Rarely, either inside or
outside the home, are you systematically rewarded as you develop these skills.
Sometimes you may have been rewarded for exhibiting poor rather than good mind
and communication skills. For example, parents unskilled at explaining cause
accurately may collude with or encourage their children when they engage in un-
called for blaming of others. Also, sometimes parents provide rewards in such
clumsy ways that children rebel and do the opposite.

Children also provide rewards for their parents. Often these rewards help parents
to continue rewarding their children for exhibiting good mind and communication
skills. On other occasions, children can reward parents for colluding in their use of
poor skills.

In addition you can acquire deficient mind skills by becoming too dependent on the
need for external reward rather than trusting and developing your skills of thinking for
yourself. Sometimes to gain or maintain parental approval, children introject or adopt
their parents' thoughts and prejudices as though they were their own.

Parental insecurities and thinking difficulties can impede helping children to think
skilfully. Psychologist Claude Steiner writes: 'When problem solving is discouraged
by parents, children develop a reaction of mindlessness, stupidity, passivity, and
incapacity to think in the face of difficult situations' (1974, p. 151). Such 'training in
mindlessness' may include providing negative consequences for the use of skills
involving awareness, intuition and rationality.

Above I focused on parents providing consequences that develop or retard your
acquisition of good mind and communication skills. However, parents are not alone
in providing consequences. Teachers, friends, relatives and many others do so too.
For young people, the peer group can exert particularly strong pressure to gain
approval by thinking and communicating in conformist ways rather than by thinking
for yourself and communicating accordingly.

Many people acquire good and poor mind and communication skills through
receiving consequences according to their biological sex. Intuition and sensitively
perceiving the needs of others may be more discouraged in boys than in girls. Skills
involving being analytical, independent, willing to take a stand, and willing to take
risks may be more discouraged in girls. Members of both sexes may possess residues
of irrational gender-related rules: for example, 'Men must always be competitive'
and 'Women must always be nurturing'. The thinking that sustains traditional sex
roles is currently being strongly challenged, but not universally so. Gradually it
becomes less likely that children will acquire mind skills deficits through receiving
inappropriate gender-related consequences for what they say and do.

In the following examples of providing consequences for mind and communication skills, the first is of encouraging good skills and the second of encouraging poor skills.

Providing consequences encouraging good skills
Julia, 28, grew up in a close-knit family. At the same time as being protective, her parents encouraged her to make her own decisions about what sort of career to have and what sort of boys to go out with. When Julia wanted to discuss any decisions, her parents rewarded her by listening closely, eliciting her ideas and sometimes, in a neutral rather than controlling way, making suggestions of their own. Julia valued the fact that her parents would leave her with the final decision, yet showed interest and concern as she talked issues through. Julia has been in a relationship with Jake for over five years, and lived with him for the last three. When Jake has an important decision to make, Julia encourages him to think and talk it through rather than either ignoring him or offering him gratuitous advice.

Providing consequences encouraging poor skills
Jim, 25, was brought up in a family where his parents had frequent fights when you could cut the tension in the house with a knife. Jim's father, Ken, was a successful engineer. Jim's mother, Christine, chose not to go out to work and, apart from socializing with her women friends, developed no interests of her own. Much of the time Christine deeply resented Ken, wallowed in aggressive self-pity, and would complain bitterly, repetitively and at length about her marital troubles to Jim, whether he wanted to hear it or not. Jim was amazed and scared at the intensity of her emotions, the red flushes she would get on her neck, and at how she emotionally bullied him to be sympathetic to her viewpoint. On the rare occasions when Jim would share his feelings, Christine might tell him 'You are far too wrapped up in your own feelings'. If Jim dared to offer an alternative perspective on the marital relationship, Christine would sigh and say 'You just don't understand women'. Jim grew up feeling thoroughly squashed by Christine. Nowadays, Jim is shy with women and very reluctant to commit himself to any ongoing relationship.

In the positive example, Julia's parents provided rewarding consequences for the good mind skills of perceiving accurately the elements of a decision and of assuming responsibility for her decisions. Julia's parents also rewarded her communication skills of talking through decisions. In the negative example, Christine had so many agendas of her own that she transmitted to Jim a false perception both of women in general and of his adequacy with them. In addition, Christine provided consequences that discouraged Jim from developing good communication skills for initiating relationships and for developing intimacy, especially with women.

Other factors can influence the impact of both positive and negative consequences. For example, Christine might try to act in the same way to another son, Brian, who was more psychologically resilient, more assertive about setting limits to her complaining, and more outgoing with girls anyway.

Consequently, the impact of her behaviour for Brian would be much less destructive than for Jim.

Instruction and self-instruction

Psychologists researching animal behaviour stress the importance of learning from example and consequences. However, humans possess the capacity for symbolic thought and communication. Consequently, instruction is a major transmitter of good and poor mind and communication skills.

Much informal communication skills instruction takes place in the home. Some of this instruction is very basic: for instance, asking children to say 'please' and 'thank-you'. Often instruction at home is insufficiently systematic. Also, it is probably the lucky few children who are openly instructed at home in how to think effectively.

In addition, much informal mind and communication skills instruction takes place in schools and colleges. However, systematic attempts to train young people in a range of skills are probably still more the exception than the rule. Nevertheless a variety of mind and communication skills programmes may be offered in educational settings inside or outside the formal curriculum: for instance, making friends, managing anger, being assertive, decision making, and moral development.

Instruction can be for better or worse. Poor as well as good mind and communication skills may be imparted. Frequently, instruction contains sex bias: for instance, teaching cooking skills to girls and not to boys. In addition, mind and communication skills may not be taught clearly enough for young people to instruct themselves afterwards. If learners are unable to talk themselves through the relevant sequences of choices, mind and communication skills have been inadequately imparted and/or learned.

Information and opportunity

When thinking about problems, it is a great help if you possess a realistic set of concepts within which to understand them. The late George Kelly, a noted personality theorist, is reported to have said that asking a psychologist to describe a problem without the concept of anxiety was like asking a jockey to win a race without a horse! If you do not possess a reasonable understanding of the concept of anxiety, you are disadvantaged in understanding both yourself and others. In all probability most of you grew up with conceptual frameworks that both helped and hindered you in effectively thinking about your relationships. This book, which reviews some central mind and communication skills required by partners, attempts to provide you with a more adequate way of thinking about how to make your relationships successful.

Often children grow up with considerable gaps in information about essential aspects of life. However, to think realistically about relationships, you require as much relevant information as is necessary to make good choices. Sometimes with the best and sometimes with the worst of intentions, children are subjected to lies, half-truths and omissions of truth. All of these blunt your awareness of life. For instance, parents may conceal information that differs from how they want their children to see them. Also, they may be too embarrassed to talk about how children are born, their own sexuality, or their financial position. Furthermore, their own anxieties about subjects like death may mean that their children get fobbed off with euphemisms rather than gently, yet honestly, confronted with reality. Governments, education and the media may also either present, or fail to present, information in ways that restrict your awareness of reality.

Children, adolescents and adults alike need available opportunities to test out and to develop their mind and communication skills. Ideally, such opportunities are in line with your maturation and state of readiness. You may have different opportunities on account of sex, race, culture, social class, physical disability, financial position and schooling, to mention but some potential barriers. Furthermore, you may be fortunate or unfortunate in having parents who open up or restrict learning opportunities. Children, adolescents and adults also have a role in seeking out opportunities. Some people have better skills at this than others.

Anxiety and confidence

Confidence is extremely important in life. Sometimes, confidence erring on the side of optimism may help you initiate and persist in tasks. Unfortunately all people suffer in varying degrees from anxiety that is harmful rather than helpful. On occasion your anxiety may be appropriately high so that you can ward off real threats to your existence. However, harmful anxiety is higher than that required to cope efficiently with life's challenges, either general or specific. As such it is disproportionate and damaging rather than useful.

A two-way relationship exists between harmful anxiety and your mind skills. If you are highly anxious, you may block your awareness of the information you require to think effectively. For instance, you may possess 'tunnel vision' in which you rigidly perceive only a few considerations in a complex situation. Furthermore, you may block your awareness of your own thoughts and feelings. Also, you may possess an inadequate sense of your identity and so lack a firm base for evaluating your inner and outer experiences. However, poor mind skills can not only result from, but may also contribute to harmful anxiety. Thinking unskilfully about problems may generate negative outcomes which in turn may cause further harmful anxiety.

A close connection exists between feelings of security and anxiety. Perhaps a good definition of feeling secure is that you are relatively free from harmful anxieties. Feelings of insecurity both manifest and cause anxiety. Children grow up having both good and bad experiences for developing self-esteem. The fortunate acquire a level of anxiety that both protects against actual dangers and also motivates them toward realistic achievements. Those less fortunate may acquire harmful anxieties through observing poor examples, receiving the wrong consequences, and from inadequate instruction. Even parents who communicate carefully can bruise children's fragile self-esteem. Far worse are parents who communicate hostilely and then become defensive. Here children's feelings and perceptions are doubly discounted: first by the initial aggression and second by being subjected to further aggression when they react. However, as indicated earlier, children differ in the extent of their genetic vulnerability to negative parental behaviour and also in terms of their coping skills.

Poor communication skills resulting from as well as manifesting harmful anxiety include unwillingness to initiate relationships, a heightened tendency to say and do the wrong things, and excessive approval-seeking. As with using poor mind skills, using poor communication skills may further raise anxiety and make future learning even more difficult.

Some people's feelings of insecurity and of harmful anxiety are very pronounced. If you fall into this category, you may require long-term counselling where, within the context of a nurturing relationship, you can be coached in the mind and communication skills required for getting on well with others.

MAINTAINING MIND AND COMMUNICATION SKILLS

All truly wise thoughts have been thought already thousands of times; but to make them truly ours we must think them over again honestly, till they take root in our personal experience.

Goethe

Earlier in this chapter I mentioned that for any good or poor mind and communication skill your past consists of two overlapping parts: acquiring the skill in the first place and then maintaining it. An important difference exists in your responsibility for acquiring skills and in your responsibility for maintaining them. In acquiring your skills the main emphasis is on what others did to you. As a child and adolescent, you were relatively powerless in relation to your parents and other adults. In maintaining mind and communication skills the main emphasis is on what you did and keep doing to yourself. Thus, you provide many of the influences for this second past. Though environmental considerations play a part, you are now the main agent in protecting your strengths and, where you have poor skills, trying to reverse the trend by developing better skills.

In the following discussion I focus on how you maintain poor mind and communication skills rather than on how you maintain good ones. Sometimes you can allow your good skills to deteriorate to poor skills because you insufficiently acknowledge that there is no magic concept of cure for mind and communication skills. Once you acquire good skills, you require vigilant effort to maintain them.

What you did and keep doing to yourself

Nearly three hundred years ago British philosopher John Pomfret wrote: 'We live and learn, but not the wiser grow.' Pomfret's message has been given a more contemporary expression by Albert Ellis (1985) in the lyrics of his rational–humorous song based on "Beautiful Dreamer".

> Beautiful hangup, why should we part
> When we have shared our whole lives from the start?

A contributing factor to your maintaining poor mind and communication skills is that you may insufficiently think about how you think and act in skills terms. You can go round in circles talking about your relationship problems in everyday terms.

Far preferable is to analyse your relationship problems in skills terms so that you then know which skills to target for change.

One possible reason for maintaining deficient mind and communication skills is that you possess insufficient awareness of your personal responsibility for making the most of your life. You are the author of your life and how successful you are depends on the quality of the thoughts and communications you create. In general being personally responsible is much easier said than done.

Much of your thinking takes place in the form of self-talk. The self-talk of many people when faced with personal problems is highly repetitive. Their thinking resembles a record player that is stuck in the same groove. Ellis (1995) points out that, if you keep repeating irrational thoughts to yourself, this habit both represents and sustains deficient thinking and communicating. Sample irrational thoughts include: 'I must get what I want immediately' and 'Life must always be fair'.

Your view of yourself may be that you are always a rational human being. Thinking of yourself this way may block you from acknowledging incoming information that differs from it. Your perceptions of yourself are what you regard as 'I' or 'me'. Your self-picture reflects your feelings of security and of competence to cope with life. The more insecure you are, the more you are likely to have rigid perceptions about the sort of person you are. Instead of having what Rogers terms openness to your experiencing, both inner and outer, you are likely to react defensively by denying and distorting information about your communication that differs from how you see yourself (Raskin and Rogers, 1995).

Your defensive reactions or self-protective mental habits take place beneath conscious awareness. One result of these defensive habits is that you retain deficient mind and communication skills since they remain unexamined. Another result is that you stay anxious and insecure. Thus you may sustain your illusion of security at the price of relinquishing some of your hold on reality. You may reduce your immediate level of anxiety at the expense of increasing your longer-term harmful anxiety. Furthermore, harmful anxiety can make you fearful of change. You may prefer the safety of your existing mind skills, however deficient, to the growth entailed in changing the way you think and, in turn, communicate.

You may also maintain deficient mind and communication skills through secondary gains and payoffs – inner rewards you get for keeping your deficient skills. For instance, you may blame everybody but yourself for your misfortunes. If you are going to attain the real gain of accurately explaining the cause of your misfortunes, you will have to relinquish the secondary gain of being able to blame others all the time. This is an easy and convenient habit that stops you from the work of having to change your own thinking and communication.

In relationships, both partners can possess the poor mind skill of creating unrealistically negative expectations about the possibility of change. Such expectations include: 'My partner is incapable of change', 'Nothing can improve our relationship', 'Things will only get worse', 'People are set in their ways and cannot change', 'Too much damage has already been done', and 'It only postpones the inevitable' (Beck, 1988, p. 197). Expectations like these can erode one another's willingness to work on improving individual communication skills for the benefit of the joint relationship.

What your environment did and keeps doing to you

The earlier section on *learning* deficient mind and communication skills focused mainly on external influences. Once you learned your skills, many of these external influences may still have persisted, thus helping you *maintain* good and poor skills. Furthermore, even now, you may continue to have insufficiently supportive relationships. Also, you may still be exposed to examples of how not to think and communicate rather than the reverse.

In addition, you may continue receiving the wrong rewards. Your poor mind and communication skills may persist because they produce positive consequences. For instance, you may be able to manipulate people into believing they are persecuting an innocent victim such as yourself when the reverse may be the case. Getting angry and the thinking that accompanies it may get you what you want. However, this may be at the expense of mutual respect. Also, you may fail to learn the necessary mind and communication skills to manage your anger better. Just as using poor skills may have positive consequences, so using good skills may have negative consequences. For instance, however well you present your ideas, thinking and speaking for yourself may threaten others. This may make it harder for you to think and communicate as an independent person.

A contributing factor to maintaining poor skills could be that you still fail to find or receive adequate instruction in mind and communication skills. For instance, you may not have access to people, such as skilled counsellors, to help you overcome your deficiencies. In addition, you may still be exposed to insufficient or faulty information and lack suitable opportunities to develop your skills and potential.

ACTIVATING MIND AND COMMUNICATION SKILLS

Good and poor mind and communication skills may be both latent and manifest. People differ in their genetic predisposition to be mentally vulnerable. Also, you may have learned some poor mind skills that leave you vulnerable to specific situations. If circumstances in your life are favourable, you may not activate these deficiencies. However, in response to adverse – and sometimes positive – life events, you may start exhibiting these previously latent poor mind skills. In couple relationships, negative triggers include infidelity, overwork, sickness, visits from demanding in-laws, and financial problems, to mention but some. Positive events that might activate poor mind and communication skills include the birth of a child and receiving a sizeable legacy.

If anything, partners' latent poor mind and communication skills tend to be activated by stressful life events or a series of negative experiences. Often these events are stressful because they relate to previous negative experiences. For instance, take the earlier example of Jim who, when growing up, felt squashed by his emotionally tyrannical mother, Christine. Now Jim is hypersensitive in his personal relationships. In the presence of any hint of a powerful and seemingly controlling woman, Jim's poor skills and harmful anxieties relating to previous events feed forward into the present situation. This transferring of past agendas contributes to Jim perceiving too negatively the behaviour of some women he now dates. On the other hand, in the presence of an openly nurturing woman, Jim is much less likely to activate his poor skills. In fact, after some initial shyness, Jim could blossom in the warmth of an approving woman.

Once one partner activates latent poor skills, this can trigger their partner's skills deficiencies, thus increasing the likelihood of both of them further activating poor skills. Their thinking can become even more biased, demanding and rigid and their communication even more hostile and counterproductive.

The good news is that you can activate good as well as poor mind and communication skills. Stress, change and crisis can bring out the best in partners. Under normal circumstances you may function moderately well, under difficult circumstances you may flourish. In addition, the stresses of adverse events can be testing grounds in which partners can develop both commitment and good mind and communication skills.

CONCLUDING COMMENT

Your past learning history has provided you with some good mind and communication skills as well as with some poor ones. I do not wish this chapter on influences from your past to be taken as an excuse to continue blaming the older generation for any poor skills you may possess. Like you, your parents may have had their difficult as well as their good times when growing up. The fact that poor mind and communication skills are largely maintained by inner considerations heightens the need for partners of all generations to assume responsibility for rising above limiting past influences.

PART TWO
EMPOWERING YOUR MIND

4

Creating Self-Talk

He who conquers others is strong:
He who conquers himself is mighty.

Lao-tse

EMPOWERING YOUR MIND

In this second part of the book, I focus on six central mind skills that you can use to empower yourself to create love and happiness in your relationship. You can live more genuinely and fully if you are able to harness your mind's potential. Throughout the ages many people have learned the advantages of disciplining their minds. However, the increases in knowledge coming from the recent 'cognitive' revolution in counselling and psychotherapy place your generation in an even better position to take control of your thoughts. Now, more than ever before, you can energize and utilize your mind as an active agent for the well-being of yourself, your partner and your relationship.

The Olympic Games provide a good analogy of the relationship between mind and communication skills. First, many of the mind skills required for top athletes are similar whether they run, row, ride horses or swim. For example, all athletes require the mind skills of clear goals, explanations of cause that stress the importance of effort and persistence, and the ability to perceive their stronger and weaker points accurately. Second, even with the most brilliant of mind skills, athletes still need to perform the required action skills – running, rowing, riding horses, or swimming – in conditions of extreme competition.

The same mind skills and communication skills connections hold true for partners in close relationships. First, your mind skills strengths and deficiencies often carry across a range of situations. For instance, perfectionist rules may inhibit you when socializing together with your partner. Also these same rules may contribute to your becoming disproportionately angry with your partner. Second, using mind skills on their own is rarely enough. If you are to manage your relationships better, you must communicate with one another better, sometimes in circumstances of extreme stress.

I lay the foundations of how you can empower yourself through developing mind skills in this second part of the book before addressing communication skills in Part Three. However, unlike in the Olympic Games where there is only one victor for each event, my assumption is that in couple relationships both partners can be victorious by conquering yourselves through using good mind skills. The rewards of your inner victory will lie in your success in creating and cultivating happiness together.

WHAT IS SELF-TALK?

There is a joke about a psychoanalyst with a client who remained silent for three sessions, at the end of each he was charged one hundred pounds. Half-way through the fourth session the client requested permission to ask a question and said: 'Do you by any chance need a partner?' In other words, the client's self-talk was: 'This analyst is in on a good racket. Let's see if I can get in on it too!'

Try a simple mind experiment. For the next thirty seconds, close your eyes and try and think of nothing. Some readers trained in meditation techniques may be successful in stilling your mind. Most readers will become conscious that thinking of nothing is very difficult and that you have a constant stream of intrusive verbalization – including telling yourself to think of nothing!

If you want, try another mind experiment. Imagine that someone gives you an expensive gift that you intensely dislike. As in cartoon drawings, what might go in your 'thinks' bubble? Clearly, many things could go through your mind: your thoughts and feelings about the gift itself, the context of your previous relationship with the giver, how you might respond both now and in future, the consequences of various responses, and so on. My guess is that few of you would blurt out: 'I just don't want this bloody gift!', though your vocal and bodily communication might give you away.

Self-talk goes by numerous other names including inner monologue, inner dialogue, inner speech, self-verbalizing, self-instructing and talking to yourself. You talk to yourself even when you remain silent. In any two-person relationship, there are at least three conversations going on: each partner's private self-talk and their public conversation. Even when alone, you may talk to yourself about your partner as well as, sometimes, engage in imaginary talk with your partner.

All verbal thinking can be regarded as self-talk. However, this chapter focuses on a specific area of self-talk, namely instructing yourself so that you may cope with specific situations in relationships better (Meichenbaum, 1977; 1983). You may be aware of much of your self-talk, yet awareness is no guarantee of skilful self-talk. In addition, some of your self-talk is preconscious or automatic. This is not necessarily bad. For instance, when you learned to drive a car, you first received instructions which you then consciously told yourself to the point where these self-instructions became automatic. In some instances, your automatic self-talk may be unhelpful. Without knowing it, you are creating unskilful thoughts that depower rather than empower you.

NEGATIVE AND COPING SELF-TALK

The real alchemist is one who learns secrets of turning everyday situations into gold, who learns how to make every situation serve him.

John Kehoe

At the end of Chapter 2, I provided the situation-thoughts-consequences (STC) example of Megan, who was eating in a restaurant on her first date with Joe. Megan's thoughts or negative self-talk included 'I must make a good impression', 'I always get tense on first dates', and 'Joe is evaluating me all the time'. Negative self-talk can be contrasted with coping self-talk. You can distinguish between coping, 'doing as well as I can', and mastery, 'I have to be perfect'. Coping emphasizes competence rather than perfection. Megan's self-talk was negative because her emphasis was more on mastery than coping. In reality, most people use a mixture of negative and coping self-talk.

Negative self-talk refers to anything that you say or fail to say to yourself before, during or after specific situations that contributes to potentially avoidable negative feelings, physical reactions and communications. When American psychologists Philip Kendall and Steven Hollon researched their anxious self-statements questionnaire, they discovered three main types of anxious statements: those reflecting inability to maintain a coping view of the future, for instance 'I can't cope' and 'I can't stand it anymore'; those reflecting self-doubt, for instance 'Will I make it?'; and those suggesting confusion and worry regarding future plans, for instance 'I feel totally confused' (Kendall and Hollon, 1989). If you create negative self-statements such as these, you weaken yourself internally through unskilful thinking. You are less in control of your feelings and thoughts. Also, you put yourself at risk of communicating externally in ways that worsen rather than improve difficult situations: for example, by persistently inhibiting showing you love your partner and only showing the bad side of yourself.

With coping self-talk, you acknowledge that you have choices, calm yourself down, become clear about your goals, and coach yourself appropriate communications to attain them. Where necessary, you cool your anger and self-pity. Also, you increase your confidence by acknowledging strengths, support factors and previous success experiences. Altering your goal from mastery to coping is likely to increase your self-support and to decrease your self-oppression. You now possess an attainable standard toward which to strive.

The fact that you choose to use coping self-talk for a problem does not preclude your using other mind skills as well. For instance, Megan needs to alter her rule about demanding acceptance from everyone. In addition, she may require better communication skills, for instance at conversing. If anything, regard coping self-talk as a necessary part of rather than as a sufficient whole for dealing with specific situations in your relationships.

For the remainder of this chapter, rather than elaborating about negative self-talk, I emphasize the positive by focusing on areas of coping self-talk in which you can develop your skills. Though I mainly present the different elements of coping self-talk separately, often you put them together: for instance, combining calming, coaching and affirming self-statements.

CHOOSING SELF-TALK

He is free who knows how to keep in his own hands the power to decide.
Salvador de Madriaga

As a general guideline, the more you can become aware that in your waking hours you are always making choices, the better. Often, in my workshops, I do an introductory activity that emphasizes choice. At first, for about a minute or so, I demonstrate waking up in the morning and putting 'I chose' before everything I did.

I chose to turn over in bed and I chose to ignore the alarm clock. However, I disliked the sound so much that I chose to switch the alarm clock off. I chose to snatch an extra five minutes in bed and then I chose to get up. I chose to go to the bathroom, chose to urinate, and then chose to shave. Then I chose to get dressed and so on.

Then I ask the workshop participants to divide into pairs and take turns, for a minute or two each, in describing a couple of hours in their recent lives, putting 'I chose' before everything they did. This activity tends to bring home to participants how much they are in the process of choosing throughout their waking lives, how many choices they make, and the fact that many of these choices have become habitual.

Often you can give away much of your power by failing to remind yourself that you have choices. Instead, like a record stuck in the same groove, you risk repeating behaviour that has not worked in the past. You may have the illusion that you are choosing, but instead just be responding according to habit. The following is a personal responsibility credo that emphasizes your inescapable responsibility for your choices.

PERSONAL RESPONSIBILITY CREDO

I am personally responsible for my choices regarding how I think, feel and act in relation to myself, others and the environment.

I am always a chooser.

Within the realistic limitations of my existence, I make my life through my choices.

My choices always have consequences for good, ill, or both.

My choices always have costs.

The sum of my life is the sum of the consequences of my choices.

If you are to create your life and relationships, you require the skill or mental attitude of being proactive rather than reactive. Reactive people wait for things to happen to them. They allow themselves to be the prisoners of their upbringing and of their current life circumstances. They do not use their capacity for 'response-ability', the ability to create their responses to what transpires inside and outside their relationships.

Keep reminding yourself in simple language that you are responsible for your choices in how you think, feel and communicate. One idea is to prominently post the Personal Responsibility Credo or an adaptation to serve as a reminder for your choosing self-talk.

When thinking and communicating, you can use verbs that indicate choice (for example, 'I won't' rather than 'I can't' or 'I choose to' rather than 'I've got to') and avoid static self-labelling (say, for example, 'I choose to be poor at forgetting birthdays' rather than 'I am poor at forgetting birthdays'). Furthermore, you can challenge restrictive self-statements that do not acknowledge choice: for instance, if you find yourself thinking: 'I have no choice but to …'. You always have choices in how you communicate, including your verbal, vocal, bodily messages and often the touch and taking action messages you send.

ALERTING SELF-TALK

Sometimes, when dealing with specific situations in your relationship with your partner, alerting self-talk provides a useful starting point. For example, you may be aware that you are becoming very anxious or angry and in danger of communicating inappropriately. To cope adequately with the situation, you need to change gear from the buzz of your usual thinking into a calmer and clearer state of mind. The basic alerting self-talk instruction is 'STOP … THINK!' To be effective, be prepared to give your 'STOP … THINK' self-instruction forcefully and possibly repeat it: for instance, 'STOP … THINK, STOP … THINK!' After 'THINK' you might give yourself a choosing statement like 'STOP … THINK … What are my choices?' Another option after you say 'THINK' is to remind yourself to use your self-talk skills: for instance, 'STOP … THINK … My anxiety/anger is a signal for me to use my self-talk skills.' You can then engage in other forms of self-talk: for instance, calming yourself down, clarifying your goals and coaching yourself in how best to communicate.

CALMING SELF-TALK

Creating calming self-talk can have many purposes in your relationships. Before, during and after specific situations, you may wish to calm your mind so that you better deal with unwanted feelings such as harmful anxiety or excessive anger. In addition, you may wish to calm and relax your mind as a way of managing stresses stemming from outside as well as inside your relationships. A third purpose for creating calming self-talk is to become more centred and focused when you wish to think through, or talk through, issues in your relationships. Your use of calming self-talk helps you clear a psychological space for getting in touch with your feelings and thinking more sharply and deeply.

Sometimes, after giving yourself a 'STOP … THINK … What are my choices?' self-instruction, you might give yourself a cue for calming self-talk such as 'I acknowledge I'm feeling agitated. This is a cue for me to use my calming self-talk skills.' Sometimes you may be wise to withdraw from a situation, calm yourself down in private, and then deal with the situation later.

Calming self-talk involves both presence of supporting and absence of negative self-talk. The following self-instructions may be especially useful immediately before or during specific situations: for example, raising a sensitive issue, receiving threatening feedback, or speaking at a family gathering. Sample calming self-statements include 'Keep calm', 'Slow down', 'Relax' and 'Just take it easy'. Additionally, you can instruct yourself to 'Take a deep breath' or 'Breathe slowly and regularly', and regulate your breathing accordingly. When giving calming self-instructions, remember to use a calm voice.

On other occasions, you may have more time to prepare yourself for an upcoming situation or want to clear a psychological space for calmly addressing a relationship issue. I suggest two methods of calming self-talk that you can use in such situations: instructing the tension to leave your body and mindfulness of breathing. I use both methods when I want to relax myself either as an end in itself or as a means to thinking more calmly.

Instructing the tension to leave your body

Sit in a comfortable chair or lie down on your back with your legs uncrossed and arms by your side. Close your eyes and remember to speak to yourself in a soft, dreamy voice. After giving yourself these relaxation self-instructions, stay in your relaxed state for as long as is useful for you.

> I'm going to count to ten in groups of two, and after each group of two relax a different muscle grouping. It's as though I'm going to be turning out the different lights in a house at night. One, two ... focus on the tension leaving my legs and feet ... the upper part of my legs, my knees, the lower part of my legs, my feet and my toes. I'm enjoying the peaceful calm sensations of relaxation as the tension leaves my legs and feet. Three, four ... focus on the tension leaving the trunk of my body ... the upper part of my back, the lower part of my back, my sides, my chest/breasts, my stomach, my buttocks. My relaxation is getting deeper and deeper and deeper. Five, six ... focus on the tension leaving my arms and hands ... the upper part of my arms, my biceps, my elbows, the lower part of my arms, my hands, and my fingers. My arms and hands feel warm and relaxed, warm and relaxed, warm and relaxed. Seven, eight ... focus on the tension leaving my head and face ... my forehead, the area around my eyes, my nose, my cheeks, my mouth, my jaw, my neck, my ears, the back of my head and the top of my head. My head feels drowsier and drowsier and drowsier. Nine, ten ... focus on the tension leaving the whole of my body ... my head and face, my arms and hands, the trunk of my body, and my legs and feet. I enjoy the sensations of peace and calm, peace and calm, peace and calm as the tension flows from the whole of my body and my relaxation becomes deeper and deeper, deeper and deeper, deeper and deeper.

Progressive muscular relaxation

Those readers wishing a more thorough approach to achieving calmness though relaxation can use progressive muscular relaxation (Jacobson, 1976). Progressive muscular relaxation involves you in systematically tensing and relaxing sixteen muscle groups throughout your body. You can go through a five-step tension-relax cycle for each muscle group. These steps are

(1) *focus* – focus attention on a particular muscle group;
(2) *tense* – tense the muscle group;
(3) *hold* – maintain the tension for five to seven seconds;
(4) *release* – release the tension in the muscle group; and
(5) *relax* – spend 20 to 30 seconds focusing on letting go of tension and further relaxing the muscle groups.

I describe progressive muscular relaxation in more detail elsewhere (Nelson-Jones, 1997).

Mindfulness of breathing

Either instead of, or before, or after giving yourself relaxation self-talk, you can calm yourself by becoming mindful of your breathing. Mindfulness of breathing or 'watching the breath' is found in all forms of Buddhism. In Buddhist mind training, the present moment is regarded as most important. By becoming mindful of your breathing, your breaths anchor your mind to the present moment. You do not recall the past or look forward to the future.

Sitting, standing, walking or lying down, you can instruct yourself: 'Breathe naturally as I always do and become aware of my breathing'. You can either focus on your breathing at the top of your nose or follow your breaths down to your stomach and out again. Do not force yourself in any way to breathe slowly and deeply. When I just let go and become aware of my breathing, I find that it becomes slower and more relaxed anyway.

In Buddhist meditation training, sometimes beginners are encouraged to recite mentally BUD, while breathing in, and DHO, while breathing out, to stop the mind from playing truant and being distracted (Thitavanno, 1995). A variation of this might be to say to yourself gently a word like either 'calm' or 'relax' as you breathe out, as a cue word for allowing yourself to become calm. Alternatively, you might say 'calm' for the in-breath, and 'relax' for the out-breath, or the other way round. Using soothing words like 'calm' and 'relax' can help still your mind. The idea is to become centred by being peacefully aware of your breathing rather than by striving to concentrate on it.

Whether you use calming self-instructions, mindfulness of breathing, or both, you can create a more tranquil state of mind. Then, with your mind more relaxed and at ease, you can address issues in your relationships better, either on your own or face-to-face.

COOLING SELF-TALK

Cooling self-talk can also provide a way to calm yourself down. You can create cooling self-talk statements as contrasted with negative self-talk that fans your anger when faced with real or perceived provocations from your partner. You can substitute cooling statements for negative self-talk that jumps to unflattering conclusions about your partner, focuses on her or his shortcomings, and contains much self-pity. As with calming statements, cooling statements can help contain your level of emotional arousal, thereby increasing your chances of being sufficiently detached to think rationally and communicate appropriately.

Part of the skill of cooling your anger is learning to become more aware when you are engaged in anger-arousing self-talk, so that then you can counteract it with cooling self-talk. Sample cooling self-statements include 'Cool it', 'Count to ten', 'Lighten up', 'I can stay in control', 'Don't let my pride get in the way', 'I can choose not to let myself get hooked', 'I can choose not to take this personally', and 'Let's try and understand the other person's viewpoint'. Further cooling self-instructions include 'No put-downs or name calling' and 'Problem solve' (Deffenbacher *et al.*, 1996). In addition, you can challenge your current thinking with statements like 'I want to look at his/her good points as well'. Also, you can use self-talk that acknowledges the negative consequences of becoming angry and the benefits of equanimity.

GOAL-CLARIFYING SELF-TALK

Sometimes you may not need to use calming or cooling self-talk, since the situations may not warrant it or, if they do, you feel sufficiently confident to cope with them. Also, in some situations your goals for yourself and your dealings with your partner may be very clear. However, in many relationship situations, you may be well advised to clarify your goals. After your 'STOP ... THINK' self-instructions, and possibly some calming and cooling self-talk, you may then ask yourself 'What are my real goals in this situation? What outcomes do I want to achieve both for myself and for my partner (insert name)?'

Often, as a practising counselling psychologist, I have found clients insufficiently flexible when thinking about goals for specific situations. Rather than latch on to the first goal that comes to mind, you can generate and consider a range of goals by asking yourself 'What are my goals options?' Then you can choose one or more suitable goals. Beware of being reactive and waiting for things to happen, when you might achieve far more by being proactive, setting goals and making things happen in ways that you want.

Take care to avoid knee-jerk reactions and behaving in habitual ways that may not be creative and appropriate to the immediate situation you face. Therefore, another question you can ask is 'What outcomes do I want to prevent?' Having some insight into your mental vulnerability can help you pinpoint characteristic unhelpful ways of thinking and communicating that might lead to these outcomes.

A further question you can ask yourself when clarifying goals is 'How committed am I to my goal?' If you are not committed to your goal or have some reservations, you can then ask: 'What's stopping me from being committed and do I want to do anything about my reservations?'

Following is a vignette about using self-talk to clarify goals.

Situation

A month ago, Adam and Judy, who were going out together and are both age 20, had a row over some money that Adam had lent Judy. Both Adam and Judy went to school together, live at home, attend a nearby college, and up until now had been close friends and prospective long-term partners. Since the row, Adam and Judy have avoided one another.

Goal-clarifying self-talk

Adam's question and answer self-talk is as follows:

Question: Am I unhappy enough about the present situation with Judy to want to do something about it?

Answer: Yes, but I don't want to make matters worse.

Question: What do I want to achieve in the situation? What are my options?
Option 1: Ending my friendship with Judy.
Option 2: Getting my money back, but doing so in a way that keeps our relationship intact.
Option 3: Forgetting about the money, and remaining friends.
Option 2 is my preferred option.

Question: What outcomes do I want to prevent?

Answer: Having another blazing row that achieves nothing.

Question: How committed am I to my goal of getting my money back, but doing so in a way that keeps our relationship intact?

Answer: Very committed because it would be nice for both of us to be friends again and, as things stand, I've got little to lose by trying.

Sometimes in specific relationship situations, you may need much more time and space to engage in a process of thinking and feeling your way to goals that are right for you. Also, whether the goal-clarifying process is simple or difficult, short or long, on many occasions you will be formulating goals by discussing them with your partner or someone else. Inevitably, this should be the case when establishing joint goals.

If your goals are going to help you most, they require being stated clearly and cogently. Following are five key questions that you can ask yourself when setting goals for yourself:

- 'Do my goals reflect my values?'
- 'Are my goals realistic?'
- 'Are my goals specific?'
- 'What is the time frame for attaining my goals?'
- 'Should I set sub-goals?'

A distinction exists between outcome goals and process goals. Process goals relate to the processes of obtaining outcomes. In the earlier example of Adam and Judy, Adam decides that to obtain his outcome goal of 'getting my money back, but doing so in a way that keeps our relationship intact', he needs to become more specific and set a time frame. Consequently Adam sets himself the process goal 'Within the next 48 hours, I will phone Judy up and ask if we can meet for a chat.'

COACHING SELF-TALK

Once, like Adam, you have decided on both your outcome goal and your process goal, you can then use coaching self-talk to help you attain your process goal. Coaching self-talk is no substitute for possessing the communication skills for achieving a task. The first step in coaching self-talk is to break tasks down. Here you need to think through a step-by-step approach to attaining your goal, including how you might handle setbacks. Once your plan is clear, you then need the ability to instruct yourself through the steps of implementing it.

Remember to emphasize vocal and bodily as well as verbal messages. When you develop self-instructions, you can coach yourself in how to put across your verbal message most effectively. For example, Adam targets that, when phoning Judy, 'My vocal messages should be calm, measured, easily audible and emphasize key words'. If Adam were then to meet Judy, he could target that 'My bodily messages should include greeting Judy with a smile and then conversing with an open body posture, using good gaze and eye contact'.

You can use coaching self-talk before, during and even after specific situations in your relationship. If before a situation, coach and train yourself diversely. By this I mean, anticipate different ways your partner might respond and develop strategies for how to handle them. During a situation, concentrate on the task at hand. Keep your goal in mind and your focus on talking yourself through the steps involved in attaining it.

AFFIRMING SELF-TALK

I prefer the notion of affirming self-talk to that of positive self-talk. The danger of positive self-talk is that you may tell yourself false positives that set you up for disappointment and failure. Affirming self-talk focuses on reminding yourself of realistic factors that count in your favour. Following are some aspects of affirming self-talk.

First, you can tell yourself you can cope. Sample self-statements include 'I can handle this situation', 'My anxiety is a signal for me to use my coping skills', and 'All I have to do is to cope'. In addition, after you have coped with a situation better, acknowledge this: 'I used my coping skills and they worked.'

Second, you can acknowledge your strengths. Often when prospective partners or partners are anxious about difficult situations, they forget their strengths. For example, when asking for a date, you may genuinely possess good points, so you do not have to boast about them. Also, you may have good conversational skills that you can acknowledge and use rather than thinking about what may go wrong. In addition, you can think about any successful experiences you may have had in the past in situations similar to the one you face. Furthermore, you can think through how you might handle worst-case scenarios and realize that you do have more strengths than you originally thought.

Third, you may become more confident if you acknowledge your support factors.

For instance, relatives, friends, spouses and helping service professionals might each be sources of support, though not necessarily so. You need to develop skills at identifying who really is supportive and of avoiding unnecessarily exposing yourself to unsupportive people. Just knowing you have supportive people to whom you can turn may be sufficient to help you cope better with some relationship difficulties.

PUTTING IT ALL TOGETHER

Coping self-talk may be used before, during and after different situations in your relationship. Often choosing, calming, cooling, goal-clarifying, coaching and affirming self-instructions are combined, though not necessarily all at the same time: for instance, 'STOP ... THINK ... I can choose how to react. Calm down. What are my goals? Just take one step at a time. I have some skills for managing this situation.' You need to think through the self-instructions that work for you.

Instead of courting failure you can court success and happiness in your relationships through creating coping self-talk to replace negative self-talk. Below are examples of possible before, during and after coping self-talk statements for Megan, about first dates, and Adam, about phoning Judy to ask for a chat.

Megan, 35, who feels shy on first dates with men
Megan's coping self-talk for stressful dating situations might include the following statements:

Before
'Now calm down. Think of some things I can talk about.'
'Some tension is inevitable on first dates and I know I can handle it.'
'This date gives us the opportunity to know each other better. If we don't hit it off, there are plenty of other fish in the ocean.'
'Remember to let him see something of the real me and not just put on an act.'

During
'Relax. Everybody is not looking at me.'
'My anxiety is manageable. I know I can cope.'
'Let's have some fun. It's better for both of us.'
'Let _____ (insert name) know something about my thoughts and feelings.'

After
'Well done. I managed to control my negative ideas.'
'I'm pleased that I'm making progress in handling dating situations.'
'I feel better when I'm honest.'
'Next time I'd like to share more of what I think.'

Adam, 20, who wants to get a loan back from Judy and keep their relationship intact
Adam's coping self-talk about phoning Judy to ask for a chat might include the following statements:

Before
'There's no point in deferring the call. I'll make it at what used to be our usual time for chats.'
'Remember, stick to the issues and avoid put-downs.'
'I can cope with this phone call if I don't let my pride get in the way.'
'Even if I don't succeed, all I can do is the best I can.'

During
'My voice should be calm, friendly and easy to hear.'
'Keep task-oriented and listen to what she has to say as well.'
'Calm down. I can feel in control so long as I keep my cool.'
'Try to arrange a specific time and place for our chat.'

After
'I'm glad I made the effort to phone Judy.'
'Now, what are my choices about how I communicate when we meet?'
'Though we didn't resolve anything, at least I handled myself well.'
'I'm learning to cope better with Judy without getting so aggressive.'

REMEMBERING, REHEARSING AND PRACTISING

So far I have attempted to increase your awareness and to clarify some of your thinking choices when creating your self-talk. Here I focus on building a bridge between knowing what to do and doing it in practice.

Remembering your coping self-talk statements is vital to implementing them in practice. Ways to enhance your memory include writing the statements down on A4 paper, making reminder cards, and making cassettes. You can post written reminders in prominent places. In addition, you can take reminder cards with you and look at them immediately before difficult situations.

Rehearsing your self-talk is important. You can use reminder cards and cassettes for rehearsal. Sometimes you may be able to rehearse coping self-talk as you role-play situations with other people. If rehearsing with others is not feasible, an effective method of learning can be to use coping self-talk as you visually rehearse how to communicate better. For instance, both Megan and Adam can imagine themselves before, during and after the difficult situations they face.

You may need to practise hard at relinquishing unskilful self-talk and replacing it with skilful self-talk. Be open to modifying your coping self-talk if you are uncomfortable with it and it does not work for you. Also, build your self-instructions into a routine. For instance, as soon as you find yourself getting anxious or angry in a specific situation, use your self-talk. Genuine learning rarely occurs without setbacks and difficulties. Use coping self-talk to encourage yourself in handling these. Also, reward yourself for using your self-instructions. Use coping self-talk to acknowledge your successes, thus motivating you to persist.

Since you use self-talk all the time in your relationship with your partner, it is important that you start *increasing* your *coping* self-talk and *decreasing* your *negative* self-talk NOW. Remember, it is not whether you talk to yourself but what you choose to keep saying to yourself that makes you crazy!

INTRODUCTION TO ACTIVITIES

At the end of this and all the remaining chapters in the book, I include learning-by-doing activities to help you and your partner develop your skills. As you see fit, do the activities either on your own, or with your partner, or with some other suitable person, such as a relationship counsellor or trainer.

Here I provide a basic STC (situation-thoughts-consequences) practice sheet that you can use for many of the activities, especially those focusing on mind skills.

CREATING HAPPY RELATIONSHIPS
STC (SITUATION-THOUGHTS-CONSEQUENCES)
PRACTICE SHEET

Situation (S) (State the relationship situation clearly and succinctly.)

Thoughts (T1) (Record your initial thoughts about the situation.)

Consequences (C1) (What are the consequences of your initial thoughts?)

Your feelings

Your physical reactions

Your communications

Thoughts (T2) (Record your revised thoughts about the situation.)

Consequences (C2) (What are the likely consequences of your revised thoughts?)

Your feelings

Your physical reactions

Your communications

ACTIVITIES

As you see fit, do the activities either on your own, or with your partner, or with some other suitable person, such as a relationship counsellor or trainer.

Activity 4.1   Exploring negative self-talk

Part A: Self-talk about a past relationship situation

Think of a past relationship situation with your partner where you thought, felt and communicated inappropriately. Close your eyes and picture the scene. Just replay the events in slow motion and try to access your thoughts, feelings, physical reactions and communication before, during and after the situation.

When you open your eyes, using the STC practice sheet format,

1. At S, describe the situation.
2. At T1, write down as much of your self-talk as you can remember. Place a minus (−) by any of your negative self-talk statements, a plus (+) by any of your coping self-talk statements and a question mark (?) by any statement about which you are unclear.
3. At C1, identify your feelings, physical reactions and communication consequences.

What have you learned from doing this task?

Part B: Self-talk about a current or future relationship situation

Think of a current or future relationship situation with your partner where you are at risk of thinking, feeling and communicating inappropriately. Close your eyes and picture the scene. Visualize in slow motion what you anticipate happening in the situation and try to access your thoughts, feelings, physical reactions and communication before, during and after it.

When you open your eyes, using the STC practice sheet format,

1. At S describe the situation.
2. At T1 write down as much of your self-talk as you can remember. Place a minus (−) by any of your negative self-talk statements, a plus (+) by any of your coping self-talk statements and a question mark (?) by any statement about which you are unclear.
3. At C1, identify your feelings, physical reactions and communication consequences.

What have you learned from doing this task?

Part C: Identifying and analysing negative self-talk

1. With regard to *either* your overall style of self-talk when faced with challenging relationship situations *or* a specific difficult relationship situation with your partner, identify with a tick whether you use or used any of the following characteristics of negative self-talk.

_____ Insufficient choosing self-talk

_____ Insufficient alerting self-talk

_____ Anxiety-arousing self-talk

_____ Anger-arousing self-talk

_____ Absence of or insufficient goal-clarifying self-talk

_____ Absence of or insufficient coaching self-talk

_____ Absence of or insufficient affirming self-talk

2. Summarize what you perceive to be your current style of self-talk when faced with stressful situations in your relationship with your partner.

Activity 4.2 Creating coping self-talk statements

1. Why are each of the following types of coping self-talk important?

- choosing self-talk
- alerting self-talk
- calming self-talk
- cooling self-talk
- clarifying goals self-talk
- coaching self-talk
- affirming self-talk

2. Create and write out two specific examples each of

- choosing self-talk
- alerting self-talk
- calming self-talk
- cooling self-talk
- goal-clarifying self-talk
- coaching self-talk
- affirming self-talk
- coping self-talk that combines one or more categories of self-instructions.

3. The examples of coping self-talk in the text focused on Megan's shyness on first dates, and Adam's ambivalence about phoning Judy. Refer back to the text and, for each of these problem areas, create one additional self-instruction for before, during and afterwards. For example, for Megan, create one coping self-instruction each for before, during and after potentially stressful dating situations.

Activity 4.3   Substituting coping for negative self-talk

Using the STC practice sheet format,

1. At S, identify and describe a specific situation in your relationship with your partner for which you consider developing and using coping self-talk might be appropriate.
2. At T1, write down as much of your current self-talk as you can remember. Place a minus ($-$) by any of your negative self-talk statements, a plus ($+$) by any of your coping self-talk statements and a question mark (?) by any statement about which you are unclear.
3. At C1, identify your feelings, physical reactions and communications consequences.
4. At T2, create and write out at least two coping self-talk instructions for each of before, during and after your specific relationship situation. Read your coping self-talk instructions at least twice daily for a week.
5. At C2, write out what you think might be the feelings, physical reactions and communication consequences of using your coping self-talk instructions in contrast to your negative self-talk instructions for dealing with the situation.
6. How can you change how you communicate along with your coping self-talk?
7. Conduct an experiment in which you try out your changed self-talk and communication in the real situation and evaluate the consequences.

Repeat this practice for other specific situations in your relationship with your partner where you could be more effective by substituting coping self-talk for negative self-talk.

5

Creating Visual Images

I have imagination, and nothing that is real is alien to me.

George Santayana

This chapter focuses on creating happiness and avoiding unhappiness by influencing your pictorial mind as contrasted with influencing your verbal mind. Do not underestimate the importance of your visual images. Noted psychotherapist Arnold Lazarus writes: 'Through the proper use of mental imagery, one can achieve an immediate sense of self-confidence, develop more energy and stamina, and tap into one's own mind for numerous productive purposes' (1984, p. 3). Also, the proper use of mental imagery can help you improve your partner skills.

Try a simple mind experiment. Think of someone you love, such as your partner. Put down the book and hold the thought for about fifteen seconds. Then think of someone you dislike – hopefully, not your partner! Again, put down the book and hold the thought for about fifteen seconds. Almost certainly, in both instances you saw visual images of these people. To use a computer analogy, you called up visual images onto your screen.

When experiencing any significant feeling or sensation, you are likely to think in pictures as well as words. In addition, your relationship with your partner takes place on a pictorial level. Not only do you see your partner face-to-face, but you store pictures about her or him in your mind and, even when absent, you relate to these mental pictures.

The human brain consists of a left hemisphere and a right hemisphere, each of which has different functions. For instance, each side of your brain controls the other side of your body. Also, the left side of your brain is responsible for rational thinking, verbal activity and speech, with the right side of your brain being more emotional, intuitive and pictorial. While the left hemisphere processes information step-by-step, the right hemisphere processes information in a more holistic, simultaneous and visual way. This difference between the two brain hemispheres in information processing echoes Goleman's proposition, mentioned in Chapter 1, that humans have two minds and two different, yet overlapping, kinds of intelligence: rational and emotional (Goleman, 1995).

One way of looking at your mind is that it is like a movie camera that is continually recording images of what you see. These images get stored in the movie vaults or picture albums of your memory. American psychiatrist William Glasser goes further than this in stating that 'all our senses combine into an extraordinary camera that can take visual pictures, auditory pictures, gustatory pictures, tactile pictures, and so forth. In simple terms, this *sensory camera* can take a picture of anything we perceive through any of our senses' (Glasser, 1984, p. 21). Thus the pictures in your picture album also contain sounds, tastes, touch and smells. Glasser asserts that throughout our lives, we develop personal picture albums consisting of detailed pictures of what we want to satisfy our needs. He considers that 80 per cent of perceptions we store in our memory albums are visual.

Awareness of visual images

Your visual images are at varying levels of awareness. Much of your pictorial mental life is conscious, including your daydreams, fantasies and imaginings. However, visual images can also be preconscious. Cognitive psychotherapist Aaron Beck writes of patients having underlying or automatic images as well as automatic thoughts. These images are below the threshold of consciousness and patients may require professional help to assist them into consciousness (Beck and Emery, 1985). In addition, many of your visual images are unconscious. For example, much of your dream work remains unconscious. Also, painful pictorial memories may be repressed.

How can you assess and become more aware of your visual images? Partners can differ not only in how much each visualizes but also in how vividly. Possessing full awareness of a visual image means that the image is very vivid. Vividness incorporates the degree to which all relevant senses — sight, smell, sound, taste and touch — are conjured up by the visual image. Lazarus (1984) presents a simple five-point imagery vividness scale, with 4 meaning very clear; 3, moderately clear; 2, fairly clear; 1, unclear; and 0, very unclear or indiscernible. I suggest you substitute the word 'vivid' for the word 'clear' if using the scale, since 'clear' tends to emphasize the sight dimension at the expense of the other senses. Another possible aspect of vividness is the extent to which visual images elicit or are accompanied by your feelings, for instance hope and sadness.

Some of you either possess well-developed powers of imagery or can develop the skills of visualizing vividly. Others of you may experience much difficulty in visualizing vividly and need to emphasize other ways of controlling your thinking. In general, the more you can experience the senses and feelings attached to your images, the better you can use visualizing as a self-helping skill.

Methods for becoming more aware of your visual images and for enhancing their vividness include the following. First, you can become calm and relaxed. You may need to clear a time and space to get in touch with your visual images. Often, you will visualize best when you close your eyes and feel at ease. Second, you can ask yourself questions that can elicit and increase the power of your images, including 'What visual images do I have about the situation before, during and after it?', 'Are people moving?', 'Do I hear anything?', 'Do I smell anything?', 'Do I taste anything?', 'Do I have any tactile sensations?', 'How vivid is my image?', and 'What feelings accompany my visual images?' Another method for increasing the vividness of your imagery is to verbalize what you see. For instance, you can imagine a past, present or future situation and describe the scene as you are doing so either silently or aloud.

NEGATIVE AND COPING VISUAL IMAGES

Were it not for imagination, sir, a man would be as happy in the arms of a chambermaid as of a Duchess.

Samuel Johnson

You can incorporate visual images into the STC framework. For instance, the T in the STC framework can emphasize visual images as well as thoughts:

S – the situation;
T – my thoughts and *visual images*;
C – my feelings, physical reactions and communication consequences.

Using the STC framework can help you become more aware not only of your visual images, but of their influence on how you feel, physically react and communicate. Furthermore, this process may increase your realization that you have choices regarding the visual images you create for yourself at T.

As with self-talk, the visual images you create at T can be negative, coping or a mixture of both. For instance, socially confident partners can have images of behaving competently and obtaining positive reactions from others that you store in your memory albums and retrieve before new social situations. In addition, happy partners tend to possess the knack of seeing one another and the world through kinder eyes than less happy partners. You have a greater readiness not only to see good things happening around you but to store happy events in your memory albums.

Whereas positive images are associated with positive feelings, negative images accompany negative feelings. For instance, in one research study of 32 anxious psychiatric patients, some 90 per cent reported visual images prior to and concurrent to their anxiety attacks (Beck and Emery, 1985). Negative images are common in everyday life and you do not need to be a psychiatric patient to create visual images about your social incompetence and other people's negative reactions to it. Sometimes, if feeling under-confident, you can both experience and see yourself as smaller than you really are, whereas others are more powerful and larger than they really are. Furthermore, you can create unnecessarily negative images about your partner and others by selectively picturing their faults rather than their virtues.

To illustrate the point about creating negative and coping images, following are examples of the differing self-talk and imagery of a socially underconfident husband, Josh, and his more socially confident wife, Julia, who are thinking about going to a party together where each knows some of the people invited, but neither knows anybody else well.

Josh's negative self-talk and imagery
Josh, 28, starts telling himself what an ordeal the party is going to be for him. He pictures going there and standing around looking like a lost sheep. When he does make conversation, he imagines other people will notice how uneasy, boring and socially inept he is and not want to continue speaking with him. He is especially hard on himself when he imagines how

disparagingly women will view him. Josh pictures party guests drifting away from him and/or only wanting to talk with Julia when he is near her. Josh imagines people criticizing him behind his back. A consequence of Josh's negative self-talk and imagery is that he continues dreading going to the party and contemplates making an excuse for Julia and him not to go.

Julia's coping self-talk and imagery
Julia, 29, starts feeling anxious when she pictures herself and Josh going into the room where the party is held. She instructs herself to 'STOP ... THINK' and then successfully calms her fears by imagining other people being in the same boat as they are at the start of the party and needing to help each other get warmed up. Julia tells herself that she has skills in social situations that she can draw on. Julia pictures herself as speaking competently with other people at the party, using good verbal, vocal and bodily messages. She pictures other guests as having smiling faces and reacting positively when she speaks. Julia tells herself that she does not have to be perfect, but just to manage as best she can. Julia imagines herself enjoying the party as the evening goes on and trying to help Josh enjoy it too. A consequence of Julia's coping self-talk and imagery is that she starts looking forward to going to the party.

CREATING COPING VISUAL IMAGES

Like Julia in the above example, you can create, as well as coping self-talk, coping visual images that increase your confidence and communication skills in specific relationship situations. Following are some suggestions for how to increase your mind power by skilfully creating visual images.

Choosing images

Your self-concept is not only what you think about yourself, but also the pictures you carry around in your mind about yourself. You can develop images of yourself as a partner who is not impulsive, but rather is calm and collected and who stops, thinks and makes choices before communicating. You not only tell yourself that you are a thoughtful partner capable of taking initiatives, you carry around in your mental picture album visual images of yourself being this kind of person. Furthermore, you may have a store of previous experiences that you can use to corroborate your current positive image. Also, where appropriate, you can access a store of visual images to remind yourself of previous negative consequences for you of communicating before giving yourself the chance to make reasoned choices about how to act.

Another approach to seeing yourself as a chooser is to imagine yourself talking either to a real person whom you really respect or to an imaginary wise guide about a relationship situation with your partner where you are at risk of self-defeating behaviour. Imagine this wise guide encouraging you to use your mind, probing your choices, and helping you to think through the consequences of your choices. Some people might hold imaginary conversations with great visionaries like Jesus Christ, Mohammed or Buddha. A related approach to increased awareness of your choices is to imagine someone you respect actually confronting your upcoming situation and observing their choices and how they communicate.

Alerting images

You can accompany your alerting self-talk with appropriate visual images. For example, you can create the visual image of a 'STOP' sign at a road junction with the words 'STOP … THINK' painted on it. You might also image a large advertising billboard with the same 'STOP …THINK' message. Alternatively, you can create the visual image of a large neon advertising sign flashing the words 'STOP … THINK'. Another possibility is to get a visual image of yourself in an upcoming potentially difficult situation with your partner and calmly telling yourself 'STOP … THINK … What are my choices?'

Calming images

You can use imagery to calm yourself down. For example, in the previous chapter I provided some self-talk about instructing the tension to leave different parts of your body as you counted up to ten in groups of two. There I suggested you use the visual image 'It's as though I'm going to be turning out the different lights in a house at night'. In addition, you were instructing yourself first to imagine the tension leaving your body and then to imagine the peaceful calm sensations of relaxation.

Another method of calming yourself is to imagine a restful scene. Such images can serve not only as a prelude to other visual imagery methods, for example visualized rehearsal, but also as a way of calming yourself down before, during or after becoming agitated or angry. In addition, imagining a restful scene can be a way of 'bringing your mind home' to a more tranquil state before you quietly think about a pressing relationship issue. Imagining such scenes can be used on its own, or follow either instructing the tension to leave your muscles or progressive muscular relaxation.

Each of you probably has one or more special scenes where you feel relaxed, for instance looking at a valley with lush green meadows or sitting in a favourite chair at home. The following is an example of a visual relaxation scene.

> I'm lying on an uncrowded beach on a sunny day enjoying the pleasant sensations of warmth on my body. I feel a gentle breeze caressing my skin. I can hear the peaceful noise of the sea lapping against the shore nearby. I'm enjoying the soft touch of my towel and the sand. Also, I'm enjoying the salty smell of the sea and the fresh air. I haven't a care in the world. I experience feelings of peace and calm, peace and calm, peace and calm as my sensations of relaxation and well-being get deeper and deeper and deeper.

You may be able to heighten your motivation to become calmer if, when excessively anxious, you visualize the negative consequences of acting in your present agitated state. Another method of becoming calmer is to imagine someone you respect with a tranquil mind, feeling at ease, and communicating calmly in situations similar to those you face. You can also develop a picture of yourself thinking, feeling and communicating calmly in specific relationship situations. Furthermore, you can use imagery to help you engage in activities that calm you down. For instance, if feeling anxious, you can imagine going for a walk or engaging in some other stress-reducing activity as a prelude to actually doing it.

Cooling images

If you can calm yourself down, you are likely to be cooling yourself down too. In addition, there are a number of imagery techniques you can use to cool your anger. One technique is to create visual images of kind things that another person has done for you in the past. For instance, if as an adult you still resent your parents, you may help yourself to let go some of these hard feelings if you can visualize the concern, care and attention that they bestowed on you when you were very young (Chodron, 1990).

Similarly, in a couple relationship, you can create images of the good things that you have received from your partner in the past. Also, you can create images of the happy and fun times you have enjoyed together. Allied to visualizing positive past events, you can train yourself to create images that recall your partner's good points. Creating such positive images can act as a corrective to dwelling on and ruminating about faults.

A further imagery method for cooling hard feelings is to create images of good things happening to people who have hurt you, which is a technique for letting go of resentment developed by the Simontons at their cancer clinic in Dallas, Texas. Patients are asked to get a clear picture in their minds of the person towards whom they feel resentment. They are then instructed: 'Picture good things happening to that person. See him or her receive love or attention or money, whatever you believe that person would see as a good thing' (Simonton, Matthews-Simonton and Creighton, 1978, p. 152). The Simontons report that as patients continue to use the process of visualizing good things happening they gain a different perspective on the persons resented. Consequently, they begin to feel more relaxed, less resentful, and more forgiving.

It is very easy for couple relationships to enter downward spirals of matching negative comments about one another. Often partners are blocked in their capacity to act positively, despite the fact that this might cool down perceptions and defuse situations. Visualizing can be a useful tool for overcoming blocks to acting positively toward your partner. First, create visual images of different ways in which you could be more positive towards her or him. These include smiling, stating appreciation, paying compliments, apologizing, showing sympathy, a phone call, a letter, an invitation, a gift, or any one of a number of other possibilities. Second, create images of yourself being positive in ways that your partner appreciates. Picture how it makes her or him feel and acknowledge your reactions to this – for instance, it may make you feel good too. Third, you may wish to take the next step of communicating positively and seeing what happens. A simple, if not invariable, rule of thumb is that the more positive you are to others the more positive they will be toward you in return.

In addition, you may cool your anger to your partner if you can visualize how you might come across as more threatening and negative than you would like. By visualizing your partner's perspective you may gain insight into your own contribution to conflicts. Also, before communicating angrily, you can create images of how another might receive your angry messages and of the possible negative consequences for you.

Sometimes you can feel angry because you fail to recognize your power to influence situations. You may have an image of yourself as being smaller and more helpless than you really are. To cool yourself down from the heat generated by feelings of powerlessness, you can create images of yourself acting competently and assertively in specific anger-provoking situations. For example, you feel bored and annoyed when your partner starts running everyone and everything down. Here, rather than staying silent, you can choose to cool your annoyance by developing coping images of how to deal best with this complaining and then act accordingly.

Goal-clarifying images

Already you possess a vast store of pictorial goals in your memory. Glasser (1984) provides the example of the baby who found out how satisfying chocolate chip cookies were, pasting the picture of the cookies in his personal picture album. For the rest of his life, whenever that baby became hungry, he would start turning the food pages of his mental picture album.

In specific relationship situations, you can accompany your goal-clarifying self-talk with visual images. When asking yourself questions like 'What are my real goals in the situation?', 'What are my goals options?' and 'What outcomes do I want to prevent?', you can create pictures that help you formulate and then illustrate your answers. You are probably creating these kinds of pictures anyway, to some extent. If the pictures are indistinct, you may function more effectively if you can develop them into clearer images of what you want to achieve. Having a clearer vision may strengthen your resolve and commitment.

Visualizing can also help you and your partner clarify your personal and relationship goals at various stages in the future. For instance, 'How would I like to see myself develop as a person over the next five years?', 'How would we like to see our relationship develop over the next five years?', 'What sort of work and leisure interests would we like to have five years from now?', 'What sort of financial position?', 'What sort of home would we like to live in?', 'What sort of social relationships would we like to have?' Visualizing your answers to these and other questions is a process in which you and your partner are likely to clarify and refine your goals. Clarifying your goals does not mean that they have to be rigid. You can still change them in light of new information and fantasies. Some of your visions may go beyond self-interest to social interest. Here you may visualize answers to the questions 'What sort of local community, country or world would we like to see?' and 'What actions are we prepared to take to bring this about?'

Coaching images

Two partners can differ in the extent and vividness of their visual images of how they come across to one another. Especially with improving your bodily communication, to coach yourself effectively you need to develop visual images of skilled performance. At the end of the previous chapter I briefly mentioned visual rehearsal. You may have limited opportunity to rehearse and practise certain targeted skills in real life. However, you have virtually unlimited opportunity to use your imagination to visually coach and rehearse yourself in targeted skills.

While no substitute for the real thing, visualized rehearsal has many advantages. These advantages include assisting you in a safe environment to break tasks down and focus on the processes of skilled performance; rehearse small units of communication before moving on to more complex ones; identify potential setbacks and ways of coping with them; and rehearse and practise coping self-talk along with your visualizing skills. When counselling, I often make up cassettes to help my clients use visual rehearsal to coach themselves through the steps of upcoming tasks. You also can make your own cassettes to assist you in visually rehearsing competent performance.

Here is an example of a husband, Ryan, using visual rehearsal to coach himself in the skills required to attain his relationship goal of showing more gratitude to his wife, Beth.

Ryan, 35, had been in a relationship with Beth, 33, for five years and married to her for three. They had two young daughters. Ryan was the strong, silent type who would reveal very little of his feelings, including his affection for Beth. However, he was a kind hearted man who worked hard for the welfare of his family. Both Ryan and Beth thought their relationship was deteriorating and wanted to do something about it. Though the feedback hurt Ryan when Beth said it, he agreed that he behaved as though he was taking her for granted much of the time.

Ryan decided to set himself the goal of showing more gratitude to Beth. Beth was a good cook and Ryan thought he could genuinely express appreciation at meal times about her cooking. Ryan thought the appropriate time to do this would be at the dinner table. He targeted the following skills: verbal skills, thanking her and letting her know what he appreciated about the meal; vocal skills, speaking in a clearly audible voice and emphasizing words like 'thank-you'; and bodily skills, looking directly at Beth, smiling and rubbing his tummy in fun. Ryan also imagined approaches to handling the different ways Beth might respond. Ryan acknowledged his anxiety over what he was about to do. However, he practised many times in visual rehearsals that served to increase his confidence as well as his skills. The following dinner time Ryan thanked Beth for the excellent meal and apologized for not expressing his appreciation enough in the past. Beth visibly warmed toward him, put her hand on his, and squeezed it with affection. Ever since, Ryan has tried much harder to use skills of showing gratitude in a number of areas of his relationship with her. When necessary, Ryan rehearses in his mind how best to do this.

Affirming images

You can accompany your affirming self-talk with affirming visual images. For example, you can not only tell yourself you can cope, you can picture yourself performing competently in specific relationship situations. Many sports people, such as Tiger Woods, use visual images of performing competently to enhance their performance (Woods, 1997).

You may be inclined to imagine the worst about how incompetently you perform in specific relationship situations. If so, visualizing communicating successfully may act as a corrective for this tendency. In addition, imagine yourself receiving rewarding consequences for your competent communication. Also, even when imagining the worst possibility, you can imagine yourself coping successfully in such adverse circumstances.

Another facet of affirming self-talk is to acknowledge your strengths. Here you can not only remind yourself of your good points and strengths, you can actually picture them as well. In addition, you can create visual images of times in the past when you have used some good skills in situations similar to the ones you may face now in your relationship.

A further way you can affirm yourself is by not only thinking of supportive people, but creating visual images of them too. For instance, you can visualize respected friends or relatives, helping professionals, or imaginary wise guides helping you as you face difficult situations in your relationships. Instead of feeling alone and vulnerable, possessing the ability to picture supportive people may make it easier for you to communicate in a relaxed and confident fashion.

CREATING VISUAL IMAGES TO BREAK BAD HABITS

I couldn't help it, I can resist everything but temptation.

Oscar Wilde

Visualizing can be a useful skill when trying to overcome bad habits. People with bad habits, instead of dwelling on negative consequences, often switch to dwelling on short-term rewards. If you sincerely wish to break bad habits, the time to reward yourself is when you have resisted temptation, not when you have given in to it.

Sometimes you may not want to face the negative consequences of giving way to bad habits. One way you can strengthen your will-power is to collect and remember visual images of realistic negative consequences of bad habits and dangerous behaviours. For instance, if you are inclined to lose your temper with your partner and then regret it, you can create images of the likely consequences of communicating rashly and angrily in an upcoming situation. You can then visualize an alerting 'STOP ... THINK' instruction and repeatedly visualize the negative consequences of losing your temper. Afterwards, you can switch to visualizing positive images stemming from treating your partner with more respect.

Joseph Cautela (1967) developed an approach to undermining and resisting temptations in which you visualize exaggerated negative consequences when you experience an unwanted temptation. For instance, if the habit you wish to break is overeating and you have targeted rich cakes as a food to avoid, you might visualize the following sequence when relaxed.

> I am at home sitting round the table at dinner and a rich cake is being served. As I see the rich cake I start getting a nauseous feeling in my stomach. I accept a piece of cake. As I take my first bite, I vomit all over the table and my clothes. I keep puking as the food I have previously eaten comes out in a disgusting smelly mess. Seeing and smelling my vomit makes me retch even more violently. I feel very weak and faint. Everybody looks at me in disgust. As I get up from the table having made up my mind to eat no more cake I feel much better. I wash, change and feel great.

Visualizing exaggerated negative consequences is not for the squeamish. You need to rehearse and practise the negative imagery until it becomes a virtually automatic response to the real-life temptation. My preference is for visualizing realistic rather than exaggerated negative consequences. The realistic consequences can be horrific enough in their own right. However, some of you may find that exaggeration increases the power of your negative images with beneficial effect on your will-power.

ACTIVITIES

As you see fit, do the activities either on your own, or with your partner, or with some other suitable person, such as a relationship counsellor or trainer.

Activity 5.1   Developing awareness of creating visual images

If possible, do these exercises in a quiet room with soft lighting and no interruptions. Relax and sit in a comfortable chair. After reading the instructions for each segment, put the book down and close your eyes. Take your time. Where appropriate, conjure up smell, sound, taste and touch sensations as well as visual images. If you experience difficulty creating visual images, verbalize either silently or out loud what you are trying to see.

Part A   Creating photographic visual images

Visualize your partner or someone with whom you are in a close relationship. Focus on her or his face and try and visualize every detail as though you are recreating a good photograph of her or him. Afterwards assess how vivid your visual image was.

Part B   Creating visual images associated with other senses

- *Smell.* Visualize looking at and smelling a rose. How vivid was your image?
- *Sound.* Visualize a thunderstorm. How vivid was your image?
- *Taste.* Visualize you are eating a favourite food, such as chocolate ice cream. How vivid was your image?

- *Touch.* Visualize yourself taking a hot shower or bath, including the sensations of the water on your skin. How vivid was your image?

   Now visualize

- one or more smell sensations associated with your partner
- one or more sound sensations associated with your partner
- one or more taste sensations associated with your partner
- one or more touch sensations associated with your partner.

Part C   Creating visual images associated with feelings

- *Happiness.* Visualize your partner or someone else who 'makes' you feel *happy.* Stay with the image and reflect on what it is that produces this happy feeling.
- *Anxiety.* Visualize your partner or someone else who 'makes' you feel *anxious.* Stay with the image and reflect on what it is that produces this anxious feeling.
- *Anger.* Visualize your partner or someone else who 'makes' you feel *angry.* Stay with the image and reflect on what it is that produces this angry feeling.
- *Relaxation.* Visualize your partner or someone else who 'makes' you feel *calm and relaxed.* Stay with the image and reflect on what it is that produces this calm and relaxed feeling.

Part D   Visualizing my past, present and future homes

- *Past home.* Picture the home that holds most meaning for you when growing up. Visit it in your imagination, remember its detail and conjure up its smells, sounds and textures.
- *Present home.* Visualize your present home. If not already there, visit it in your imagination, remember its visual detail and conjure up its smells, sounds and textures.
- *Future home.* Visualize a home you and your partner might like to have five years from now. Picture its details and conjure up its smells, sounds and textures.

Activity 5.2   Creating coping visual images

1. How and why do you, or might you, use each of the following types of coping visual imagery when dealing with specific situations in your relationship with your partner?

- choosing images
- alerting images
- calming images
- cooling images
- goal-clarifying images
- coaching images
- affirming images

2. As vividly as you can, create at least one visual

- choosing image
- alerting image
- calming image
- cooling image
- goal-clarifying image
- coaching image
- affirming image
- coping imagery that combines one or more categories of visual images.

Activity 5.3   Substituting coping for negative visual images

Though the focus of this activity is on visual images, you can incorporate self-talk as appropriate.

Using the STC practice sheet format (see page 47),
1. At S, identify and describe a specific relationship situation with your partner for which you consider coping visual images might be appropriate.
2. At T1, write down as many of your current visual images as you can remember. Place a minus (−) by any of your negative visual images, a plus (+) by any of your coping visual images and a question mark (?) by any visual image about which you are unclear.
3. At C1, identify your feelings, physical reactions and communications consequences.
4. At T2, create and write out at least two coping visual images for each of before, during and after your specific relationship situation. Imagine your coping visual images at least twice daily for a week.
5. At C2, write out what you think might be the feelings, physical reactions and communication consequences of using your coping visual images in contrast to your negative visual images for dealing with the situation.
6. How can you change how you communicate along with your coping visual images?
7. Conduct an experiment in which you try out your changed visual images and communication in the real situation with your partner and evaluate the consequences.

Repeat this practice for other specific situations in your relationship with your partner where you can be more effective by substituting coping visual images for negative visual images.

Activity 5.4   Using visual rehearsal to communicate competently

1. Think of a specific relationship situation with your partner that is not too difficult and that you would like to handle better by communicating competently, as with Ryan's wish to express appreciation to Beth about her cooking.
2. Think through how you would like to behave in the situation by clarifying your goals and breaking the task down into its component parts (verbal messages, vocal messages, bodily messages). Also think through how you might cope with setbacks.

3. During the next 24 to 48 hours, spend time relaxing and then visually rehearsing communicating competently in the situation. Adjust your performance if you get better ideas for how to handle it. As appropriate, use coping self-talk along with your visual images. During this period you may also engage in live rehearsal and practice, though not in the actual relationship situation you have targeted.
4. Perform your changed behaviour in the actual relationship situation.
5. Assess whether and how creating and rehearsing coaching visual images helped you to communicate more competently with your partner.

You may repeat the above activity for as many other situations in your relationship with your partner as you find useful.

Activity 5.5   Creating visual images to break bad habits

Part A   Visualizing realistic negative consequences

1. Think of a bad habit relevant to your relationship with your partner that you wish to break.
2. What graphic images of the realistic negative consequences of your bad habit might serve as a turn-off for you?
3. Play the negative images through your mind for five to ten minutes each day for at least a week whether or not you feel tempted that day. Additionally, at any other time you experience temptation, instruct yourself to 'STOP ... THINK!' and switch to visualizing your negative images.
4. Practise, practise, and practise visualizing the negative consequences of your bad habit until you become able to resist the temptation to give in to it.

Part B   Visualizing exaggerated negative consequences

Repeat the exercise in Part A above, but this time include visualizations of exaggerated negative consequences.

6

Creating Rules

The Golden Rule is that there are no golden rules.
George Bernard Shaw

One of the main ways in which you can create happiness in your relationships is to possess rules that affirm rather than negate yourself, your partner and others. Perhaps the most prominent advocate of analysing the effect of your rules on communication is American psychologist Albert Ellis, who mostly uses the term beliefs instead of rules (Ellis, 1996).

Rules are the 'do's and 'don't's by which you lead your life. You have an inner rule-book that guides how you relate. An illustrative personal rule might be 'I must never make mistakes'. In addition, you and your partner will jointly form relationship rules to guide communication between you. An illustrative relationship rule is 'In our relationship it is important that we let one another know where we are emotionally'. Both your personal and your relationship rules may be either constructive, destructive or a mixture of both. For instance, the rules that make up your conscience could either help you to function as a caring human being or cripple you with self-righteousness and guilt, or have mixed consequences.

Tolerance and acceptance are relevant to creating and implementing your rules. Try to accept yourself and your partner as human beings worthy of respect and understanding. However, you can still decide how accepting and tolerant you are about specific behaviours. Most partners strive to find a middle way between being too judgemental and having no standards at all.

You may be aware of some of your personal and relationship rules, but there are others of which you are unaware. Some of these latter rules are preconscious and moderately accessible to awareness. However, others may be more threatening and anxiety-evoking. Consequently, you may have even more difficulty acknowledging them.

CREATING AND MAINTAINING UNREALISTIC RULES

Who sets your rules? The answer is that you probably think you do, but frequently this is not the case. Influences from your past and present have helped create and sustain your rules: for example, your family, religion, gender, culture, race, peer group, age, exposure to the media and so on. You may have altruistic and rational reasons for creating and sustaining your rules.

In addition, you may sustain some rules through less rational factors. Habit, or persisting communicating in the same old unexamined way, is one such factor. Fear is another important factor. You may be afraid that you will lose out in some significant way if you examine and change your rules. Wanting immediate gratification is a third factor keeping you stuck in unproductive rules. Like a child you may demand that you must have what you want NOW, NOW, NOW, rather than balance longer-term with shorter-term considerations.

Ellis considers that people create and maintain much of their distress and unhappiness through demanding and absolutistic thinking, making demands, rather than through preferential thinking, having preferences. He uses the term 'musturbation' to refer to rigid personal rules characterized by 'must's, 'ought's and 'should's. Ellis has identified three major clusters of irrational beliefs or unrealistic rules that create inappropriate feelings, physical reactions and communications consequences (Ellis, 1996, p. 13):

1. 'I (ego) *absolutely must*, at practically all times, be successful at important performances and relationships ...' ;
2. 'Other people *absolutely must* practically always treat me considerately, kindly, fairly, or lovingly...';
3. 'Conditions under which I live *absolutely must* be comfortable, pleasurable, and rewarding ...'.

Perhaps it is easier to explore first how demanding others are, before looking at yourself! Following are three caricatures of people with unrealistic rules. I use exaggeration to make the point about how unrealistic rules can work against genuinely loving communication that comes from the heart as well as from the head. First, I present Selfish Sam who makes demands on her/his partner. However, you can also possess demanding rules in regard to yourself. You can tyrannize yourself with your own 'must's and 'should's. The second example of Martyr Toni/Tony focuses on making excessive demands on yourself. The third example is that of the Distressed Daleys, a couple whose unrealistic relationship rules seriously undermine the quality of their partnership.

Selfish Sam
In her/his couple relationship, Selfish Sam (Samantha/Samuel) possesses what might be termed a psychology of entitlement. S/he constantly focuses on what s/he is entitled to as contrasted to what s/he can contribute. S/he is a getting rather than giving person. Selfish Sam is narcissistic, power-conscious and hypersensitive to her/his dominant position and to any real or imagined threats to it.

Following are some unrealistic rules contributing to Selfish Sam's negative feelings consequences of stress, rage, self-pity, resentment and anxiety; negative physical reactions consequences of hypertension and high blood pressure; and negative communication consequences of fighting and complaining. Selfish Sam is resented and either openly and/or subtly resisted and undermined by her/his partner.

'You must always put my career first over your work and personal interests.'
'You must provide sex for me when and how I want it.'
'You must constantly look after me without praise and with constant criticism.'
'You must be available to entertain my friends, relatives and work colleagues whenever I want.'
'You must be overly solicitous of my stress and hard work while I create and ignore yours.'
'You must allow me as much personal space as I want.'
'You must not have personal interests and friendships, unless I say so.'
'You must never enjoy the company of other men/women.'
'You must turn a blind eye to my flirting and extracurricular activities.'
'You must make me feel happy at all times, even when I am moody and demanding.'
'You must not make important decisions for yourself, even though I will criticize you for being too dependent.'
'You must never challenge my decisions.'
'You must always make me look good.'
'You must never make me feel threatened in any way.'
'You must never comment on my inconsistencies.'
'You must laugh uproariously at my jokes.'

Martyr Toni/Tony
Martyr Toni/Tony possesses compulsive caring habits.

Martyr Toni/Tony's negative feelings consequences include anxiety, irritability and moderate depression. Martyr Toni/Tony's negative physical reactions consequences include physical exhaustion, migraine headaches and lower back pain. Martyr Toni/Tony's negative communication consequences include hostile bodily communication, sighing, and withdrawal from and avoidance of any meaningful personal relationship.

Following are some of the unrealistic rules, albeit sometimes contradictory, that Martyr Toni/Tony applies to herself or himself. Some of these rules, in turn, may make demands on her/his partner to fulfil them.

'I must receive appreciation for everything I do.'
'I must be selfless in my concern for others.'
'I must know what others want without them telling me.'
'I must always take responsibility for keeping our home tidy.'
'I must never ask for appreciation.'
'I must never hurt anyone's feelings.'
'I must never feel resentment when I am not appreciated.'
'I must never ask for more personal space.'
'I must always be available for my partner.'
'I must fit my schedule around my partner's.'
'I must always support my partner, even if s/he does not support me.'
'I must do it myself, if I want it done right.'

'I must not let my needs and preferences interfere with helping my partner.'
'I must never show how tired I am.'

The Distressed Daleys
The Distressed Daleys are a couple whose relationship is heading for, if not on, the rocks because they have created and maintain a set of unrealistic relationship rules.

The Distressed Daleys' negative feelings consequences include hostility and alienation. Their negative physical reactions consequences include lowered energy and heightened muscular tension. Their negative communication consequences include difficulty showing affection, insufficient assertion, and unnecessarily aggressive verbal, vocal and bodily communication.

These are some of the Distressed Daleys' unrealistic relationship rules:

'We must solve problems competitively.'
'We must punish one another for wrongdoings.'
'We must never admit that we are wrong.'
'We must automatically know one another's thoughts and feelings.'
'We must never seek help for our problems from outside.'
'We must do everything together.'
'We must have the same needs for emotional closeness.'
'We must not be open about discussing our intimate feelings.'
'We must not talk openly about sex.'
'We must make one another into better persons.'
'We must stay in a loveless relationship.'

DETECTING UNREALISTIC RULES

People are disturbed not by things, but by the views which they take of them.
Epictetus

The first step in relinquishing unrealistic personal and relationship rules is to become aware that you possess them. You may remain unaware of how much of the time you make unnecessary judgements, be they positive or negative, rather than just accept yourself, others and the environment just as you and they are. Possibly most of us blunt our awareness of ourselves and others by placing too much emphasis on judging rather than experiencing. Often our minds contain a pathological tendency to criticize rather than to accept and prize.

You may experience difficulty identifying specific unrealistic rules. The rules can be so much a part of you that you are unaware that many of them exist. Your mind is not going to flash a large picture, with accompanying soundtrack, on your mental screen that says 'LOOK ... LISTEN CAREFULLY ...YOU POSSESS THIS UNREALISTIC RULE (specify) ... DO SOMETHING ABOUT IT NOW!' Instead, you need to develop skills of becoming your own mind detective who looks for clues.

Characteristics of unrealistic rules

An issue in detecting unrealistic rules is the degree to which there are certain central themes that occur again and again. Ellis has suggested on different occasions ten, eleven or twelve central irrational beliefs that fall into his three major headings: demands on self, others and the environment. Beck and Emery (1985) consider that their patients' maladaptive beliefs often focus on one of three major issues – acceptance, competence and control.

Selfish Sam's, Martyr Toni/Tony's and the Distressed Daleys' rules contain common characteristics of unrealistic rules. When attempting to detect your unrealistic personal and relationship rules, look out for the following characteristics (Ellis, 1995):

- *'demandingness'*, which involves thinking of your wants and wishes as demands rather than as preferences;
- *perfectionism* – putting pressure on yourself and others to be perfect. Nobody's perfect;
- *rigidity* – making rules for all situations rather than allowing flexibility for specific situations;
- *self-rating*, which involves globally rating yourself as a person and not just evaluating how useful are specific characteristics for achieving your goals – for example, 'Because I was not successful in making up with my partner after a row, not only do I not possess the skills for the task but also I am a failure as a person';
- *'awfulizing'* or thinking that it is or will be absolutely awful, horrible or terrible if you, your partner or the environment are not as they should be;
- *'I-can't-stand-it-itis'* – telling yourself that you cannot stand the anxiety or discomfort arising from you, your partner or the environment not being as they should be.

Clues for unrealistic rules

What are some clues, signals or signposts that guide you to becoming aware of unrealistic rules? First, you can be sensitive to inappropriate language. Rigid personal and relationship rules tend to be characterized by 'must's, 'ought's, 'should's and 'have to's. Such language signals 'musturbatory' or demanding thinking. Also, look out for words that indicate perfectionism, self-rating, making out that things are awful, and 'I-can't-stand-it-itis'.

Second, you can attend to inappropriate feelings, for instance flashes of rage. I find tuning into inappropriate feelings the best clue to knowing whether I'm upsetting myself unnecessarily. The dividing line between appropriate and inappropriate feelings is not always clear. Life can be difficult, so appropriate feelings cannot simply be equated with 'positive' feelings like happiness, joy, and accomplishment. Some 'negative' feelings like sadness, grief, fear and anger can be entirely appropriate for the contexts in which they occur. You have to ask yourself questions like 'Is this feeling appropriate for the situation?', 'Is keeping feeling this way helping or harming me and my partner?' and 'Am I taking responsibility for my feelings or allowing them to be determined by my partner's behaviour?'

Third, you can attend to inappropriate physical reactions. For instance, if you have any of the physical symptoms mentioned in the caricatures of Selfish Sam, Martyr Toni/Tony, or the Distressed Daleys, you can explore whether their cause is medical, psychological or both.

Fourth, you can attend to inappropriate communication. Inappropriate feelings, physical reactions and communication are interrelated. If you feel excessively angry, your physical level of arousal can impair your judgement to the point where you communicate violently and worsen rather than help your position. Relevant questions are 'Is my communication helping or harming me and my partner?', 'Am I overreacting?' and 'Am I taking responsibility for my communication or allowing it to be determined by my partner's behaviour?'

If you are uncomfortable with the way you feel, physically react and communicate, your self-talk can take the form of 'I feel/physically react this way because ...' or 'I communicate in this way because ...'. These self-statements can initiate your search for relevant personal or relationship rules contributing to your distress. I do not suggest that on every occasion you backtrack from inappropriate feelings and communications to looking for unrealistic rules. Life is too short. It is a useful self-help skill for when you experience persistent and/or major distress.

Fifth, you can attend to your family of origin. Understanding the origins of your rules can help you to realize that, though they may have had a purpose in the past, they have long outlived their usefulness. Take the rule 'I must be polite at all times'. While you were growing up either or both of your parents may have created a similar rule that in public they applied to themselves as well as to you. Thus not only were you being constantly told to be polite, but also either or both of them were demonstrating a 'being polite' lifestyle to you. Because of the potency of your parents both as examples and as purveyors of rewards to you, your childhood decision to be polite may have been realistic under the circumstances. Understanding the origins of your 'be polite' decision and the fact that you have unthinkingly internalized it since then may make it easier for you now to redecide to be polite only when it suits you. In general, in close relationships, tactful honesty rather than politeness is the best policy.

Sixth, you can look for the real agenda. Try to identify which rules are most important in a given situation. For example, you may be getting irritable at home because of distress in your working life. If so, examining your work rules may be more use than exploring your relationship rules.

Putting unrealistic rules into the STC framework

You can use the STC framework to clarify the interrelationships between your rules, feelings, physical reactions and communication. Also you can use the STC framework for questioning and challenging unrealistic rules and restating them into more realistic rules. At risk of some repetition, below are two examples of unrealistic rules put into the S, situation, T, thoughts, and C, feelings and communication consequences, framework.

Martyr Toni/Tony allows herself/himself to be used as a doormat.

S   Toni/Tony is feeling increasingly stressed by doing most of the household chores.

T1   'I must always take responsibility for keeping our home tidy.'

C1   Negative feelings consequences include anxiety, irritability and moderate depression. Negative physical reactions consequences include physical exhaustion. Negative communication consequences include hostile bodily communication, sighing and withdrawal of affection.

The Distressed Daleys are in an unhappy relationship.

S   The Daleys are getting increasingly bored with their sex life.

T1   'We must not talk openly about sex.'

C1   Negative feelings consequences include boredom and frustration. Negative physical reactions consequences include loss of libido. Negative communication consequences include unskilled lovemaking – just 'going through the motions', making excuses for avoiding sex, infrequent sex with one another, and solitary masturbation.

CHANGING UNREALISTIC INTO REALISTIC RULES

There is nothing good or bad but thinking makes it so.

William Shakespeare

How can you create more realistic rules to replace your unrealistic rules? Usually unrealistic rules contain realistic as well as unrealistic parts. For example, it may be realistic to want to keep your house clean and tidy, but unrealistic to continually be striving for perfection, especially if you have children. Consequently, when altering your 'clean and tidy house' rule, focus on discarding the 20 to 30 per cent of the rule that is irrational rather than getting rid of it altogether.

Questioning and challenging unrealistic rules

Ellis (1995; 1996) considers disputing to be the most typical and often-used method of his rational emotive behaviour therapy (REBT). Disputing means challenging unrealistic rules. The main skill in challenging is that of scientific questioning. Use reason, logic and facts to support, negate or amend your rules. Challenging questions you can ask yourself include the following: 'What unrealistic rule or rules do I want to dispute and surrender?'; 'Can I rationally support this rule?'; 'What evidence exists for the truth of this rule?'; 'What evidence exists for the falseness of this rule?'; 'Why is it awful?'; 'What can't I stand about it?'; and 'How does this make me a rotten person?'

Examples of questioning and challenging unrealistic rules

Following are two examples of how to challenge or dispute unrealistic personal and relationship rules. You can record your questions and challenges on paper. I have changed the nature of each example to provide you with a broader insight into how to go about the task. In the first example, I have listed *scientific questions* for eliciting evidence or reasons to challenge Martyr Toni/Tony's personal rule about always taking responsibility for keeping the home tidy. In the second example, I have listed the *challenges* or reasons that the Distressed Daleys themselves might use to dispute their relationship rule that restricts honesty in their sex life.

Martyr Toni/Tony allows herself/himself to be used as a doormat.

S   Toni/Tony is feeling increasingly stressed by doing most of the household chores.

T1   'I must always take responsibility for keeping our home tidy.'

Questions

Questions that Martyr Toni/Tony might use to challenge her/his 'I must always take responsibility for keeping our home tidy' personal rule include:

'Are my standards for how tidy our home is too perfectionist?'

'What are the negative consequences of always taking responsibility for keeping our home tidy?'

'How much does the marginal 5 per cent, 10 per cent, 15 per cent of extra effort contribute to keeping our home tidy and is it worth it?'

'What is the effect on my health of my holding down a job and then working so hard at home?'

'Would I be happier if I did less tidying up?'

'What cultural and sex-role rules contribute to my tidying behaviours and should I be challenging some of these rules?'

'If I were advising a close friend on how to go about sharing household chores with her/his partner, what would I recommend?'

'Do I have a double standard by which I expect myself to work harder at household chores than my partner?'

'Is my doing it myself a strategy for avoiding confronting my partner about the issue of keeping the house tidy?'

'Is there another solution to keeping the house tidy, for instance hiring a cleaner?'

'If I were to ask my partner to contribute less to making a mess and more to tidying up, what communication skills would I use?'

'What is the worst-case scenario if I were to ask my partner to take more responsibility for tidying the house and could I handle these consequences?'

'Were there any harmful caring habits demonstrated and rewarded in my family of origin that make me vulnerable to being a doormat now?'

'Why would I be less of a person if the house were less tidy?'

The Distressed Daleys are in an unhappy relationship.

S   The Daleys are getting increasingly bored with their sex life.
T1   'We must not talk openly about sex.'

Challenges

The Distressed Daleys' challenges, reflecting answers from questioning their relationship rule 'We must not talk openly about sex', include:

'Our parents never talked about sex to us in a relaxed and open way, but we can choose to be different.'
'Talking openly about sex is useful, not dirty.'
'There is no such thing as perfection in lovemaking.'
'It is unreasonable to expect ourselves to be experts in lovemaking.'
'Each couple can create its own sexual relationship rather than think that there is only one standard relationship.'
'We cannot expect one another to know the things we like unless we are honest.'
'When we each are more honest about what we like in bed, we can have more fun together.'
'Talking more openly about sex can help us to be more open in other areas of our relationship as well.'
'We can talk about sex using words with which we are both comfortable.'
'We can communicate our likes and dislikes about making love and still be tactful.'
'We can use other ways than words, for instance by touching, to communicate what we want and don't want in bed.'

Creating realistic rule statements

Vigorously and repeatedly challenging key unrealistic rules should have the effect of loosening their hold on you. An added way of reducing the hold of unrealistic rules is to restate them succinctly into more realistic rules. Your disputations or challenges can be too many and varied to remember easily. Create replacement statements easy to remember and recall.

Here I alter the characteristics of unrealistic rules to become characteristics of realistic rules. You can express preferences rather than demands. An example is 'I'd PREFER to do very well but I don't HAVE TO' (Sichel and Ellis, 1984, p. 1). You can replace rules about mastery and perfection with rules incorporating competence, coping and 'doing as well as I can under the circumstances'. Your rules can be appropriately flexible and amenable to change and updating. However, since such flexibility is based on inner strength, you can still hold firmly to well-thought-through core beliefs and values.

You can avoid rating your whole self rather than evaluating how functional specific communications of yours are. Your underlying thinking is 'I am a PERSON WHO acted badly, not a BAD PERSON' (Sichel and Ellis, 1984, p. 1). Also, attempt to avoid awfulizing by accepting that the world is imperfect and by refraining from exaggerating negative factors and possibilities. In addition, endeavour to eliminate 'I-can't-stand-it-itis'. Tell yourself that you can stand anxiety and discomfort arising from yourself, your partner and the environment not being as you would prefer them to be. Indeed, even in genuinely adverse circumstances, you may have many strengths and people who can support you.

Examples of creating realistic rule statements

In the examples provided here, previous unrealistic rules are indicated by **T1** and realistic restatements by **T2**. In addition, I have provided revised consequences, **C2**, for successfully adhering to the restated rules.

Martyr Toni/Tony allows herself/himself to be used as a doormat.

S   Toni/Tony is feeling increasingly stressed by doing most of the household chores.

T1   'I must always take responsibility for keeping our home tidy.'

T2   'Though I prefer to have our home looking tidy, this is a joint responsibility rather than mine alone.'

C2   Positive feelings consequences include less anxiety and greater happiness. Positive physical reactions consequences include being less tired. Positive communication consequences include assertively requesting partner to share more tasks, and setting limits on own contribution.

The Distressed Daleys are in an unhappy relationship.

S   The Daleys are getting increasingly bored with their sex life.

T1   'We must not talk openly about sex.'

T2   'Talking more openly about sex helps us to be affectionate and to enjoy sex.'

C2   Positive feelings consequences include happiness and pleasure. Positive physical reactions consequences include increased libido. Positive communication consequences include more give and take in bed, and more frequent sex.

Unrealistic rules tend to be deeply ingrained habits of relating to yourself, others and the world. You usually have to fight hard both to lessen their influence and to avoid losing the gains you have made. There is no concept of cure in overcoming unrealistic rules. Maintaining restated rules requires practice, practice, practice. Remember that, since you possess well-established habits of reindoctrinating and recontaminating yourself, you need practice challenging the same unrealistic rule again and again.

You can prominently post reminder cards with your restated rules. Also, you can make cassettes of their restatements and keep playing them back until they sink in. In addition, you can use visual rehearsal in which you imagine yourself in a specific situation experiencing the negative consequences arising from your unrealistic rule. Then imagine yourself switching over to your more realistic rule and visualize the positive consequences.

Changing your communication along with your rules

Changing your personal and relationship rules may make it easier for you to communicate effectively. For example, Toni/Tony finds it easier to develop assertion skills now s/he is no longer pressurizing her/himself to be the perfect home help. In turn, communicating effectively is perhaps the most powerful way of generating evidence with which to dispute self-defeating rules. For instance, if the Distressed Daleys change to communicating more honestly about sex and then obtain positive consequences, they have collected invaluable evidence to combat their rule 'We must not talk openly about sex'.

Ultimately there is no substitute for real-life practice for changing your rules and communication. Sometimes, latent in your repertoire, you may already possess the relevant communication skills to handle specific situations with your partner. If so, by changing your rules, you can free yourself to use these communication skills. On other occasions, changing your rules is insufficient. You need to develop your communication skills along with developing more realistic rules.

ACTIVITIES

As you see fit, do the activities either on your own, or with your partner, or with some other suitable person, such as a relationship counsellor or trainer.

Activity 6.1   Detecting unrealistic rules

Part A   Characteristics of unrealistic rules

Examine the following list of characteristics:

- demandingness
- perfectionism
- rigidity
- self-rating
- awfulizing
- I-can't-stand-it-itis.

To what extent does each characterize how you think in your relationship with your partner? Illustrate with a specific situation each characteristic that you acknowledge as true of you.

Part B   Clues for unrealistic rules

If possible, generate one or more unrealistic rules relevant to how you communicate in your relationship with your partner by using each of the following as the starting point for your search:

- attend to inappropriate language
- attend to inappropriate feelings
- attend to inappropriate physical reactions
- attend to inappropriate communication
- attend to your family of origin.

Part C   Understanding the consequences of unrealistic rules

1. Identify a specific situation in your relationship with your partner where you may be sabotaging your happiness because of one or more unrealistic *personal* rules. Put the situation into the STC framework.

S	The relationship situation
T1	Your unrealistic personal rule or rules regarding the situation
C1	The consequences both of the situation and your unrealistic rule(s) regarding it:

       (a)   feelings consequences
       (b)   physical reactions consequences
       (c)   communication consequences.

2. Identify a specific situation in your relationship where you and your partner together may be jointly sabotaging your happiness because of one or more unrealistic *relationship* rules. Put the situation into the STC framework.

S	The relationship situation
T1	You and your partner's unrealistic relationship rule or rules regarding the situation
C1	The consequences both of the situation and your unrealistic rule(s) regarding it:

       (a)   feelings consequences
       (b)   physical reactions consequences
       (c)   communication consequences.

3. Repeat the above activities for other situations in your relationship with your partner in which you possess either unrealistic personal rules or unrealistic relationship rules.

Activity 6.2   Questioning and challenging unrealistic rules

Part A   Questioning common unrealistic rules

In the context of your relationship with your partner, use scientific questioning to question and create challenges for each of the following unrealistic rules.

'I must perform to perfection.'
'I must always be liked by my partner.'
'My partner must always openly recognize my worth.'

Part B   Question and challenge specific unrealistic rules

1. For the situation you put in the STC framework in Activity 6.1 and/or for another situation in your relationship with your partner,

(a)   generate and list questions that you can use to challenge your rule (see Martyr Toni/Tony example in text)
(b)   list the most important answers for challenging your rule (see Distressed Daleys example in text, but use the first person singular)

2. Repeat the above questioning and challenging activity for one or more other unrealistic rules. If appropriate, you can do this activity together with your partner to question and challenge one or more unrealistic relationship rules.

3. Identify any specific questions that you think particularly useful for challenging unrealistic rules in future and that you might like to remember. An example might be 'Do I expect the same standard of other people?'

Activity 6.3   Creating realistic rule statements

Part A   Restating common unrealistic rules into more realistic rules

In the context of your relationship with your partner, restate each of the following unrealistic rules that you questioned and challenged in Activity 6.2 into a more realistic rule.

'I must perform to perfection.'
'I must always be liked by my partner.'
'My partner must always openly recognize my worth.'

Part B   Question and challenge specific unrealistic rules

1. For a specific situation in your relationship with your partner that you put into the STC framework in Activity 6.2 or for another situation,

S   Identify the relationship situation
T1   State your unrealistic rule
T2   Create a realistic rule statement to replace your unrealistic rule
C(2)   Indicate what the new consequences might be if you were to discipline yourself to use the realistic rule:

    (a) feelings consequences
    (b) physical reactions consequences
    (c) communication consequences.

What steps can you take to remember your realistic rule?

How, if appropriate, can you make how you communicate more in line with your realistic rule?

2. Using the format above, question and challenge other unrealistic rules pertinent to how you communicate. If appropriate, you can do this activity together with your partner to create realistic rule statements to replace one or more unrealistic relationship rules.

Activity 6.4   Changing communication along with restated rules

For any of the situations in your relationship with your partner for which you created realistic rule statements to replace your unrealistic rules,

1. Specify realistic goals for changing the way you communicate in this situation. Remember to focus on vocal and bodily as well as verbal communication.
2. Use visual rehearsal in which you imagine yourself in a specific situation experiencing the negative feelings, physical reactions and communication consequences arising from your unrealistic rule. Then, imagine yourself switching over to your more realistic rule and visualize the positive consequences for your feelings, physical reactions and communication.
3. Face the situation in real life and change how you communicate as best as possible. If and as you detect any further unrealistic rules concerning the situation, question and challenge them, and then create realistic rule statements with which to replace them.
4. Practise, practise, practise.
5. Use self-talk to recognize and reward yourself for any gains you make.

7

Creating Perceptions

If only we could pull out our brains and use only our eyes.

Pablo Picasso

Think of yourself as a computer processing information. All the time you are bombarded with internal and external stimuli, even when you are asleep and dream. However, unlike when you sleep, during your waking hours you can choose how you perceive and assign meaning to these stimuli. If you see the stimuli reasonably accurately on your computer screen, you have a better information base for relating to your partner successfully. However, if you distort, deny or misinterpret significant information, you increase your chances of creating and maintaining communication problems.

Partners' perceptions permeate all couple relationships: for instance, your perceptions of yourself and of one another. In addition, each of you has perceptions about one another's perceptions. Furthermore, you have perceptions about relationships in general and yours in particular. You can empower your mind and gain more influence over your communication if you become more skilled at creating your perceptions.

Your unrealistic rules based on habit, fear and wanting immediate gratification can introduce mistakes in how you perceive. Because of unexamined habitual 'musts', you may perceive some people and some things far too rigidly. If you believe in an unrealistic rule like 'I must be in control at all times', then you are always at risk of perceiving real and imagined threats to your sense of control. Similarly, if you have a rule like 'I must get what I want immediately', then you may fail to perceive possible negative longer-term results.

REALITY-TESTING YOUR PERCEPTIONS

Castles in the air — they're so easy to take refuge in. So easy to build too.

Henrik Ibsen

Perhaps the most influential approach to cognitive psychotherapy is that of American psychiatrist Aaron Beck. He considers that the assignment of meaning is the key to understanding self-defeating behaviour and positive therapeutic processes

(Alford and Beck, 1997, p. 11). Whereas Ellis encourages *preferential* thinking, based on realistic rules, Beck encourages *propositional* thinking, based on testing the reality of your perceptions. Both preferential and propositional thinking are useful mind skills.

Becoming aware of the influence of perception on feelings

Partners interpret one another's communication all the time. Beck observes that partners frequently have automatic thoughts and are unaware of the thoughts and perceptions that influence emotions (Beck, 1976; 1988). You may tend to jump to unhelpful conclusions that contribute to your own and your partner's negative feelings, physical reactions and communications. In distressed relationships, partners erode goodwill through continued misinterpretations of the thoughts and feelings behind one another's communications. In fact, partners can develop a 'negative cognitive set' about one another in which the level of mistrust is so high that they each interpret virtually everything the other does or says in a negative way.

In Chapter 2 I introduced the STC framework to help you see relationships between thoughts, feelings, physical reactions and communications. Below is a simple example of creating a possibly inappropriate perception based on the STC framework.

S	Charlie says to his wife Fiona: 'I've decided we need a new car.'
T1	Fiona perceives: 'Charlie doesn't respect my judgement.'
C1	Fiona feels hurt, gets angry and says: 'I don't see why we need a new car. What's wrong with the one we've got?'

You can use the STC framework to monitor upsetting perceptions in situations in your relationship with your partner. Ideally, monitor them as they happen. Develop the skill of accessing and listening to the self-talk that accompanies your inappropriate feelings. You can set aside some time each day to monitor and record upsetting perceptions. One way of doing this is to fill in a log with the following three column headings. In the feelings/physical reactions column, you can rate intensity of your feelings and physical reactions on a scale of one to ten.

S The situation (with date and time)	T My perceptions	C My feelings/ physical reactions

Understanding the difference between fact and inference

Your perceptions of the world are your subjective facts. They are the points on the map by which you steer your course through life. However, subjective facts do not necessarily correspond to the objective facts of reality. Your perceptions may be based on inference rather than fact. For instance, a favourite illustration of one of my Stanford University professors was 'All Indians walk in single file, at least the one I saw did.' That I saw one Indian is fact; that they all walk in single file is inference.

Facts are the true data of experience; inferences are deductions and conclusions drawn from those data. Inferences may be useful so long as the assumptions on which they are based are recognized and accurately evaluated. However, all too often inferences are mistaken for facts. Doing this gives you inaccurate information on which to base further thoughts, feelings and communication.

Inferences can be about yourself, your partner and the environment. They can be both positive and negative. They relate with varying degrees of accuracy to the factual data on which they are based. Below are two examples of the difference between fact and inference. In each instance, I assume that the inferences are wrong.

Example 1	
Fact:	My partner fails to congratulate me effusively on the good news that I have just had a promotion.
Inference:	My partner is not proud of me.
Example 2	
Fact:	My partner comes home late from work three evenings in a row.
Inference:	S/he is more concerned with her/his career than with me.

I stress the distinction between fact and inference because it is a theme that underlies most perceptual errors. You may both jump to conclusions and also be unaware that you have taken the leap. Illusion then becomes your reality, in whole or in part.

Identifying characteristic mind tricks

Try to become aware of your characteristic perceiving errors or mind tricks. Beck observes: 'These cognitive distortions occur automatically, often in a fraction of a second, and the number of distortions that can take place in that short period is considerable' (Beck, 1988, p. 159). Especially under stress, partners are likely to perceive inaccurately. If you are aware of your characteristic ways of distorting information you have a start in knowing where to look and what to avoid.

Using the STC framework, here are six mind tricks you may use at T that lead to negative feelings, physical reactions and communication consequences at C:

- *Making unsupported inferences*. Drawing conclusions without adequate supporting evidence.
- *Using tunnel vision*. Narrowly focusing on only a portion of the available information in a situation rather than taking into account all significant information. For example, you focus only on the caring things you do for your partner and fail to recognize when you are selfish.

- *Thinking in black-and-white terms* . Perceiving in all-or-nothing terms, for example, 'Either my relationship with my partner is a total success or a total failure'.
- *Magnifying or minimizing relevant information.* Seeing things as far more important or less important than they really are – magnifying minor upsets into disasters or minimizing negative events – for instance, exaggerating or downplaying the implications of the illness of your partner.
- *Overgeneralizing.* Making general comments that you probably would not be able to support if you bothered to check the evidence: for example, 'My partner *never* appreciates me' and 'I *always* try to understand my partner's viewpoint'.
- *Being excessively negative.* Attaching unduly negative and critical labels to yourself and your partner. Overemphasizing the negative at the expense of the positive or neutral. Going beyond useful ratings of specific characteristics to devaluing your own or your partner's whole worth as a person. Take the earlier example of Charlie saying to Fiona 'I've decided we need a new car'. When Fiona feels vulnerable about herself, she tends to see Charlie as more overpowering than he really is and then perceives what he says and does far too negatively.

Stopping, questioning, creating, evaluating and choosing the 'best-fit' perception

Think of your perceptions as propositions you can investigate to see how far they are supported by evidence. Beck and Weishaar (1995) give the example of a resident who insisted 'I am not a good doctor'. Psychiatrist and patient then listed criteria for being a good doctor. The resident then monitored his behaviour and sought feedback from supervisors and colleagues. Finally, he concluded 'I am a good doctor after all'.

Similarly, partners might start with the proposition either 'I am not a good partner' or 'I am a good partner'. Then you could list some criteria for being a good partner. Next you could monitor your behaviour and seek feedback from your partner and others to reality-test the accuracy of your initial perception.

Questioning yourself

Remember that you have choices in how you perceive. When you become aware that you are feeling and communicating, or at risk of feeling and communicating, in inappropriate ways, run a reality check on the accuracy of your information base. You can calm yourself down and ask yourself the following kinds of questions.

'STOP ... THINK ... am I jumping to conclusions in how I perceive?'
'Are my perceptions based on fact or inference?'
'Where's the evidence for my perceptions?'
'Are there other ways of perceiving the situation?'
'What further information might I need to collect?'
'Does my way of perceiving this situation reflect any of my characteristic mind tricks?'
'What perception can I choose that best fits the available facts?'
'What if the worst happens and how might I handle it?'

When questioning your perceptions you conduct a logical analysis of the accuracy with which you constructed them. This process involves both analytic and creative skills.

Creating different perceptions

One of the ways in which you may disturb yourself is by jumping to conclusions. You unnecessarily stick to your first perception rather than be more creative and flexible. Many partners lack skills of generating different perceptions to better understand the reality of the specific situations in your relationship. Remember the earlier example of Fiona and Charlie (see p. 79).

You do not always need to create and evaluate different perceptions on the spot. Sometimes you can ask for or make time to consider alternative perceptions away from the heat of the moment. Let us assume that Fiona chooses to respond to Charlie's remark about getting a new car with a neutral communication like 'I'd like to think about your suggestion'.

When Fiona makes the time to consider, she says to herself 'Are there any other ways I might see Charlie's remark about deciding to get a new car?' This time Fiona acknowledges she has choices in how she perceives Charlie and herself: for example, 'Charlie is really suggesting that we now have two cars, so we can each have one of our own', 'Charlie is trying to make me happy by suggesting we get a new car', 'I wish Charlie had worded his statement differently, but I know he will listen to my opinion if I state it assertively', 'Just because Charlie wants a new car, it doesn't mean that we have to rush out and buy it immediately', 'What about the new carpet and curtains for the living room? He is ignoring that they are more important to me', and 'Just like a man to want to have a new, expensive toy. I can treat that as humorous rather than serious.'

Evaluating and choosing from different perceptions

Another element of the skill of perceiving accurately is evaluating different perceptions and choosing the 'best-fit' perception. For instance, when Fiona evaluates the perception 'Charlie is really suggesting that we now have two cars, so we can each have one of our own', she asks herself questions like 'How closely does the inference fit the facts?' and 'What is the evidence for and against this idea?' Fiona remembers that Charlie and she went over their finances two weeks ago, so Charlie knows such a purchase is impossible within the limitations of their budget. Therefore Fiona discards this perception. Having evaluated other perceptions, Fiona decides the perception that best fits the available facts is: 'I wish Charlie had worded his statement differently, but I know he will listen to my opinion if I state it assertively'. Following is a revised STC based on this 'best-fit' perception.

S	Charlie says to his wife Fiona: 'I've decided we need a new car'.
T2	'I wish Charlie had worded his statement differently, but I know he will listen to my opinion if I state it assertively'.
C2	The feelings consequence of this perception is that Fiona is not angry with Charlie and in turn Charlie does not get angry with Fiona. The

communication consequences include not starting a fight, Fiona's acknowledging Charlie's wish for the car but saying they need to talk about it more since she wants some new curtains and carpets, and both agreeing to set aside a time to talk the issue through.

Questioning perceptions with communication experiments

Sometimes the sequence is that you change your perceptions through logical analysis, communicate differently and then get feedback that confirms your changed perceptions. On other occasions, changes in perception can follow from carrying out communication experiments. In communication experiments, instead of logically analysing *existing* evidence, you change how you communicate to see if this generates *new* evidence to confirm, negate or modify the accuracy of your perceptions.

Following is an example of a communication experiment.

Ian, 29, is married to Sarah, 32. Sarah is a very busy computer engineering consultant, who makes frequent business trips. Ian has a less demanding job as a local council executive. Sarah is getting increasingly resentful at the contribution Ian is making to the household chores. In particular, she would like him to do more of the cooking. However, until recently, Ian has responded with the perception 'I am no good at cooking'. Ian and Sarah have a lot going for them and he does not want to lose her. Consequently, Ian sets up the communication experiment (communicating through his actions) that 'If I spend the next three months genuinely trying to improve my cooking skills and cooking at least half of our meals together, **then** I will get better at cooking and Sarah and I will be much happier together'.

What are some considerations when designing, carrying out and evaluating communication experiments? Be as clear as possible about your 'If ... then ...' hypothesis. Also, state your hypothesis in the positive, as with Ian's example above. Set yourself clear and realistic goals and avoid taking on too much. Furthermore, consider a gradual approach, using intermediate tasks, if attaining your ultimate goal is difficult.

Remember to give yourself a thorough opportunity to implement your different communication. You can identify and rehearse the requisite skills for communicating effectively, focusing on vocal and bodily as well as verbal messages. Also, you can use coping self-talk as necessary. In addition, use self-talk that encourages you to persist through setbacks and to learn from experience.

Endeavour to evaluate accurately the information generated from your communication experiments by being sensitive both to the difference between fact and inference and to your characteristic tricks of the mind. Last, but not least, make sure you change your perceptions to take into account any new evidence from your communication experiments and remain open to accurately perceiving future new evidence.

Following are some further relationship perceptions that might lend themselves to reality testing through conducting appropriately designed communication experiments: 'I'm too nervous to call someone I scarcely know for a date'; 'He will not want a serious relationship with me if he finds out I've had an abortion in the past'; 'I cannot speak at dinner parties without making a fool of myself'; 'I don't understand money, so my partner has to take care of our finances'; 'If I discuss a difference with a partner/friend, it will only make matters worse'; 'My family and friends will reject me if they find out that I am gay'; 'It's always safer to hold back on expressing emotions'; 'By acting jealously, I am more likely to strengthen my partner's commitment to me'; and 'Relationships function more smoothly where wives do the laundry and husbands mow the lawns'.

PERCEIVING YOURSELF MORE ACCURATELY

Two-thirds of what we see is behind our eyes.

Chinese proverb

Your perceptions of yourself are a crucial area in which you may be creating unnecessary psychological pain for yourself and your partner. You can choose to see yourself too positively and alienate your partner with your arrogance and boasting. More often than not such communication masks deeper insecurities. Alternatively, you can use labels to devalue yourself and lower your confidence. It is paradoxical that, despite preferring to have others' approval, many people are extremely reluctant to approve of themselves. At varying levels of awareness you may be engaging in harsh self-criticism that interferes with your happiness and success in relationships. On the assumption that the more confident you are, the better you will relate, here my focus is on helping you to view yourself more positively. Much more damage is done to relationships by underconfidence, based on false perceptions, than by confidence, based on realistic perceptions.

Perceiving yourself too negatively

McKay and Fanning use psychologist Eugene Sagan's term 'pathological critic' to describe the pathological inner voice that attacks and judges you. They write: 'Everyone has a critical inner voice. But people with low self-esteem tend to have a more vicious and more vocal pathological critic' (McKay and Fanning, 1992, p. 15). While all partners have areas on which they need to work, when in pathological critic mode you can label yourself far too negatively. Such negative labels are unrealistically negative perceptions either of your specific characteristics or of yourself as a person. They are overgeneralized perceptions rather than useful evaluations that help you to attain your goals. Negative labels that you may apply to your intelligence include stupid, dumb, an idiot, a fool, a klutz, slobbish, moronic, and thick. You can also apply negative labels to aspects of your body, sexuality, tastes and preferences, leisure pursuits, and communication skills.

Last, but not least, you may label your whole worth as a person negatively part or all of the time. In a study on vulnerability to depression, British researchers Teasdale and Dent (1987) selected the following self-devaluing adjectives from a list of words associated with depression: deficient, failure, inadequate, incompetent, inferior, pathetic, stupid, unloved, unwanted, useless, weak and worthless. Be careful not to fall into the trap of talking yourself into feeling low.

Affirming your strengths

A number of the mind skills discussed so far are relevant to altering your negative perceptions of yourself to more affirming perceptions. You can test the reality of your negative labels by searching for evidence and conducting communication experiments. Also you can use affirming self-talk when dealing with specific situations. In addition, you may develop specific communication skills, for instance conversational skills, that help counteract thinking negatively about yourself.

Reducing being negative about yourself

There are some further skills that may stop your tendencies to perceive yourself negatively. You can use 'thought-stopping' which consists of creating alerting self-talk and visual images to stop unwanted thoughts. When you catch yourself in an unproductive negative train of thought, shout to yourself 'STOP!', possibly with an accompanying visual image such as a 'STOP' sign. Try to stifle your negative labels as soon as you become aware of them. The thoughts are likely to return, but you then repeat the procedure again and again as necessary.

Another skill is that of 'mental vacuuming', a visualization skill advocated by Kassorla (1984). She gets her clients to visualize a tiny toylike vacuum cleaner sweeping across their foreheads vacuuming up all their negative words and images.

Yet another skill is 'thought-switching'. When you find yourself dwelling on negative self-labels, you can replace them with affirming perceptions and appreciation of positive experiences. For instance, if you perceive that you rarely help anyone in your relationships, you can switch to thinking of a helping achievement that had personal meaning for you. If you dwell on something unpleasant in the future, you can switch to thinking of a positive future event.

Thought-switching can be combined with thought-stopping and mental vacuuming. When you find you are labelling yourself too negatively you can:

(1) instruct yourself to 'STOP!';
(2) mentally vacuum the negative self-label away; and
(3) switch either to an affirming perception of yourself or to an appreciation of a positive experience.

Increasing affirming perceptions

Why wait for negative thoughts before you switch to affirming thoughts? Be ready to own your personal strengths and any successes you achieve in your relationships. If anything the insecurity that leads to conceit comes from under-confidence rather than from owning realistic positive perceptions. Following are some ways in which you can increase affirming thinking.

One approach is to list your strengths. Do this in the first person singular: for instance, 'I am a good financial provider' or 'I am good at giving parties'. Some people find difficulty making a list of their strengths. You may dwell on your failures and insufficiently own your resources and successes. Consequently, you may need to search hard for ways of perceiving yourself positively. Another approach is to keep a journal in which you record daily your accomplishments, however small. A further approach is to write an essay in the first person singular, based on positive themes and actions in your life, and find in your essay positive statements about yourself (Lange *et al.*, 1997).

Once you have a strengths list, you may do a number of things to help it sink in. For example, you can record your strengths list on a cassette, and play it back. You can post the list in prominent places. You can put items on cards and shuffle the deck and read them back to yourself either as self-talk or aloud. Whether reading silently or aloud, always speak your strengths with conviction.

In addition, you can pair affirming thoughts to things you do often. Lewinsohn and his colleagues write: 'remind yourself to think a positive thought each time you eat, brush your teeth, talk on the phone, read something, get in your car or on the bus, and so on' (Lewinsohn *et al.*, 1986, p. 150).

Also, be careful not to mentally punish yourself when you notice you do something well. You are neither boasting nor egotistical, merely acknowledging using your skills well. Reward and encourage yourself for using your strengths. For instance, you can use self-talk like 'Well done', 'I'm pleased with how I coped', 'I feel proud about this' and 'I actually did it'. In addition, especially if you have a strong pathological critic, reward yourself for reminding yourself of your strengths and achievements.

Reducing your self-protective habits

Frequently, you can retrieve the negative consequences of poor communication if you are honest enough to admit your mistakes. What damages relationships far more is poor communication accompanied by defensively protecting yourself at the expense of your partner.

There is an old British saying, 'There's nowt so queer as folk'. Perhaps this refers to the human animal's huge capacity for psychological self-protection. 'Defensive reactions', 'defence mechanisms', 'security operations', and 'self-protective habits' are terms for the ways in which you may 'operate' on incoming information in order to reduce high anxiety. Your objective is to maintain consistency in how you perceive yourself, your partner and others.

All humans, in varying degrees, have vestiges of childish ways of handling anxiety that have now become mental habits which help to lose rather than gain power. Your self-protective habits reflect your lack of mental development when as a child you needed to protect yourself against a stronger and sometimes frightening world. Since these defensive habits distance you from reality, they may have serious consequences for yourself and others.

Here are some self-protective habits that can block you from thinking and communicating to the best of your ability (Freud, 1949; McKay, Fanning, and Paleg, 1994):

- *Avoiding.* You may avoid people and situations that you find threatening: for example, situations involving confronting problems with partners and friends.
- *Withdrawing.* When situations become emotionally charged, you may lower the temperature by either psychologically or physically withdrawing or both.
- *Engaging in compulsive activity.* You avoid genuine human contact by always doing things. For instance you can take refuge in work rather than devote adequate time to relationships.
- *Becoming dependent.* You allow yourself to become dependent on another person, for instance a possessive and controlling spouse, rather than acknowledge and confront your anxiety and then develop your own strengths.
- *Denying.* You repress significant aspects of yourself: for instance, anger, concerns about death, or altruistic feelings. You may also deny certain aspects of the feedback you receive from others: for instance, accurate 'home truths' from your partner about you.
- *Distorting.* You selectively filter incoming experiences: for example, only partially acknowledging the full extent of a compliment or criticism.
- *Projecting.* Rather than acknowledge aspects of yourself that you do not like, you become very conscious of these qualities in your partner or others: for instance, *their* need to control or *their* manipulativeness.
- *Rationalizing*: excuses, excuses, excuses. You are adept at finding reasons for your less acceptable thoughts, feelings and communications in your relationships with your partner and with others.
- *Competing.* You need to see yourself in a competitive relationship to your partner, relatives and friends. To feel superior you exaggerate your virtues and your partner's faults.
- *Attacking.* You avoid acknowledging your own hurt and inadequacies by attacking your partner in your mind. Also, outwardly you may criticize, ridicule, nag and blame her or him. Furthermore, you may accompany your verbal abuse with physical abuse.
- *Defensive lying.* You tell stories about yourself and your partner intended to have the outcome of making you seem in the right and her or him seem in the wrong. Defensive lying differs from deliberate lying in that you believe the distortions of reality entailed in your dishonesty.
- *Playing roles and games.* You may play various roles, for instance acting the clown, and psychological games, for instance 'Why don't you ... yes but', that create distance in your intimate relationships (Berne, 1964; Powell, 1969).

Letting go of childish ways of thinking can be hard for a number of reasons. You may have an illusion of rationality. You may not know what mental habits to look for. These self-protective habits may be partially or totally submerged below your awareness. Your relinquishing self-protective habits reveals a different you. These emerging perceptions may be highly threatening, even sometimes if the new information is positive.

The first step in relinquishing your self-protective habits is to realize their existence in almost all people, including yourself. The second step is to know what the various defensive habits are. The third step is to review and monitor your thoughts and communication to see if you possess any of these self-protective habits. Since the habits are rarely fully in your awareness, you may only get glimpses of them. For instance, if you catch yourself reacting aggressively to criticism, you may question the justification for this. When you calm down, you may realize the criticism was accurate, though you did not wish to hear it. You may then become aware that attacking is one of your ways of protecting your picture of yourself. If you catch yourself blaming other people for characteristics you are unhappy with in yourself, then you may become aware that projecting is one of your self-protective habits.

Once you become aware of a self-protective habit, tell yourself 'I can get by without this childish way of thinking'. Then work hard to identify the triggers for your hypersensitivity and try to catch them early on. For instance, if you know that you have a tendency to get self-protective when your partner questions whether you are being consistent, calm down, acknowledge your tendency to overreact, and think through what is the most appropriate response given the available evidence. Use your skills of distinguishing inference from fact and of evaluating the realism of your inferences. In addition, it is much easier for you to acknowledge and fight against your self-protective habits if you can overcome certain demanding rules, including 'I must be rational at all times', 'I must be perfect', 'I must never make mistakes', and 'Others must see me as I see myself'.

Once you have identified your characteristic self-protective habits you need constantly to guard against them. These habits represent well developed ways of distorting reality. Sometimes the habits may perform a benign function in allowing you to acknowledge information at a time and rate when you feel strong enough to process it. However, most often self-protective habits weaken rather than empower you. In addition, they can be very hurtful to others: for instance, you may act aggressively towards your spouse and then attack her or him for noticing you have acted aggressively and then further attack her or him for reacting negatively to your attack. The fact that you may once have identified and overcome a self-protective habit does not mean you are immune to it recurring. The probability is that the habit will recur, especially when your relationship with your partner becomes heated, and you will have to work and practise to keep on top of the habit.

ACTIVITIES

As you see fit, do the activities either on your own, or with your partner, or with some other suitable person, such as a relationship counsellor or trainer.

Activity 7.1   Monitoring upsetting perceptions and mind tricks

Part A   Monitoring upsetting perceptions

1. Identify a specific situation in your relationship with your partner where you may be jumping to unwarranted conclusions.

2. Monitor and record your upsetting perceptions relating to the situation by making an STC log with the column headings shown below. Fill the log out for at least the next 48 hours. Rate the intensity of your main feelings and physical reactions on a scale of one to ten.

S The situation (with date and time)	T My perceptions	C My feelings/ physical reactions

3. Assess the extent to which each perception is based on fact or inference.
4. Assess how any inaccuracies and inconsistencies between fact and inference in your perceptions influence your feelings and physical reactions.

Part B   Identifying mind tricks

To what extent does your perceiving either in the above relationship situation with your partner or in your overall relationship contain any of the following errors or mind tricks?

(a)   making unsupported inferences
(b)   using tunnel vision
(c)   thinking in black-and-white terms
(d)   magnifying or minimizing relevant information
(e)   overgeneralizing
(f)   being excessively negative.

Activity 7.2   Creating and evaluating different perceptions

1. Make an activity sheet similar to that illustrated below, but with more space in the columns.

S The relationship situation	C1 My feelings (before and during)	T1 My perceptions (before and during)	T2 Different perceptions I create

2. Think of a recurring situation in your relationship with your partner where an inaccurate perception may contribute to your feeling and communicating negatively. In column S state the situation; in column C1 state your inappropriate feelings and physical reactions; and in column T1 state your inaccurate perception. Also in column T1 state any mind tricks your perception contains, such as overgeneralizing.

3. In column T2, create at least five different perceptions relevant to the situation. Evaluate each perception to assess how closely each corresponds with the available facts.
4. Put a star (*) by the perception that you consider best fits the facts and assess how you might feel, physically react and communicate differently as a result of using this best-fit perception.
5. Repeat this exercise until you consider you have developed some lasting self-helping skills at creating and evaluating different perceptions in your relationship with your partner.

Activity 7.3   Conducting a communication experiment to reality-test a perception

Think of a current situation in your relationship with your partner in which you can reality-test a perception by changing how you communicate. Conduct a communication experiment to test the reality of your perception. Go through the following steps.

1. Clearly state your hypothesis in 'If ... then ...' terms.
2. Make a careful plan of how you intend to go about changing your communication, including your verbal, vocal and bodily messages. Rehearse and practise the skills you require to communicate effectively in the situation.
3. Implement your plan.
4. Assess the consequences for yourself and for your partner of changing your communication. Have you generated new evidence to alter your original perception?
5. Clearly state any changed perceptions you have resulting from the findings of your communication experiment.
6. Practise conducting communication experiments to test the reality of your perceptions in other situations in your relationship with your partner where your perceptions may be interfering with your happiness.

Activity 7.4   Affirming strengths

Part A   Monitoring negative labelling

1. Take a small note-pad and, for a 24-hour period, jot down the negative and positive perceptions of how you relate to your partner that enter your awareness. The emphasis is on *your* perceptions so only include feedback from your partner or others if you agree with it.
2. At the end of the 24-hour period, transfer your perceptions onto a master sheet with NEGATIVE PERCEPTIONS in one column and POSITIVE PERCEPTIONS in the other.
3. Put a star (*) by each perception that you consider may be a negative label rather than a realistic assessment of yourself.

Part B   Affirming strengths

1. Where appropriate, use the following ways to reduce any negative labels you place on the way you relate:

- thought-stopping
- mental vacuuming
- thought-switching.

2. Conduct a strengths review. Using the first person singular, list your strengths:

(a) in your relationship with your partner
(b) in other areas of your life.

As part of this process of generating statements about yourself, you may find it helpful either to keep a journal or to write an essay.

3. Where appropriate, use the following ways to remember your affirmations about yourself:

- using visual prompts, such as written lists and cue cards
- using audio prompts, such as cassettes
- using frequent activities as cues
- noticing your achievements
- rewarding yourself for using your skills and strengths.

Activity 7.5   Reducing self-protective habits

1. Make out an activity sheet in which you list the following self-protective habits. Do this at the left-hand margin and leave a space under each.

Avoiding
Withdrawing
Engaging in compulsive activity
Becoming dependent
Denying
Distorting
Projecting
Rationalizing
Competing
Attacking
Defensive lying
Playing roles and games

2. Write out your assessment of the extent to which you engage in each of these self-protective habits in your relationship with your partner. Where possible, cite specific examples.
3. Spend some time each day for the next week reviewing your thinking and communicating that day and seeing if you can add information to your activity sheet about your self-protective mental habits.
4. Develop and implement a plan to let go of each of your self-protective habits.
5. Work hard to stop being so self-protective in your relationship with your partner both now and in the future.

8

Creating Explanations

You cannot prevent the birds of sorrow from flying over your head,
but you can prevent them from building nests in your hair.

Chinese Proverb

Partners who have good skills of explaining cause accurately possess one of the main keys to creating happiness and avoiding pain when living together. As Beck observes, 'It is crucial that people recognize that they *do* have choices – that they are *not* simply the victims of a bad relationship, no matter how hopeless it may seem' (Beck, 1988, p. 10). When explaining cause, be very careful about unnecessarily seeing yourself as the victim of your partner's persecution. In choosing to allow the starting point for your explanations of cause to be your partner, you weaken yourself in two significant ways. First, you may be inadequately acknowledging your own contribution to starting and sustaining problems in your relationship. Second, by focusing from outside to inside, you may conclude that it is up to others to address the problems rather than for you to do so. Conversely, if you take yourself as the starting point for your explanations of cause, you should be in a better position both to analyse issues in your relationship clearly and to do something about them.

COMMON ERRORS OF EXPLANATION

Often errors of explanation make partial truths seem like whole truths. You can use the STC framework to help identify not only your errors of explanation, but their negative consequences as well. Following are some general errors of explanation that erode personal responsibility and have the potential to help you stay stuck in unproductive patterns of feeling, physically reacting and communicating.

- '*It's because of my genes.*' Undoubtedly your genetic endowment has limited your physical characteristics, for instance height, and abilities, for instance intellectual and musical ability. However, your relationship problems are to a large extent created by your and your partner's inability to use sufficient mind and communication skills rather than by any genetic inability to learn them in the first place.

- '*It's because of my mental illness .*' For most psychological problems, be they connected with relationships or otherwise, the explanation of mental illness overemphasizes the role of heredity and physical factors and underemphasizes the roles of learning and choice.
- '*It's because of my unfortunate past .*' Albert Ellis advises people to 'Forget Your "Godawful" Past!' (Ellis, 1988, p. 69). Your unfortunate past, or what others did to you, may have contributed to your mind and communication skills deficits that make you prone to relationship problems. However, you sustain your skills deficits mainly by what you do to yourself. Some people with unfortunate pasts require counselling help to give them the nurturing and healing they never received from their natural parents. Many people, either with or without professional help, have learned to overcome the skills deficiencies caused by their unfortunate pasts.
- '*It's because of my bad luck.*' Undoubtedly luck does play a part in life. However, you can either wait for your luck to change, which may be for ever, or sometimes you can make your luck. As one very successful golfer put it, 'The more and more I practise, the luckier and luckier I get.' Similarly, the more partners practise mind and communication skills, the happier and happier you get.
- '*It's because of my poor environment.*' You may see yourself as a helpless victim of circumstances. Adverse cultural, social, and economic conditions may make it more difficult for you and your partner to fulfil yourselves. Nevertheless, as the Austrian Jewish psychiatrist Viktor Frankl observed about his experiences in Nazi concentration camps, you still have choices regarding how you cope with deprivation and suffering (Frankl, 1997).
- The reverse is also possible in that you can think '*It's never because of environmental circumstances*' and, consequently, attribute too much of the cause of problems to yourself. Wars, natural disasters, unemployment, poor housing, and inadequate medical facilities are a few of the many unfavourable external events that partners can face in relationships. Discrimination – for instance, racial, sexist, homophobic or ageist – provides other examples of environmental stresses. Furthermore, cultures may have practices, for instance arranged marriages, that interfere with free choice. In short, it is possible to personalize problems by explaining their causes too internally. Such over-personalization of problems can impede your effectiveness in coping with them both in your own mind and in the external environment.

EXPLAINING YOUR PAST

It is important that you live your life in the present and the future, rather than in the past. It is good to get hurt and anger out of your system in an appropriate context, but persistent wallowing in self-pity over past hurts achieves no positive objectives. You cannot sit on the so-called 'pity pot' for ever. Nevertheless, I disagree with Ellis's advice to 'Forget Your "Godawful" Past'. However unfortunate your past may have been, you can understand and possibly cherish it as an important part of your journey in life. Furthermore, you can learn from your past, so that you do not repeat the same mistakes. Also it is preferable, where necessary, to create different and better explanations for your experiences in your family of origin. Then, without damaging yourself, you can integrate those experiences into your present life rather than pretend that the past never happened.

Assuming you genuinely have suffered from an unusually negative upbringing by your parents or parent substitutes, how can you prevent yourself becoming a victim a second time around? This second time you would be the victim of your own insufficient mind skills rather than those of your parents. You cannot go back and undo your past, but you can alter the way you think about your past so that you become stronger and freer in how you communicate in your present and future. You may need to challenge explanations that contain unwarranted self-blame. For instance, if you are inclined to explain your parents' problems or any of their clearly unjustified actions as your own fault, you can work on challenging and replacing these guilt-engendering inaccurate explanations.

More often than not you will need to challenge explanations that contain excessive blame of your parents. For example, you may explain parental negative behaviour as the consequence of their being basically bad or unloving people. If so, you can create a different explanation by viewing it as the result of their insufficiently possessing mind and communication skills strengths that would have prevented their negative behaviour. An important reason for their not possessing such skills strengths is that, like you, they may have been victims of their parents (your grandparents) who themselves possessed insufficient mind and communication skills.

You are not being asked to forget the negative things that have happened to you, but to understand their origins more deeply. You can still remember negative events in your past, but your different explanations may help you to gain emotional distance from them. The risk of remaining angry at past hurts is that you damage yourself as well as other people. If you carry around the unpleasant emotions of anger and resentment, you can lower your self-esteem. Furthermore, you may, knowingly or unknowingly, transfer your anger into current relationships where it is inappropriate. If possible, use your anger at past hurts as a stimulus to moving beyond it. The danger of the advice to forget your past is that this can be a superficial approach that does not allow you to work through to a mature acceptance of past wrongs rather than a denial of them.

Further ways that you can challenge excessively blaming your parents for past hurts include the following reality checks. First, you can do a reality check and try to remember many of the positive and nurturing things your parents did for you. As Chodron observes, 'Whatever their motives, they cared for us to the extent that they were physically and mentally capable. If we can appreciate this and forgive them for their weaknesses, our hearts will open towards them' (1990, p. 91). For some people, acknowledging parental kindness and expressing gratitude may create discomfort because it challenges seeing yourself as a victim. In addition, you can do a reality check and see if your behaviour as a daughter or son may have contributed to your own early unhappiness.

In this section I have challenged you to look at how you may be holding on to unhelpful explanations of your parents' behaviour and to assume responsibility for creating more helpful explanations. You can also examine your current communication and see whether you are still reacting as a psychological child towards your parents rather than being strong enough to relate to them as an autonomous adult. However, do not assume that all people can get on with their parents and that it is your fault if you do not. In extreme instances, you may be better off not seeing parents who persist in exhibiting obnoxious mind and communication skills deficiencies.

EXPLAINING RELATIONSHIP PROBLEMS

It is the act of an ill-instructed man to blame others for his own bad condition; it is the act of one who has begun to be instructed to lay the blame on himself; and of one whose instruction has been completed, neither to blame another, nor himself.
Epictetus

One approach to dealing with problems is to deny that they exist. As the saying goes, 'No problem is so big or so complicated that it cannot be denied'. For instance, in relationships, either or both partners may, at varying levels of consciousness, pretend that little or nothing is wrong, when this is not the case. Some partners find it psychologically more comfortable to deny or minimize rather than to acknowledge anger and conflict. However, the risk here is that your negative emotions fester and worsen. Then your feelings may 'come out sideways' in activities like gossip or subtly frustrating one another. Alternatively your pent-up feelings may come out directly, for instance in aggressive outbursts.

Another approach is to accept that some problems are inevitable in relationships. The problem may be that either or both of you are insufficiently accepting of problems as part of life. In such instances, each of you needs to develop greater tolerance of the existence of problems. Then you may be in a better position to choose which problems are worth addressing together and which are not worth bothering about.

Explaining the cause of problems

Assuming you acknowledge the existence of problems between you, how you and your partner explain them influences how constructive or destructive an approach you will take to resolving them. Your explanations for the cause of problems can be at varying levels of awareness: sometimes, you may need to access 'automatic' or preconscious thoughts.

Blaming your partner is probably the most common way of explaining cause wrongly. By blaming one another, couples not only create but sustain unhappiness by staying stuck in destructive patterns of communication. The following vignette illustrates the way mutual blaming can freeze rather than allow flexibility into how partners address relationship problems.

Connor and Kevin, a couple in their late twenties, blame each other for the breakdown of trust in their relationship due to Kevin's one-night stand with George, an older divorced businessman. Kevin blames Connor for his inability to show affection and poor performance in bed. Connor blames Kevin for his sexual demandingness, selfishness and devotion to his career. Both Kevin and Connor play the blame game, rather than look more deeply at their own contribution not only to the breakdown of trust in their relationship, but also to what they might jointly do to repair the relationship, assuming that it is worth repairing. The feelings consequences of Connor's and Kevin's explanations include mistrust, anger and resentment. Also, Connor has become increasingly anxious about having sex with Kevin. The communications consequences include less sex and frequent rows followed by emotional withdrawal.

Though you can blame yourself, most commonly in close relationships blaming involves externalizing the cause of your problems and anger onto your partner. Blaming can be a deficient explanation of cause for many reasons. First, you fail to acknowledge your own contribution to problems. Almost invariably, the causes of relationship problems are not simple. Also, usually when you blame you explain cause defensively. Either unintentionally or intentionally you may possess a self-serving bias in which you tell yourself stories intended to make you seem totally right and the other person seem totally wrong. Second, when you blame you may make your partner responsible not only for the problem but for your angry reactions as well: for instance, by thinking, and possibly saying, 'It's all your fault. Look how angry you've made me.' Third, blaming can elicit unwanted negative consequences: for instance, your partner reacts defensively and counterattacks. Fourth, blaming mainly addresses the past rather than the future. You can stay stuck because you blame your partner both for creating a problem and then for failing to solve it.

How can you explain the cause of your relationship problems more accurately? You can become more mindful of the risks of blaming. Also, you can monitor the frequency, duration and intensity of your blaming thoughts. Whenever you catch yourself blaming, you can ask yourself the following questions:

(1) 'What is/are the real problem(s)?';
(2) 'How have I contributed to their creation?';
(3) 'How am I contributing to their maintenance?';
(4) 'What is the outcome I would really like for myself and for our relationship?'; and
(5) 'What can I do to achieve that outcome?'

Identifying the real problems or agendas and neutrally defining problems are skills that can help partners avoid destructive patterns of mutual blaming. For instance, Tony may be pressuring his wife Debbie not to go out to work and both of them start arguing. Tony blames Debbie and states 'You don't care enough about the children and me'. Debbie blames Tony by stating 'If you really loved me you would help me find happiness in work'. However, Tony's real concerns are about seeing that the house and children are well looked after. At heart Tony wants Debbie to feel more fulfilled.

Tony and Debbie can neutrally redefine their problem as an 'it' rather than become personal and use language that involves blaming one another. A neutral definition of their problem might be 'How can we best see that the house and children are well looked after?' Then Tony and Debbie can address the real issues.

Cooperation to solve a common problem replaces antagonism based on pursing individual agendas. In other words, a correct explanation of Tony and Debbie's blaming one another and then arguing is more that they lacked the mind and communication skills to address their problem effectively than the problem itself.

Explaining the causes of not changing

Always blaming your partner for any problems between you represents an 'It's all your fault' mentality which can make it harder to strive for changes in your relationship. Even if your partner genuinely is in the wrong, you still have a responsibility for trying to make the relationship work. For example, instead of becoming angry, you could try providing her or him with some corrective feedback in a tactful way.

Another way to put the responsibility for problems onto your partner is to explain: 'It's because of his/her poor personality'. The explanation of cause becomes a permanent and pervasive negative label applied to your partner. Why should you ever change if you perceive yourself, despite your own best efforts, as a victim of your partner's personality problems? Surely you are a saint for putting up with your partner's poor personality. One of the values of thinking in skills terms is that it encourages partners to be specific rather than talk in vague and general terms about 'poor personality'.

You can lose much of your influence in a relationship if you say that your willingness to work for change depends upon what another does. If you explain 'S/he must change first' you allow your feelings, thoughts and communications to be dependent on your partner's actions. This may be in neither of your best interests.

You can also ascribe attitudes and intentions to your partner that give you an excuse for not working on the problems between you. For instance, you may make the following statement about your partner: 'If s/he loved me, s/he would not communicate like that.' Such a simple explanation can ignore how you interact – for instance his/her unlovable communication may be in response to yours. You conveniently overlook the influence of your own communication. Also, you may assume that loving is a black-and-white phenomenon rather than a fluctuating emotion frequently tinged with ambivalence.

Another explanation that helps justify not changing is 'S/he deliberately wants to hurt and humiliate me'. You explain to yourself that malicious intentions stimulate your partner's negative behaviour and so you justify your anger toward her or him. It is naive to deny the existence of malicious motives. However, often partners in distressed relationships exaggerate one another's negative motives and play down their own. In most instances, it is better to give the benefit of the doubt, or at least gain more evidence, rather than jump to negative explanations about one another's intentions.

Partners can use defeatist explanations that create resistances to attempting changes in how you relate. Such explanations include 'Our relationship is beyond repair', 'I can't stand the pain of trying to make things better', and 'Nothing is likely to work'.

In addition, 'tit-for-tat' explanations are a major way that partners can become stuck and foil genuine attempts to address problems. Such explanations include 'I won't make an effort unless my partner does', 'After all the effort I've made, it's my partner's turn to do the work', and 'It takes two to tango – I don't see why I should be the one to change' (Beck, 1988, p. 198). You can challenge both defeatist and 'tit-for-tat' explanations and, where appropriate, replace them with more realistic explanations.

EXPLAINING SPECIFIC RELATIONSHIP SITUATIONS

Your perceptions of situations heavily colour how you explain their causes. In the previous chapter, I described skills of reality-testing your perceptions. Many of the skills of reality-testing your explanations of cause overlap with those for perceptions. To prevent undue repetition, I mention such skills briefly.

Stopping, questioning, creating, evaluating and choosing the 'best-fit' explanation

You can examine the evidence for your explanations and see how closely they fit the facts. Where possible, start by calming yourself down and asking yourself questions like 'STOP ... THINK ... am I jumping to conclusions in how I explain?'; 'Are my explanations based on fact or inference?'; 'Where is the evidence for my explanations?'; 'Are there other ways of explaining the situation?'; 'Does my way of explaining this situation reflect any of my characteristic explaining errors?'; and 'What explanation can I choose that best fits the available facts?'

Where appropriate, create and evaluate different explanations. Following are some different explanations for common situations in relationships. As you read through the list for each situation, think how you might feel and communicate differently as a result of each explanation.

Explanations for your partner's silence at the dinner table
'S/he is angry with me.'
'S/he is not interested in how I am.'
'S/he's worried about a work problem.'

Explanations for your partner's lateness for an appointment
'S/he is caught in a traffic jam.'
'S/he has forgotten our arrangement.'
'S/he is a poor timekeeper.'

Explanations for your partner not finishing a household chore
'S/he is lazy.'
'S/he is extremely tired from overwork.'
'S/he is getting back at me.'

Explanations for your partner's offer of help
'S/he knows that I'm feeling down.'
'S/he has no confidence in my ability.'
'S/he wants something from me in return.'

Explanations for your partner not offering to help
'S/he does not care. If s/he cared s/he would know what I want without my needing to ask.'
'S/he thinks I'm capable of doing it on my own.'
'We have a prior agreement that doing this job is my responsibility.'

The likelihood is that already you possess some skills in creating and evaluating different explanations. However, some readers may use poor cause-explaining skills across a range of situations. Others of you may use good cause-explaining skills in most situations, but regress to using poor skills in situations where you feel threatened. In general, partners who feel good about themselves, their partner and their relationship are more likely to explain one another's communication and intentions kindly than those with lower self-esteem and greater relationship distress.

One of the most important ways that you can cultivate love in your relationship is to be kind and tolerant in how you explain cause in particular situations. Be careful about mind-reading your partner and ascribing negative intentions. Instead, you can politely ask your partner for explanations and then use good listening skills when she or he responds. In general, you will have a happier relationship if you can give your partner the benefit of the doubt for good intentions, unless you have genuine evidence for the contrary.

Reality-testing explanations with communication experiments

Beck provides an example of a communication experiment for Marjorie, who felt insecure in her marriage of some years' standing with Ken, who was devoted to her. Marjorie had come from an unhappy home in which her domineering and critical father had frequently attacked her mother. Marjorie, who identified with her mother, was afraid of parental history repeating itself in her own marriage. Consequently, Marjorie was always emotionally holding back and watching out for Ken's flaws, which she would then magnify. Instead of explaining either Ken's flaws or her fears of being treated like her mother as the reason for her insecurity, Beck set up the following three-month experiment with Marjorie to test the following 'if … then …' hypothesis: *'If I totally commit myself to the relationship, look for the positive instead of the negative, [then] I will feel more secure'* (Beck, 1988, p. 224). After three months of communicating on the basis of this different explanation, Marjorie discovered that she did indeed feel more secure.

You too can use communication experiments to challenge your explanations. For example, your explanation for your anger in a specific recurring situation, 'It's all my partner's' fault', can be restated along the lines of 'Even though I may not like how my partner behaves, her/his negative communication is the result of my waiting for him/her to change first'. You can then design a communication experiment in an 'If … then …' statement format. The 'if' part of the statement outlines specific verbal, vocal and bodily messages by which you will communicate differently toward your partner. The 'then' part of the statement outlines your predicted consequences. You may need to rehearse and practise communicating more positively or assertively towards your partner before conducting your experiment. Also, you may have to persist in your experiment despite initial setbacks. Your partner may take time to adjust his or her communication in relation to yours. Even if he or she does not change, you may still have used good communication skills. You can have a process success without necessarily having an outcome success. Whatever the outcome, you should have collected useful information for how to relate to your partner in future.

EXPLAINING ALTRUISM

Seek not good from without: seek it within yourselves, or you will never find it.
Epictetus

Genuinely loving relationships, despite their ups and downs, are characterized by a high degree of altruistic communication between partners. In its pure form, altruism is unselfish concern for the welfare of others. Characteristics of an altruistic mind include sensitively perceiving others' feelings and a desire to help others. Characteristics of altruistic communication include engaging in kind, affectionate, considerate and benevolent actions.

Numerous explanations exist for altruism. One is that humans are altruistic by nature. This explanation has two main versions. One is that humans instinctively possess capacities for good and evil and, over the species, neither capacity is more fundamental than the other. However, differences can exist between individuals. A more religious version of this explanation is that human nature is in the image of God. For all humans, selfish thoughts and acts represent ignorance, repression and alienation from the underlying purity of their intrinsic nature. The purpose of human life is to strive for a fundamental reconnection to this underlying godlike nature.

Much evidence exists in children, adults and animals of the presence of altruistically cooperative communication (Argyle, 1991). An important reason for altruistic communication is that it possesses a survival value for the species. Also, the idea that people are at their most human when they transcend themselves is related to the explanation that humans are naturally altruistic. Frankl sees such self-transcendence in fulfilling a meaning or encountering another person lovingly (Frankl, 1988; 1997). Arguably happiness and a sense of fulfilment comes even more from loving than being loved.

Another broad category of explanation is that humans are altruistic by nurture. It is possible to bring up humans so that they think and communicate unselfishly. Loving communication towards others can be demonstrated to children, who are then rewarded for behaving likewise. The mind is trained so that sympathetic feelings and communication towards others are influenced, if not enforced, by pride and by the prospect of a guilty conscience when others' welfare may be insufficiently attended to. Furthermore, current rewards and social pressure, for instance pressure on parents to care for their offspring, can influence humans to continue showing altruistic behaviour. With the nurture explanation for altruism, unrealistically negative thoughts about others and destructive communication result from individuals being brought up in – and possibly continuing to be exposed to – insufficiently loving environments.

A further category for explaining altruism relates to reciprocity. There are two main versions of this explanation (Gouldner, 1960). One is that reciprocity represents a utilitarian pattern of social exchange. Partners exhibit enlightened self-interest by exchanging positive thoughts and feelings towards one another. However, problems may start when it appears to either or both partners that they are doing more of the giving than the getting. The second version is that there is a moral norm or rule that directs that 'what one party receives from the other requires some return'. In relation to this rule, partners may be just as worried about doing too little of the giving as too much (Uehara, 1995).

Another explanation for altruism in relationships relates to individuals taking responsibility for their mental development. Unfortunately, most people are unwilling to take this seriously. The noted humanistic psychologist Abraham Maslow observed that 'What we call normal in psychology is really a psychopathology of the average, so undramatic and so widely spread that we don't even notice it' (Maslow, 1968, p. 16). Increasingly people can learn to take more control of their thoughts.

Whether insufficient altruism results from nature, nurture or a breakdown in reciprocity, the responsibility remains for partners, both as individuals and as couples, to develop their capacity for altruistic intentions and communication. The emphasis on striving for enlightenment in Asian psychology and religion seems relevant to any person seeking to become a more compassionate human being in her or his everyday relationships. A major purpose of my writing this book is to help you in the universally difficult struggle to assume responsibility for developing more altruistic mind and communication skills. Your achievements in attaining this objective are for the sake of your own mental wellness as well as of the wellness of others and of your relationships.

ACTIVITIES

As you see fit, do the activities either on your own, or with your partner, or with some other suitable person, such as a relationship counsellor or trainer.

Activity 8.1   Exploring errors of explanation

Part A   Common errors of explanation

To what extent do you inappropriately use the following explanations of cause in your relationships?

Never	0
Sometimes	1
Frequently	2

Your rating	Error
_____	It's my genes
_____	It's my mental illness
_____	It's my unfortunate past
_____	It's my bad luck
_____	It's my poor environment
_____	It's never environmental circumstances

Part B   Explaining your past

1. When you think about unfortunate experiences for you growing up in your family of origin, to what extent do you inappropriately use the following explanations of cause?

(a) Explanations of cause located in yourself (please specify explanations)
(b) Explanations of cause located in your parents or parent substitutes (please specify explanations)

2. Either as part of answering Question 1 above, or on their own, carry out the following reality checks:

(a) Try to remember and list many of the positive and nurturing things that your parents did for you.
(b) Examine the extent to which your behaviour as a son or daughter may have contributed to your unhappiness.

3. If necessary, create one or more new and better explanations for unfortunate experiences that happened to you in your family of origin.

4. To what extent might or do the explanations you created in Question 3 above help you to

(a) let go of past hurts;
(b) be more understanding and forgiving of your parents or parent substitutes;
(c) if appropriate, be more understanding and forgiving of yourself; and
(d) communicate better in the present with your parents or parent substitutes?

Part C   Explaining your current relationship problems

1. When you think about any problem or problems in a current close relationship, to what extent do you inappropriately use the following explanations of cause?

(a) Explanations of cause located in yourself (please specify explanations)
(b) Explanations of cause located in your partner (please specify explanations)

2. If necessary, create one or more new and better explanations for your current relationship problem(s).

3. To what extent might or do the explanations you created in Question 2 above help you to

(a) let go of past and current hurts;
(b) be more understanding and forgiving of your partner;

(c) if appropriate, be more understanding and forgiving of yourself; and

(d) communicate better with your partner?

Part D Explaining the cause of not changing

1. Using the following rating scale, to what extent do you use the following errors of explanation to sustain relationship problems?

Never	0
Sometimes	1
Frequently	2

Your rating	*Error*
_____	It's all your fault
_____	It's because of her/his poor personality
_____	S/he must change first
_____	S/he does not love me
_____	S/he deliberately wants to hurt and humiliate me
_____	Our relationship is beyond repair
_____	Nothing is likely to work
_____	I won't make an effort unless my partner does
_____	After all the effort I've made, it's my partner's turn to do the work

2. Challenge your inaccurate explanations and, where appropriate, replace them with more realistic explanations.

3. As part of this activity, you can also rate your partner's explanatory errors that may be sustaining your relationship problems.

Activity 8.2 Creating and evaluating explanations in specific situations

1. Make an activity sheet similar to that illustrated below, but with more space in the columns.

S. The relationship situation	C1 My feelings (before and during)	T1 My explanations (before and during)	T2 Different explanations I create

2. Think of a recurring relationship situation where you think one or more inappropriate explanations of cause may be contributing to inappropriate negative feelings and adversely affecting your communication. Write the situation in column S, the inappropriate feelings and physical reactions in column C1, and your faulty

se in column T1. Also in column T1, write any common errors of
ɔu consider your explanations contained.
reate at least five different explanations of cause relevant to the
each explanation of cause to assess how closely it corresponds with

4. Put a star (*) by the explanation of cause that you consider best fits the facts and assess how you might feel, physically react and communicate differently as a result of using this best-fit explanation.
5. Repeat this exercise until you consider you have developed some lasting self-helping skills at creating and evaluating different explanations of cause.

Activity 8.3 Conducting a communication experiment to reality-test an explanation

Think of a situation in your relationship with your partner in which your current explanation of cause may be unsatisfactory. Create a different explanation of cause and reality-test it by changing how you communicate. Go through the following steps.

1. Clearly state:

(a) your original explanation of cause;
(b) your different explanation of cause.

2. Based on your different explanation of cause, clearly state your hypothesis, involving changing how you communicate, in 'if ... then ...' terms.
3. Make a careful plan of how you intend to go about changing your communication, including your verbal, vocal and bodily messages (if appropriate). Rehearse and practise the skills you require to communicate effectively in the situation.
4. Implement your plan.
5. Assess the consequence of changing your communication, based on your revised explanation of cause, for yourself and for others. Have you generated new evidence to alter your original explanation of cause?
6. Clearly state, and if necessary refine, any changed explanations of cause you have created resulting from the findings of your communication experiment.
7. Practise conducting communication experiments based on changed explanations in other relationship situations where your current explanations of cause may be decreasing your chances of success and increasing your chances of failure.

9

Creating Expectations

The triumph of hope over experience.
Samuel Johnson, referring to a man who remarried immediately
after the death of a wife with whom he had been very unhappy.

You can empower yourself if you learn to create realistic expectations both inside and outside of your relationships. Imagine two married couples, the Joneses and the Smiths. The Joneses are happily married and each thinks 'We made the right decision to get married'. The Smiths are on the brink of a messy divorce and each thinks 'Why on earth did I let myself in for this disaster?' Both were confident when they got married that it would be 'till death us do part'. However, the expectations of the Joneses turned out to be far more accurate than those of the Smiths. Arguably, the Smiths would have avoided much unhappiness if, prior to getting married, either or both partners had possessed better skills of creating accurate expectations about their joint future.

You lead your life into the future. However, your future cannot consist of facts, since it has not happened. Instead, from the vantage point of the present, your future consists of a series of expectations of varying degrees of accuracy. Often these expectations are in visual images as well as words. In addition, your expectations are influenced by your self-talk, rules, perceptions and explanations.

Relationships can be viewed as processes of creating expectations. Starting out with your attempts to circulate and meet a partner, on to deciding whether or not to spend more time together, to cohabiting and/or getting engaged, married and possibly divorced, all your decisions involved expectations about various outcomes for yourself, your partner and others. Furthermore, every act of communication within a relationship – for instance, whether to talk or listen and, if talking, what to say next – entails you in creating expectations. For example, you can predict both the processes of your communication, for instance how well you will perform, and its outcomes, what the consequences of your communication will be for yourself and others. Furthermore, since relationships involve interaction, you create expectations about your partner's reactions to your communication and yours to theirs. In addition, you create expectations in your partner's mind regarding what sort of person you are both in general and in specific situations.

EXPECTATIONS ABOUT CONSEQUENCES

Like the prototype of the scientist that he is, man seeks prediction.

George Kelly

Consequential thinking

Humans seek to predict their futures so that they can influence and control them (Kelly, 1955). Consequential thinking entails creating expectations about the consequences of your communication and actions. For good or ill, you create and influence your own consequences, including your own and others' feelings, physical reactions, thoughts and communications.

Consequential thinking can be overdone. Harmful anxiety is a feeling generated by excessive preoccupation with dangerous consequences. Also, you can freeze yourself with indecision if you spend too much time trying to predict consequences. Furthermore, in daily life, you can lose all spontaneity if continually preoccupied with the consequences of your communication.

The opposite to indecision is impulsiveness in which you act without adequate consideration of consequences, for instance rushing into a new relationship on the rebound from your previous relationship or 'shooting your mouth' when conversing. As a general guideline, strike a balance between being mentally present in the here-and-now and being conscious of future consequences. Consequential thinking can be very difficult. Most of us, at one time or another, predict consequences insufficiently accurately. Nobody has 20/20 foresight!

Although you also create expectations about others' communication and the environment, here I focus mainly on creating expectations about the positive and negative consequences of your own communication. Since your expectations about the consequences of your communication and actions can either help you increase your chances of creating happiness in your relationships, by being accurate inferences, or increase your chances of unhappiness, by being insufficiently accurate, they are very important. Sometimes you make accurate inferences concerning consequences. On other occasions you may overestimate or underestimate the probability of loss or gain.

Inaccurately expecting negative consequences

Expectations about negative and positive consequences are interrelated. However, here I first treat them separately before treating them together in the section on creating better expectations.

Underestimating loss

The following examples are of people in relationships who make the mistake of underestimating the negative consequences of their communication.

Olivia, 26, married Josh, 25, after cohabiting with him for two years. Despite getting feedback from Josh that, in the six months since their marriage, he felt increasingly taken for granted, Olivia did not really listen and failed to change her pattern of communication. Olivia did not understand the true extent of Josh's resentment at her attitude. She brushed off as hysterical nonsense his comments about seeking couples counselling for their relationship. Olivia was much more dependent on Josh than she realized, both practically and emotionally. Josh's leaving her 'out of the blue' came as a huge shock to Olivia.

Since he was a teenager, Cal, now 43, thought it amusing to make suggestive comments around women whether they liked it or not. Cal also was prone to touching women whom he found attractive without their permission. Cal's crudeness and lewdness were constant sources of friction in his marriage with Maureen, 38. Eventually Cal, the manager of a supermarket firm, faced a sexual harassment charge for stroking the bottom of a young female sales assistant. In addition to Maureen's contempt for his behaviour, negative consequences for Cal included the loss of his job, the costs of litigation, and the difficulty of getting reemployed with the stigma of a sexual harassment episode in his past.

In the above examples, both Olivia and Cal found that their expectations about getting away with unsatisfactory patterns of communication were damagingly inaccurate. Each inaccurately assessed the 'downside' of their communication. Both persisted in creating expectations that failed adequately to take into account how their communication was perceived by others. Furthermore, such is the human capacity for self-deception that even now Olivia and Cal may still have limited insight into their poor mind and communication skills.

Overestimating loss

Many people overestimate loss through creating unrealistic expectations both about failing and about the negative consequences of failing. For example, often when shy people start to date they create exaggerated predictions about not being liked and about their inability to deal with any form of rejection. Furthermore such shy people may talk to themselves as though their expectations are both permanent ('It will always happen in future') and pervasive ('It will happen across many situations with many different people').

Even in well established relationships, partners can overestimate the negative consequences of communicating positively — of, for example, showing care, being a good companion, managing anger well, being assertive and solving relationship problems cooperatively. For instance, you may wrongly expect that your partner will take advantage of you if you are more conciliatory. Here is an example of a couple, Alex and Leslie, who put themselves through agony by overestimating the negative consequences of some positive behaviour.

Alex and Leslie, a couple in their mid thirties, were thinking of giving a party for their friends. However, they became extremely anxious and nearly did not invite their friends because they created the expectation that few of them would want to come. On the days leading up to the party, Alex and Leslie were very nervous and created catastrophic visual images of people not coming, of the food and drink being unsatisfactory, and about their own social unattractiveness and incompetence as hosts. Furthermore, they told themselves that they would never be able to live with the shame when this happened. They created the expectation that, if the party was unsuccessful, they might be permanently dropped by their friends. In the event, their fearful predictions were unjustified because the party went well and they were even able to enjoy it, though they both rushed about too much and were insufficiently relaxed.

You can also overestimate negative consequences in your relationship with your partner through fear of change. You may have built up a way of dealing with the world based on the assumption 'The known ways are safest and best'. Change involves the risk of moving beyond the safety of the known. As such you may see it as a bad consequence in its own right. An example of exaggerating the negative consequences of change is that of couples afraid to confront problems for fear of altering the existing equilibrium in their relationship, however unsatisfactory it might be. Fear of change may have some basis in reality. However, creating distortions that overemphasize loss can lead to passivity, inhibition and a failure to take realistic opportunities to become happier in your relationship.

Inaccurately expecting positive consequences

Overestimating gain

Overestimating good consequences frequently accompanies underestimating bad consequences. When courting, you may create unrealistic expectations about riches, romance and living happily ever after with 'Mr or Ms Right'. Overestimating gain may have disastrous consequences for your health, happiness, independence and financial security if you engage in rash actions based on these false expectations. Overestimating gain differs from underestimating loss. For instance, you may underestimate the negative effects on your health of smoking, without thinking that smoking will positively benefit your health.

A mind skills deficiency that contributes to overestimating gain is that of selectively perceiving the positive events in a relationship at the expense of a more balanced appraisal. For instance, those searching for and badly wanting a long-term partner can all too easily create rosy expectations about potential partners that ignore warning signs of eventual problems. Such warning signs include the potential partner being a flirt, needing a lot of attention, having ongoing credit problems, nursing anger towards past lovers, and still being in frequent contact with one or more exes (De Angelis, 1997).

Other areas in which you can create expectations that overestimate gain include talking too much and talking too positively about yourself; listening too much rather than revealing more of yourself; giving gratuitous advice; engaging in too many caring behaviours so that your partner becomes dependent on you; and, when feeling insecure, coming on too strong.

Underestimating gain

There are two issues in regard to underestimating gain. First, some of you may be poor at generating expectations of the potential gains from your proposed communication. You may be much better at thinking up risks than rewards. Second, even when gains are identified, you may not give them the weighting that they deserve.

Pessimists tend to underestimate good consequences. Underestimating good consequences can be risky. For instance, in your relationship with your partner you can underestimate the good consequences of developing and using such communication skills as being more assertive, showing more gratitude, and solving differences cooperatively rather than competitively. Consequently you lose out on the potential gain from communicating differently.

Darren, 38, is married to Laura, 32, and they have two young children. Darren is emotionally unexpressive and thinks that Laura should know how much he loves her. He sees himself as a kind husband and father who is willing to put the needs of his family above his own. What Darren has great difficulty in seeing is that Laura and the children need more open shows of affection and appreciation. Laura encourages him to be more demonstrative, but Darren thinks he is a good husband and father as it is and that it is soft for men to show too much emotion. Darren has wrongly created the expectation that being more openly affectionate would not make much difference to their happiness and to his own. A more accurate expectation is that Darren's relationships with Laura and his children, which are mildly satisfactory, would blossom if Darren could reach out more and show them how much he loved them both by words and by hugs.

EXPECTATIONS ABOUT PERFORMANCE

Only those who risk going too far can possibly find out how far one can go.
T.S. Eliot

In relationships, you create expectations of varying degrees of accuracy about your competence and coping ability. Such expectations influence how confident you feel and how you communicate.

Expectations about competence

Communicating competently is not simply a matter of knowing what to do. You need both to possess the necessary communication skills and also the confidence to use them. Expectations about competence differ from expectations about outcomes. Expectations of competence involve your predictions about your capability to accomplish a certain level of performance. Outcome expectations are your predictions about the likely consequences your performance will produce. A competence expectation is that you can skilfully 'chat up' a potential partner. An outcome expectation is that this person will then want to spend more time with you.

Expectations about your competence influence what activities you engage in and how you communicate. For instance, your competence expectations influence to whom you relate. If you lack confidence in your conversational ability you may avoid social situations where you might meet interesting people. Furthermore, if you attend social functions, you may be less active than if you had greater confidence about your competence at conversing. For instance, you may take solace in seeking out other wallflowers rather than risk conversing with those more socially skilled and popular.

Expectations about competence are highly relevant to the extent and quality of your engagement in life. For example, competence expectations influence how willing women are to take initiatives in asking for dates, assertively contribute to discussions on how to spend recreation time, and perform household chores and duties that in former times would have been the preserve of men. In addition, positive expectations about competence are important in helping women manage the demands of family and work. A strong sense of confidence in competence to manage dual roles not only protects women against distress, but contributes to positive well-being. On the other hand, women beset by self-doubts about their competence to manage dual roles can suffer both health problems and emotional strain (Bandura, 1995).

Frequently misjudgements of competence are damaging. However, optimism rather than total accuracy may be helpful. Probably the level of competence expectations that are most useful are those that slightly exceed what you can do at any given moment. Such expectations can encourage you to initiate feared tasks and keep going.

Expectations about your level of competence also influence how much effort to expend and how long to persist in face of setbacks and difficulties. Unlike self-doubt, strong expectations of competence strengthen your resilience when engaging in difficult tasks. In addition, expectations about your level of competence influence how you think and feel. If you judge yourself insufficiently competent in dealing with relationship demands you tend to exaggerate your personal deficiencies, become disheartened more easily and give up in face of difficulties. If you possess a strong sense of personal competence, though you may be temporarily demoralized by setbacks, you are more likely to stay task-oriented and to intensify your efforts when your performance in your relationship with your partner falls short of your goals: for instance when trying to resolve problems between you.

Expectations about coping ability

Related to your expectations about your level of competence are your expectations about your ability to cope with difficult relationship tasks and people, unexpected events, perceived physical threats and unwanted feelings. In regard to the latter, depressed people are inclined to expectations that they are helpless and life is hopeless. For example, an Australian study found suicidal behaviour related to insufficient confidence about one's ability to cope with and survive life's stresses (Steele and McLennan, 1995). Beck and Weishaar observe of depression: '*Paralysis of the will* is created by the belief that one lacks the ability to cope or control an event's outcome. Consequently, there is a reluctance to commit oneself to a goal. Suicidal wishes often reflect a desire to escape from unbearable problems' (Beck and Weishaar, 1995, p. 239). The same authors observe that anxious people not only overestimate the danger of situations, but minimize their ability to cope.

In your relationships, lack of confidence about your ability to cope with difficulties, crises and critical incidents can worsen how you handle them, if and when they occur. Difficulties can be turned into crises then disasters. Ironically, at the times when you need to be at your most realistic and rational, your emotional brain can take over and strong feelings can overcome reason (Goleman, 1995).

CREATING BETTER EXPECTATIONS

Experience is the name everybody gives to their mistakes.

Oscar Wilde

Many of the mind skills already discussed in this book influence how accurately you create expectations. For example, the self-talk you create can increase rather than decrease your anxiety, which in turn interferes with how well you create expectations. Catastrophic visual images of negative consequences or visual images of unduly positive consequences require correcting. If you possess perfectionist rules about performing specific communication tasks, you risk lowering your confidence in carrying them out. If you perceive information inaccurately, you have a less adequate information base on which to create accurate expectations. For instance, when angry, you may possess insufficient awareness of how you communicate and, hence, be disadvantaging yourself in predicting another's responses to your anger.

Seven approaches to empowering your mind by creating better expectations are:

- assessing probability better;
- tuning in to your intuition;
- increasing your expectations about performing competently;
- identifying strengths and supportive people;
- time projection;
- creating and evaluating additional potential losses or gains;
- carrying out communication experiments to test the reality of your predictions.

Assessing probability better

Assessing probability involves reviewing your assumptions concerning the likelihood of risks or rewards occurring. Wherever possible, use your skills of distinguishing fact from inference and seeing that your expectations are as closely as possible related to the available facts.

Questions that you might ask yourself in assessing probability fall into two categories. First, 'What *rational* basis do I have for creating particular expectations about events in my relationship with my partner?' You can assess the number and similarity of previous events as a basis for creating expectations about future events. Also, you can collect further information which may help this process. In addition, you can try to identify relevant factors that are not immediately apparent and anticipate the unexpected.

The second category of question is 'What *irrational* considerations might interfere with the accuracy of my expectations?' Strong emotions can bias the accuracy with which you create expectations, as can your physical condition, for instance being very tired. If you are conscious that you are agitated, you can instruct yourself to 'STOP ... THINK ... and calm down'. You may then be in a better position to create more rational expectations. In addition, your mind tricks, self-protective mental habits and characteristic explaining errors, might each interfere with your ability to predict. You can take such factors into account when assessing probability. Also, you can monitor your style of creating expectations. Do you have tendencies to overestimate or underestimate gain and loss?

Tuning in to your intuition

Your intuition is a powerful source of information within you for creating better expectations, if you allow yourself to listen to it properly. You can develop skills of listening to your 'still small voice within'. Your hunches, gut feelings, insights and 'eureka's can help you to create accurate expectations about yourself, potential partners and partners. For instance, at the start of your relationship with your current partner, you may have had a gut feeling that you should phone for your first date. You may also have had gut feelings, which at first you found difficult to explain, that certain potential partners were not suitable for you. Also, on occasions during a relationship you may intuitively feel that you are drawing closer or apart from your partner.

Where time allows, Kehoe (1996) suggests that there are two stages in getting answers from your intuition. The first stage is that of preparation in which you immerse yourself in all the available facts and information so that you give your subconscious as much material to work with as possible. The second stage is that of incubation. Having gathered relevant information you now relax and let it simmer. Your subconscious mind operates whether you are awake or asleep. You require skills of being receptive to the answers it produces. For example, at first you may only get glimpses of your hunches and gut feelings which you may then need to acknowledge more fully.

There is a difference between recognizing real signals from your subconscious and wishful thinking. You can develop intuitive maturity in which you learn through experience when to trust your judgement. Part of such intuitive maturity is learning from experience to apply reason and logic to refine the accuracy of the expectations that your intuition creates for you.

Increasing your expectations about performing competently

The most effective way to increase your confidence about specific communication tasks is to experience success in performing them. Success raises your expectations about your level of competence, whereas failure tends to lower them. Once established, enhanced expectations about your competence can become both more pervasive, by generalizing to other situations in relationships, and more permanent, with repeated successes.

Observing other people behave competently and gain rewards from doing so can also increase your expectations about your own competence. Partners can learn from observing one another's communication skills strengths. Demonstrations of competent communication transmit knowledge and teach you effective skills and strategies for managing various situations. However, the effects of observing your partner's performance tend to be weaker than succeeding yourself.

Another way to increase your beliefs about your competence is to obtain support when learning to communicate in new and better ways. Couples are in a unique position to support and encourage one another in developing communication skills. Further ways in which you can increase your expectations about your competence include visualizing yourself, or even others, competently and successfully performing relevant communication tasks.

Identifying strengths and supportive people

Your expectations about coping may reflect an inaccurate assessment of your skills at coping with particular situations. For instance, you may have been applying negative labels to your attributes. If so, try to counteract this tendency by affirming your resources. In addition, you may have underutilized the contributions of many supportive people. For example, you may have a partner whose support you can enlist more when you experience difficulty socializing, trusted advisers with whom you can discuss relationship problems, and friends and relatives who can encourage your efforts to communicate better.

If you feel discouraged about aspects of your relationship, sometimes you can increase your confidence about coping by associating with friends relatively happy with their lot rather than those perpetually complaining. Furthermore, you may feel more confident about coping if you develop self-care skills, for instance engaging in recreational activities with friends not directly involved with your relationship.

An inverse approach to increasing your confidence by obtaining support is to identify unsympathetic or counterproductive people. You are then left with various choices: getting such people to accept, if not support, your efforts; seeing less of them; or stopping seeing them altogether. If these people are partners or family members, avoiding them altogether may be difficult. Here, you can consider damage control strategies, such as spending less time with them and setting limits on their negative comments.

Time projection

Time projection, which entails imaginary mind tripping into the future, is a useful visualizing skill which can help you to create more accurate expectations (Lazarus, 1984). You can both visualize how the present might look from the vantage point of the future and also visualize looking into the future. Also, you can visually project how to deal with worst-case scenarios.

If you visualize relationship difficulties from a vantage point three, six, or twelve months 'down the track', it may be easier for you to see their true significance. This may help you to create more accurate expectations now, so that you can feel and communicate more appropriately in the present. For instance, you may be reeling from the fact that someone has broken off a relationship with you. However, if you take a mind trip six months into the future and look back on this break-up, you can get much more perspective on it. For instance, you will probably realize that, although life can be painful, this set-back is one with which you have the resources to cope. Consequently, you can adjust your expectations both about the disastrous consequences of the break-up and also about your not having sufficient resilience to cope with it.

The ability to visualize how your life might be different at some point in the future is a useful skill for creating more accurate expectations. You can attempt reality checks by mind tripping into the future. For example, lovers thinking of forging permanent commitments with people they are still getting to know can visualize how it might be to spend each hour of a representative day with that person at some stage in the future, say five years from now. You can then imagine this representative day repeated, with minor variations, day after day. You could add to this visualization by imagining how you might both look, what sort of home you might have, your circle of friends, relating to your 'in-laws', your potential partner as a parent, how he or she might react in a crisis, your future financial circumstances and so on.

Visualizing the worst possibility is another form of time projection that may help you create more accurate expectations. Ask yourself 'So what if the worst were to happen?' and then visualize it happening at some stage in the future. Then visualize what you might do to cope with your worst-case scenario. Once you actually face in your imagination having to deal with your worst fears, you may find that you have sufficient resources to cope if they were to happen in real life.

Creating and evaluating additional gains or losses

If, when creating expectations, you err more in the direction of overestimating the potential for gain and underestimating the potential for loss, you may need to develop skills of generating ideas about additional risks. However, many of you are likely to be overestimating potential risks. If so, you should develop your skills of creating and evaluating additional gains. Below is a vignette in which a counsellor helps a client, Sean, to generate additional gains, so that Sean creates more useful expectations.

Sean, aged 30, had little experience of dating women; his longest experience had lasted for three dates. In his church group, Sean was on a committee with Suzanne who had been friendly to him and whom he wondered if he should ask out. Sean questioned 'Why bother to take the risk of seeking the gain?' With his counsellor, Sean generated both the potential risks and gains of taking this initiative. He was already expert at acknowledging risks and needed to learn that 'It is in my interests to look at gains as well as risks in my decisions'. His list of potential gains for asking Suzanne out included the following:

'I might have a chance of a strong relationship.'
'I might gain more experience in developing relationships.'
'This might contribute to helping me become happier.'
'I might gain confidence and a more positive self-image.'
'I might develop my ability to express my feelings more.'
'I might give myself the opportunity of Suzanne taking some of the initiative too.'

Sean evaluated that the gains of asking Suzanne out outweighed the risks. He then acted on his revised prediction that there was a good chance that Suzanne would want to spend more time with him. Subsequently, Suzanne became Sean's first steady girlfriend.

Reality-testing expectations through communication experiments

The most conclusive way of gauging the accuracy of your expectations is, like Sean, to put them to the test. Reality-testing expectations is similar to carrying out communication experiments to test the accuracy of your perceptions (see Chapter 7) and explanations (see Chapter 8). Sometimes you can reality-test expectations by 'testing the water' before committing yourself to a major course of action.

Below are two examples of people who might benefit from reality-testing their expectations through communication experiments.

Sheila, 28, is afraid to tell her husband Jon, 37, how she would like him to make love. She expects that 'Jon'll never listen to me and I will only make matters worse'.

Amy, aged 47, feels trapped in a loveless marriage, especially now that her children have grown up and left the nest. She wants to develop a life of her own, yet creates the expectation 'I will never find the courage to get more education or to find a job'.

Reality-testing expectations may become easier if you carefully break tasks down, take small steps before larger steps, rehearse what you are going to do and, where appropriate, enlist the support of other people. Be careful to perceive the results of your communication experiments accurately. For instance, be careful not to engage in black-and-white thinking in which you mentally transform partial successes or failures into brilliant achievements or total disasters. Those of you whose unrealistic expectations are deeply embedded in your style of relating to the world might consider seeking professional counselling.

ACTIVITIES

As you see fit, do the activities either on your own, or with your partner, or with some other suitable person, such as a relationship counsellor or trainer.

Activity 9.1   Exploring expectations about consequences

1. When you create expectations about the consequences of your communication you can

- underestimate the bad consequences (loss)
- overestimate the bad consequences (loss)
- overestimate the good consequences (gain)
- underestimate the good consequences (gain).

Write down the extent to which you consider each of the above ways of predicting loss and gain and describe how you create expectations in your relationship with your partner. Where possible, give specific illustrations.

2. Select a particular skills area in your relationship with your partner where you consider you may have been creating expectations about consequences that contribute to your losing influence and effectiveness. Areas that you might choose include: being more outgoing; listening; having sex together; sharing intimacy; companionship; showing you care; managing anger; being assertive; and managing relationship problems.

Using the above fourfold classification for overestimating or underestimating loss and gain, write out how you think you have been creating inaccurate expectations in the area you selected.

What have been the consequences for you and your partner of your inaccurate expectations?

Activity 9.2 Exploring expectations about performance

1. When you create expectations about how competently you are going to communicate in your relationship with your partner, in the main are your expectations

(a) very overconfident;
(b) overconfident;
(c) neither overconfident nor underconfident;
(d) underconfident;
(e) very underconfident?

To what extent does your level of confidence interfere with how competently you perform?

2. On the scale below, please rate your confidence that, where appropriate, you can perform competently in each of the following communication skills areas.

1   Cannot do at all
2   Slightly certain I can perform competently
3   Moderately certain I can perform competently
4   Certain I can perform competently
5   Very certain I can perform competently

Rating	*Communication skills area*
_____	Being outgoing
_____	Listening well
_____	Showing and receiving caring
_____	Developing intimacy
_____	Enjoying sex
_____	Managing anger and asserting myself
_____	Managing relationship problems

For each skills area

(a) give reasons for your rating;
(b) indicate how your degree of confidence helps or hinders your level of performance;
(c) indicate how resilient and persistent you are when faced with potentially manageable difficulties and setbacks.

Activity 9.3   Creating better expectations

1. Think of a situation in your relationship with your partner in which your unrealistic expectations may be interfering with or blocking you from achieving an important goal.

2. Review the realism of your expectations in the following ways:

- assessing probability;
- tuning into my intuition;
- assessing my expectations about performing competently;
- identifying my strengths and supportive people;
- using time projection skills;
- creating and evaluating additional gains and losses.

As a result of using the above methods, do you consider you have managed to create new and better expectations? If so, state them clearly to help you remember them.

3. Design a communication experiment that tests the accuracy of your previous unrealistic expectations. If possible, carry out and evaluate your experiment and then, if appropriate, create new and better expectations in light of any additional information.

4. Repeat the above steps for other situations in your relationship with your partner in which creating unrealistic expectations may be interfering with or blocking you from creating happiness and/or avoiding unhappiness.

PART THREE
DEVELOPING YOUR
COMMUNICATION

10

Becoming More Outgoing

Gather ye rosebuds while ye may
Old Time is still a flying.
And this same flower that smiles today
To-morrow will be dying.

Robert Herrick

This third part of the book directly explores how you can create your own and others' happiness by using better mind and communication skills in seven central areas of relating skills. In each chapter, after some introductory observations, I aim to provide a 'nuts and bolts' overview of the main verbal, vocal, bodily, touch and action skills for communicating better in that chapter's area of partner skills. However, the question remains: 'If these communication skills are so simple and straightforward, why don't all partners just use them?' The world is a vale of tears, broken hearts and blighted hopes along with being a land of happiness, smiles and promising vistas. There are biological, social and cultural reasons, as well as those relating to your past, why partners do not possess better mind and communication skills. In each chapter, after focusing on communication skills, I then discuss how partners can use each of the mind skills reviewed in Part Two of the book to communicate better. You can create thoughts that support your communication instead of using your mind to trip yourself up and sabotage your own and your partner's happiness.

WHAT IS SHYNESS?

Shyness is just egotism out of its depth.

Penelope Keith

I have been told that when I was a little boy I was very outgoing, with the attitude that 'life is a hoot'. Then, partly because of receiving too many of life's hard knocks before I was tough enough to withstand them, I became very shy. However, I only partly acknowledged the extent of my shyness. I used to defend myself both inwardly and outwardly: inwardly with various self-protective habits, for instance hiding my sense of inferiority with a compensatory sense of superiority; and outwardly with various communication skills deficiencies, for example withdrawing and revealing little about myself. Feeling vulnerable and unlovable, I failed to reach out enough to others and also to allow them to reach inside the protective shell of my fragile self-esteem. Now that I have been helped, and have helped myself, to become more outgoing again, my heart goes out to those readers who suffer badly from shyness. I have been there myself and, even now, I sometimes struggle to prevent myself slipping back into my former self-protective ways.

When you are shy, you can feel, physically react, think and communicate shyly. However, some who feel and think shy are very good at covering it up: they are privately rather than publicly shy.

Words that you can associate with feeling shy include timid, anxious, insecure, bashful, lonely, confused, mistrustful, embarrassed, ashamed, afraid, tense, humiliated, and vulnerable. Physical reactions that can accompany your shy feelings include blushing, nausea, faintness, perspiring, knotted stomach, pounding heart, shaking, dry mouth, and shallow breathing.

The art of living is to be able to strike that delicate balance between detachment and involvement. In moments when you achieve that balance you are both mentally alert and emotionally present. This is much easier said than done. Shy people tend to become overinvolved with negative thoughts about both themselves and what others think of them. Examples of negative thoughts about themselves include 'I am uninteresting', 'I lack confidence', and 'I lack social skills'. Examples of negative thoughts about what others think include 'They think less of me because I am shy', 'They are very concerned about my behaviour', and 'They may reject me'. For a person who thinks shy, the world can be a dangerous place. Often, if you are shy, you possess insufficient insight into how you create your mind in ways that sabotage your happiness.

You can also communicate shyly. Illustrative verbal messages associated with shyness include staying silent or speaking only when spoken to, disclosing little about yourself, and being too ready to agree. Illustrative vocal messages include speaking softly, stammering and, sometimes, loudness masking insecurity. Illustrative bodily messages include avoiding situations, averting your gaze, smiling too much and a tight body posture. In addition, shy people can have problems in touching and being touched by others. Furthermore, you can fail to reach out to others with actions: for instance, sending cards, flowers, or gifts.

Some readers may be shy with all people in all situations. However, others of you vary in how shy you feel, physically react, think and communicate depending on whom you are with and in what situations you find yourself. There are a range of situations in which you may experience shyness. Potentially difficult situations include conversing with strangers, dating, requesting help, going to a party, situations requiring assertiveness (for example, returning something to a shop), going to a dance/disco, showing your body in either non-sexual or sexual situations, and starting to go out again after a relationship break-up.

If you are shy and wish to become more outgoing, what can you do about it? People differ in the degree to which they are extroverted or introverted. Nevertheless, there is a large learned component in how your shyness was acquired and is currently maintained. As was true in my case, if you are seriously underconfident you may need long-term counselling to help rebuild your shattered self-esteem. However, I hope that most of you are sufficiently confident to learn from this chapter which helps you understand your shyness in terms of the adequacy of your mind and communication skills.

DEVELOPING YOUR COMMUNICATION

Venus favours the bold.

Ovid

There are different stages in starting and developing relationships. Here the main focus is on helping you to make effective choices when first meeting people. This is the important time in which you make and receive first impressions. During this period you may plant the seeds for relationships to grow later. Alternatively, you may curtail opportunities either by choice or by mistake.

Putting yourself in circulation

Some people are 'stay-at-homes' and wait for the world to come to them. However, there are many things you can do to increase your chances of making contact with potential friends, lovers and partners. First, without being crass about it, you can let appropriate people in your existing social network know you are interested in making friends and, possibly, meeting eligible partners. Second, you can entertain people. Do not expect all the invitations to go one way. Your friends are more likely to help you if you are rewarding for them. Depending on your resources and entertaining preferences, you can take people out for drinks and meals, hold dinner parties, give parties or whatever it takes to show clearly that you are in circulation.

Third, do not play hard to get to know. Be prepared to accept invitations to social events and dates graciously, if this will help you achieve your objective. Often it is a good idea to give others the benefit of the doubt, rather than turn them down too quickly. Some people improve on further acquaintance – when both of you may feel more relaxed.

Fourth, you can be active about joining clubs, going on outings, and attending social events where you may meet potential friends and partners. Fifth, you can take advantage of chance encounters. If you find someone looks attractive or interesting, you can try to catch her or his eye and strike up a conversation: for instance, at a bus stop or in the supermarket. If you use good judgement, tact, and diplomacy, and do not push your luck, the risks can be minimal.

Introducing yourself

Some people are absolutely wonderful at breaking the ice. With a smile, a casual comment, a compliment, they draw others out of their shell to the point where they respond. One way to develop you skills of breaking the ice is to practise showing an interest in other people in your daily life by making brief pleasant comments or, if appropriate, striking up conversations with them. As well as at social events, such interactions may take place in restaurants, parks, and shopping centres, on public transport, and in classrooms. The idea is that through practising being friendly in low-level situations, it becomes easier for you to break the ice when more is at stake. In addition, if you are currently rather withdrawn, being friendly on a daily basis should make your life more pleasant.

Skills of introducing yourself are very important. If you are competent in meeting and greeting people, you get off to a good start. When meeting people for the first time try to communicate a sense of relaxed competence, liking and interest, absence of threat, an initial definition of yourself, and that you are a rewarding person to get to know.

Following are some central verbal, vocal and bodily communication skills for introducing yourself in a range of situations. With verbal communication, you can give a brief greeting and clearly state who you are: for example, 'Hello. I'm Jack/Sophie (and possibly add your surname).' If others have not introduced themselves already, now they will probably do so without your needing to ask their name. If somebody else is introducing you to a third party, you can say 'Hello' followed by the third party's name. Saying another person's name makes remembering it for future use easier.

With vocal communication, speak at a comfortable volume, clearly and fairly slowly so others can hear you first time. Be careful to avoid being monotonous by using emphasis in appropriate places. Also, speak with some enthusiasm and do not let your voice trail away at the end. In addition, pay attention to your bodily communication. If standing, pull your shoulders back and do not slouch. Adopt an open position to the speaker, but avoid getting too close. Hold out your hand in a relaxed way and give a moderately firm handshake. Smile and look other people in the face.

Starting conversations

Starting conversations is easier if you have developed a repertoire of appropriate opening remarks. You can then choose conversational openers appropriate to the different situations in which you find yourself. Making initial contact is usually done by way of small talk as you 'feel' each other out psychologically to see if you want the contact to continue and on what level. Safe talk is another way of describing small talk. The level of disclosure is usually low in terms of intimacy. You have yet to establish trust and mutual acceptability. However, in situations where you are unlikely to meet again, a 'strangers on the train' phenomenon can occur in which disclosures may be surprisingly intimate.

Often shy people insufficiently acknowledge that the process of starting conversations with new people involves uncertainty on both sides. You can place yourself under unnecessary pressure to be fluent. Some of you may have your favourite opening gambits that have worked well for you in the past. If so, why change? Others of you may wish to build up your repertoire. For instance, you can exchange basic information: 'What brings you here?'; 'Where do you live?' and 'What line of work are you in?' Another suggestion is to pass comments relevant to the occasion, perhaps following them up with a question: 'It's a great party. Do you agree?'; 'I've just arrived. What's happening?' You can also bring up topical events, again perhaps following them up with a question: 'I like this hot weather. Do you?' If you are nervous, sometimes it is best to admit it: for instance, 'I feel nervous because this is the first time I've been here.' Also you can encourage others' attempts to make conversation with small rewards like 'That's interesting', 'Really?', and head nods.

Your vocal communication is very important. Good speech is easy to hear and relaxed. Shy people often need to work on speaking louder. For instance, Adrian is a shy student who talks very softly so as not to draw attention to himself. Sometimes, without being fully aware, you may show your nervousness by speaking very quickly or by slurring your words. Even those without obvious impediments may need to work on the quality of your speech.

Holding conversations

Argyle (1992) lists six types of rewarding verbal utterances that are conducive to developing friendships:

- *Paying compliments*. Examples are for instance, 'I like your tie' or 'I like your dress'.
- *Engaging in 'pleasure talk'*. You stick to cheerful, pleasant topics of conversation. There are a number of obvious ways in which you can keep yourself informed about various 'pleasure' topics: reading newspapers and magazines; looking at the TV news; and keeping up to date on the latest developments in your specific areas of interest, for instance by watching your local football team or the latest movies.
- *Emphasizing agreement* with the other person.
- *Using the other person's name* and also using 'we' to signal shared activities and group membership.
- *Being helpful*, for instance with information, sympathy or practical help.
- *Using humour* to break down barriers and increase mutual enjoyment. You may need to rehearse your jokes in advance so as not to blow the punch line.

Meeting new people involves searching for common ground. This is partly to find safe talk with which to fill or structure time. In general, people find silences awkward when they do not know each other well. However, this searching for common ground is also part of the exploration of whether you later wish to become friends, lovers or marital partners. You can find out specific information, for instance a shared hobby, a mutual friend, and similarity of interests and beliefs. When asking questions, respect another's privacy by not probing too deeply. When talking about yourself, a general rule is that you should match or even go slightly beyond the intimacy level of the speaker's disclosures.

A basic conversational sequence involves three steps: speaking, switching and listening. When switching, you coordinate who has the floor by sending and receiving vocal, bodily and verbal cues (Argyle, 1992). When speakers finish they often use a prolonged gaze and stop gesturing with their hands. When not asking questions, the pitch of their voice may fall at the end of sentences. Politeness requires that listeners wait for speakers to finish sentences. When listeners wish to discourage speakers from continuing, they may avert their gaze, stop making 'uh huh' and verbal listening responses, and even raise their hands.

Often shy people possess poor skills of taking their turns. They leave others to do most of the work in bringing up topics and keeping conversations going. Also, shy people often reveal too little about themselves. Saying too little about yourself, as well as interfering with the search for common ground, can leave speakers with the feeling that they are the only ones willing to risk revealing themselves. You have allowed the giving and getting of personal information to become too one-way.

Ending conversations

All people need to develop exit skills – the skills of ending conversations tactfully. Often, shy people, and even those not so shy, have trouble ending conversations. There are numerous reasons why you may choose to end a conversation. Such reasons range from boredom, or heeding a call of nature, to having to go when you would really rather stay conversing with someone you find attractive. Breaking eye contact, starting to edge away, making your body orientation less open, and holding out your hand are all body messages that you wish to go.

How you end the conversation can have positive or negative consequences for your subsequent relationship. If you wish to meet again, you can show appreciation with words like 'I very much enjoyed talking with you', said with a smile and with sincere vocal communication. You could also reinforce your initial statement with a follow-up comment like 'I hope we meet again'. If your feelings are even more positive you might ask 'I wonder if we could get together again some time?', 'Can I have your phone number?' or 'Here is my phone number if you want to get in touch sometime'.

If your feelings are negative, your disengaging bodily communication can become more pronounced, even to the extent of holding out the palm of your hand as a stop signal. You can make closure comments like 'Well, that's about the sum of it' and 'I must be off now' said in a firm voice. Also, you avoid smiling too much. If nothing else works, just leave.

Making a date

Since an assumption of this book is that of equality between the sexes, both women and men are encouraged to take the initiative when they want to meet somebody again. Receiving messages from another that they might be interested in dating involves using your decoding skills. Even then you may get it wrong. Men especially may be too ready to read sexual messages into the friendliness of women.

Verbal communication that conveys interest in future dating includes compliments, making it clear that you have noticed the other person in the past, reflecting the other person's feelings, being helpful, and asking them questions about themselves. Vocal communication includes animated speech and variations in emphasis. Bodily communication includes eye contact, absence of arm and leg barriers, smiling and laughing, and light touching – for instance on the hand, arm or upper back.

Often asking for a date is done on the telephone. Telephone communication skills start with clearly identifying yourself: for example, 'Hello, this is Jack Smith/Sophie Jones. You may remember we met at Chloe's party.' You may then move on to a conventional ice-breaker, such as exchanging 'How are you?' You may then make further small talk.

When you decide the time has come to request a date, you may sound more positive if you speak in the first person singular, what is known as sending an 'I message'. For example, you can say 'I'd like it if we could get together sometime' or 'I was wondering whether you would like to come out with me this weekend?' If the answer is favourable, be prepared to offer specific alternatives – for example, different movies or places for coffee. Make suggestions in such a way that the other person feels safe discussing them. Also, you can ask for their suggestions. At the end it can be useful to summarize your agreement: 'Just to confirm, I'll pick you up at your flat at 8 p.m. to go for a meal and then to a disco. I look forward to seeing you then.' A misunderstanding over the first meeting is not the best way to start a relationship.

A final observation is that the other person has a perfect right to turn you down. With any luck, she or he will use tact. People can have numerous reasons for not wanting to pursue contact with you, for instance an existing relationship or just thinking you are not their type. Another person's thoughts and feelings about refusing you merit respect and you can politely end the conversation. If necessary, use appropriate self-talk to cope with your feelings about the refusal – it certainly is not the end of the world!

EMPOWERING YOUR MIND

I am afraid to tell you who I am, because, if I tell you who I am, you may not like who I am, and it's all that I have.

John Powell

Being outgoing is a state of mind at least as much as a set of communication skills. Many of you who are shy possess reasonably good communication skills in situations in which you do not feel particularly threatened. However, in socially threatening situations, most of you could improve your communication skills. In addition, you can become more outgoing by empowering your mind.

At the end of Chapter 2, I introduced the situation-thoughts-consequences (STC) framework. There, I made the point that, in specific situations (S), you heavily influence your feelings, physical reactions, and communication consequences (C) by the thoughts (T) you create in your mind. In this section, I review each of the mind skills covered in Part Two of the book with specific reference to creating more happiness for yourself and others by becoming more outgoing. I refer those of you wishing to learn more about specific mind skills back to the previous chapter or chapters focused on them.

Creating self-talk

Coping self-talk is a very useful thinking skill for managing feelings of shyness. The goals of coping self-talk are to calm your anxieties, set yourself goals, and to help you deal effectively with the task at hand. If you are shy, probably you create anxious feelings by creating anxious thoughts that are overly focused on yourself, for instance on what you will say or do next, the impression you are making, your anxiety level, your internal bodily reactions, and on your past social failures (Woody, 1996).

The following example contrasts Mick's negative self-talk with Rob's coping self-talk before going to a party. No prizes for guessing which of the two creates his own shyness and communication difficulties.

Mick's negative self-talk
'I know that I am going to find this party difficult. Everybody is looking at me. I feel unattractive. I don't want to make a mistake. I'm feeling tense and, when this happens, I know it will only get worse.'

Rob's coping self-talk
'I enjoy parties and meeting new people. Though I get a little anxious with strangers I know I can overcome this. I can use my skills of relaxing, selecting interesting-looking people, introducing myself, conversing and, if appropriate, arranging to meet people again. I'll give it my best shot.'

You can create coping self-talk before, during and after stressful social situations. Beforehand, you might say 'Calm down. Develop a plan to manage the situation.' During the situation, you might say 'Relax. Smile. Disclose as well as listen'; and afterwards, 'Each time I use my coping self-talk skills it seems to get easier.'

Another area in which you can use coping self-talk is if you are prone to potentially destructive self-doubt when starting close relationships. For example, if you had a very successful date a couple of evenings ago, but have had no further contact with your date since then, you may handle your insecurity by devaluing yourself. Later possibly you may either avoid making contact altogether or come on too strong when you do. Instead, tell yourself to calm down, realistically appraise the feedback you received (much of which may have been very positive), and either initiate contact or wait and see what happens. If you cannot trust yourself to remember the positive feedback, write it down.

Creating visual images

Many shy people who want to become more outgoing create negative visual images of how incompetent they are going to be in future social situations and how appalled others will be by their behaviour. Instead, you can focus on the processes and outcomes of competent performance. Say, like Mick and Rob, you have an upcoming social situation which you fear you will handle poorly. Before going, you can take the opportunity to rehearse in your imagination how you will communicate. Break the tasks down and focus on the skills or processes of competent performance. In addition, identify potential set-backs and develop ways of coping with them. Also, rehearse your coping self-talk skills along with your communicating skills. Furthermore, visualize some realistic outcomes of skilled performance. For example, you can imagine a specific situation in which other people enjoy your company as you converse with them.

Here is an example of using visualized rehearsal to become more outgoing in a specific situation.

> Hannah, 43, was married for 19 years to Fred, but they split up about a year ago. Hannah is just getting her confidence back after the break-up and feels very nervous about going out with men again. Last weekend, at her tennis club, Hannah had a long conversation with Alex, 46, whose own marriage ended six months ago. Alex asked her if she would like to have another chat with him sometime and said he would phone her tonight. Hannah uses her visualized rehearsal skills to imagine herself behaving competently when Alex phones, for instance both sitting and talking calmly. She also visualizes succeeding in arranging to meet Alex again. A side effect of Hannah's visualized rehearsal is that she now feels less anxious about relating to Alex.

Creating rules

Four important unrealistic or demanding rules that people create to sustain their shyness are:

Unrealistic rule 1:   'I *must* be liked and approved of by everyone I meet.'
Unrealistic rule 2:   'I *must* never reveal anything about myself that might be viewed negatively.'
Unrealistic rule 3:   'I *must* never make a mistake in social situations.'
Unrealistic rule 4:   'I *must* never have set-backs in learning to overcome my shyness.'

If you wish to become more outgoing, perhaps of all the above demanding rules the one you should challenge and replace most is unrealistic rule 1, about needing other people's approval all the time. You might ask some of the following questions to challenge this self-sabotaging rule. You can challenge the rule either in general or in relation to a particular individual whose approval you may be irrationally seeking too much of.

'What evidence exists that supports the truth of my rule?'
'What evidence exists that reveals the falseness of my rule?'
'What are the worst possible things that might happen to me if I were not to be liked and approved of by this individual?'
'What exactly can't I stand about not being liked and approved of by this individual?'

'Do I demand the same standards of being liked and gaining approval for other people as I apply to myself?'
'How exactly might not being liked and approved of by this individual make me worthless as a person?'
'What are the negative consequences to me of my demand that I must be liked and approved of by everyone I meet?'

Once you have challenged your rule about approval, restate it simply so that you can remember it easily. *Unrealistic* rule 1, 'I must be liked and approved of by everyone I meet', can be restated to become *realistic* rule 1: 'Though I might prefer to be universally approved, it is unreasonable and unnecessary to demand that this be the case. I can meet my needs for friendship and affection if I only meet some people who like me and whom I like.' The consequences of increasingly believing in your realistic rule can be greater ease in becoming more outgoing.

Following are realistic rule restatements of the second, third and fourth demanding rules cited above as common among shy people.

Realistic rule 2:   'Nobody's perfect. If I am to have honest and open relationships I need to reveal my vulnerabilities as well as my strengths.'

Realistic rule 3:   'To err is human. Though I would prefer not to make mistakes I can use them as learning experiences.'

Realistic rule 4:   'Set-backs are part of learning any new skill. They are challenges with which I can cope.'

Many shy people stay shy because of what Ellis (1988) calls low frustration tolerance. Unrealistic expectations about the learning process and smoothness of life can make you vulnerable to set-backs. Also, sometimes your level of performance may be good, but you do not get the outcomes you wish. As you work on becoming more outgoing, you can develop skills of supporting yourself and persisting through set-backs rather than giving in to them.

Creating perceptions

Some of you who really might be better off being more outgoing are too anxious to acknowledge your problem. However, more frequently, those who are shy perceive yourselves too negatively, perceive others inaccurately, and jump to conclusions unfavourable to yourselves in specific situations.

Creating more accurate perceptions of yourself and others

If your self-esteem is low you risk filtering out positive messages and magnifying negative messages from others about your social attractiveness. Many shy people inhibit themselves from becoming more outgoing because they underestimate their performance in social situations (Stopa and Clark, 1993). Also, as in the following example, you can develop skills of perceiving yourself more accurately by reducing unrealistic negative perceptions and owning realistic strengths.

Charlotte is a first-year college student just starting to date men. She is fearful about both approaching men and being approached by them. Charlotte perceives that she will have difficulty finding and keeping a boyfriend because she is neither beautiful nor rich. In addition, she perceives that she does not perform well on dates. In reality, Charlotte is pleasant-looking, with a warm personality, and excellent career prospects because she is bright and industrious. Charlotte needs to challenge and replace her negative self-perceptions with more accurate ones. Also, Charlotte will take the pressure off herself if she perceives that finding suitable boyfriends is a process rather than pinning all her hopes on finding 'Mr Right' too soon.

Shy people can also inhibit themselves from becoming more outgoing by perceiving others as more competent, witty, 'together' than they are (Alden and Wallace, 1995). For instance, De Angelis observes that a basic perception that women should carry into all their interactions with men is that, 'contrary to popular belief, men are just as sensitive as women, and need just as much love and reassurance as we do' (De Angelis, 1997, p. 30). The reverse is also true. As a protection against your own insecurities, if you are shy you can be too ready to pass hasty negative judgements about others. If so, you can challenge tendencies to be too critical too soon. In addition, you can carry out communication experiments in which you use your skills of breaking the ice and introducing yourself to gather more information about others before writing them off.

Perceiving situations more accurately

If you are shy, the way you perceive many situations is likely to sustain your discomfort. Each person carries within them some pain and insecurity. Without necessarily knowing it, you can be so influenced by your self-doubts that in specific situations you jump to unwarranted conclusions and then treat these conclusions as facts. As in the following example, often people are unaware that they may jump to conclusions rather than say to themselves 'STOP ... THINK ... what are my choices in how to view this situation?'

S	Sandy talks to Claire at a party and then circulates.
T	Claire perceives: 'Sandy does not like me.'
C	Claire feels depressed and leaves the party early.

However, Claire might have had many other perceptions at T, including the following.

'Sandy is sensible in wanting to circulate at a party.'
'Sandy liked me enough to come and talk to me.'
'I need to improve my conversational skills if I am going to hold the interest of men like Sandy.'

'There are plenty of other men at the party so why keep worrying about Sandy?'

'I quite liked Sandy but I didn't find him that fascinating.'

If, like Claire, you tend to jump to conclusions that are negative for you, you can use the stopping, questioning, creating, evaluating and choosing the 'best-fit' perception skills presented in Chapter 7.

Let's assume that Claire has some skills in choosing the most realistic perception. She went back in her mind over her contact with Sandy and assessed the evidence for her 'He does not like me' perception. On doing this Claire discovered that there were no facts to support this conclusion and that it was an inference on her part. She created alternative perceptions such as the five perceptions listed above. Claire decided that the most realistic perception was: 'I need to improve my conversational skills if I am going to hold the interest of men like Sandy.' She did not feel devalued by this perception which left her feeling still in control of her life.

Creating explanations

How you explain your shyness influences whether you either work to overcome it or stay stuck. There are a number of faulty explanations for shyness which can weaken motivation for change. These explanations are often partial truths; the error is to treat them as whole truths. Some research suggests that people who attribute their social successes and failures to controllable causes experience less shyness and anxiety than those who do not (Bruch and Pearl, 1995). Below are four common inaccurate explanations concerning shyness replaced with more realistic explanations that can help you to become more outgoing.

Faulty explanation for not being more outgoing: 'It's my genes.'
More realistic explanation: 'Though like many people I'm naturally sensitive, I've mainly learned to be shy.'

Faulty explanation for not being more outgoing: 'It's my unfortunate past.'
More realistic explanation: 'Though others undoubtedly contributed to my becoming shy, I currently sustain my shyness through some poor skills that I can work to overcome.'

Faulty explanation for not being more outgoing: 'It's up to others to draw me out.'
More realistic explanation: 'It is not up to others to make the first move to help me out of my shyness since I am responsible for making the choices in my life that work best for me.'

Faulty explanation for not being more outgoing: ' It's all my fault whenever things go wrong.'
More realistic explanation: 'I am only responsible for my own behaviour in social situations rather than needing to accept total responsibility for what happens.'

Creating expectations

In a study of depressive future thinking, mildly depressed undergraduates showed a greater belief in the likelihood of future negative events than non-depressed undergraduates (MacLeod and Cropley, 1995). Such future negative events included feeling rejected, feeling inferior, finding yourself rather irritated, people getting annoyed with you, people acting hostilely toward you, not handling problems well, letting someone down, and making an important mistake. Also, in another study, depressed undergraduates were significantly less likely to perceive the potential gains of acting in social situations and significantly more likely to assign weight to the potential risks (Pietromonaco and Rook, 1987).

If you are shy and not very outgoing, this does not necessarily mean that you are depressed. However, I have cited the above studies because many shy people have similar patterns of overestimating the risk of negative events, underestimating gain and hence being less prepared to make contact with others. Furthermore, some shy people can become very lonely and, hence, depressed. One explanation for depression is that it stems from people possessing inadequate social skills.

When counselling, I have found that I can help some people to overcome their shyness by building up their skills of creating and evaluating the gains of being more outgoing. For an example of how to do this, I refer you to the case of Sean described on p. 115. The most conclusive way of testing the accuracy of your more positive expectations is, like Sean, to put them to the test. As mentioned previously, reality-testing expectations may become easier if you carefully break tasks down, take small steps before larger steps, rehearse what you are going to do and, where appropriate, seek the support of other people.

You may have tried to overcome your shyness and become more outgoing before and been unsuccessful. Now, your expectation is negative: 'I've tried before. What's the use?' However, your past is not necessarily a guide to your future. Unnecessary pessimism may result from expectations that are permanent, 'I have my shyness problem for all time', and pervasive, 'I have my shyness problem in every situation' (Seligman, 1991). You require realistic optimism. For instance, this time you may try harder, understand your shyness better, possess improved mind and communication skills for being more outgoing, and be more skilled at enlisting the support of others. Following is a more optimistic prediction than 'I've tried before. What's the use?' that you might tell yourself.

'Though I've tried before, present circumstances are different and I understand better how I maintained my shyness. Now I can develop new and better skills to become more outgoing.'

A FINAL WORD

If you are reasonably socially confident and either starting a relationship with a prospective partner or in a relationship with a partner who is shy, you can help one another. For instance, the more socially confident person can support the shy person's attempts to think and communicate in more outgoing ways. In addition, the shy person can indicate to the less shy person what sort of help is most useful. In successful relationships, you lovingly try to bring out the best in one another.

ACTIVITIES

As you see fit, do the activities either on your own, or with your partner, or with some other suitable person, such as a relationship counsellor or trainer.

Activity 10.1   Assessing problems in being outgoing

Fill in the activity sheet below by assessing whether you have any problems concerning being outgoing in each of the dimensions listed. Give specific illustrations where possible.

Dimension	My assessment
My feelings	
My physical reactions	
My thoughts	
My verbal communication	
My vocal communication	
My bodily communication	
People with whom I'd like to be more outgoing	
Situations in which I'd like to be more outgoing	

1. To what extent do you see that any problems in being outgoing you possess are influenced by considerations relating to your biological sex and to your culture? If so, please explain.
2. Summarize how outgoing you currently perceive yourself to be. What are the consequences for yourself and for others?

Activity 10.2 Developing conversation skills

When doing these activities, you may find it useful to video-record your rehearsals to obtain feedback.

Part A: Skills of ice-breaking and introducing yourself

1. Assess how good you currently are at breaking the ice with people and making brief, casual small talk with them. These may be people you meet for the first time or people you meet more regularly in a range of daily situations. Pay attention to your vocal and bodily as well as to your verbal communication. Also, observe other people's skills at breaking the ice and making casual small talk with others.
2. Assess how good you currently are at introducing yourself. Pay attention to your vocal and bodily as well as to your verbal communication. Also, observe other people's skills at introducing themselves.
3. Specify the verbal, vocal and bodily skills of introducing yourself you want to develop.
4. Rehearse with a partner skills of introducing yourself and give one another feedback.
5. Practise your skills of breaking the ice and introducing yourself in real life, evaluate their impact, and make changes as necessary.

Part B: Skills of starting conversations

1. List comments and topics that you could use when starting conversations.
2. Take turns at demonstrating specific conversation-starting comments to a partner, including focusing on vocal and bodily messages. Provide one another with feedback.
3. Rehearse starting a conversation with a partner, focusing both on initiating topics and on responding to his/her agendas. Afterwards, hold a feedback session.

Part C: Skills of holding conversations

1. List ways that you can be rewarding during conversations.
2. Hold a conversation with a partner in which each of you takes turns in listening, switching and talking. Make sure that both of you take responsibility for keeping the conversation going.
3. Now, without interrogating each other, both of you can ask questions as you search for common ground. Remember to show that you have heard what your partner says and, if necessary, clarify what you have heard. Where appropriate, respond to a personal disclosure by your partner with a relevant personal disclosure of your own. Afterwards, hold a feedback session.

Part D: Skills of ending conversations

1. Assess how good you currently are at ending conversations. Pay attention to your vocal and bodily as well as to your verbal communication. Also, observe other people's skills at ending conversations.

2. Specify the verbal, vocal and bodily skills of ending conversations that you want to develop.
3. Rehearse with a partner your skills of ending conversations and give each other feedback.
4. Practise your skills of ice-breaking, introducing yourself, and starting, holding and ending conversations in real life, evaluate their impact, and make changes as necessary.

Activity 10.3   Developing date-making skills

1. Assess how good you currently are at making dates, either in person or on the phone.
2. Specify the date-making skills that you want to develop.
3. Rehearse your date-making skills with a partner. Role-play both face-to-face requests and telephone requests. Provide each other with feedback. You may find it useful to audio-record or video-record your rehearsals and play them back.
4. Where appropriate, practise your date-making skills in real life, evaluate their impact, and make changes as necessary.

Activity 10.4   Developing mind skills for becoming more outgoing

Address the mind skills that you identify as most important to help you to become more outgoing. Consult the text if in doubt about any of the mind skills.

Mind skill 1:   Creating self-talk

1. Think of a situation in which you might be less outgoing than you would like.
2. Identify any negative self-talk that contributes to your being less outgoing.
3. Specify a clarifying-goals statement for the situation and create two each of calming and/or cooling, coaching and affirming statements. Then, if appropriate, develop self-talk that puts together clarifying goals, calming and/or cooling, coaching and affirming statements.
4. Put your statements on reminder cards or on a cassette and rehearse them daily for as long as necessary to learn them properly.
5. Implement your self-talk in real life and assess its consequences.

Mind skill 2:   Creating visual images

1. Think of a situation in which you might be less outgoing than you would like.
2. Think of the verbal, vocal and bodily communication skills you will need to perform competently in the situation.
3. Visually rehearse yourself communicating competently in the situation, including coping with any difficulties and set-backs that occur.
4. Accompany your visual rehearsal with appropriate coping self-talk.
5. Practise your visual rehearsal plus coping self-talk skills daily for as long as you find it helpful, then practise communicating effectively in the real-life situation.

Mind skill 3:   Creating rules

1. Detect any unrealistic rules that contribute to your being less outgoing than you would like to be.
2. Use disputing and challenging skills to question the most important unrealistic rule that you detected above.
3. Restate the unrealistic rule you disputed above into a more realistic rule.
4. Put your realistic rule on to a reminder card or cassette and rehearse it daily for as long as you need to learn it properly.

Mind skill 4:   Creating perceptions

Part A: *Creating more accurate perceptions of yourself*

If you consider your being insufficiently outgoing is partly maintained by unnecessarily negative perceptions of yourself,

1. Identify your negative perceptions of yourself and of how you communicate.
2. Use questioning skills to challenge your negative perceptions.
3. Restate your negative perceptions with more realistic perceptions.
4. Put your more realistic perceptions on to a reminder card or a cassette and rehearse them daily for as long as is necessary to learn them properly.

Part B: *Creating more accurate perceptions in specific situations*

1. Detect a particular situation where you may jump to a self-devaluing conclusion.
2. Dispute your self-devaluing conclusion by creating and evaluating different perceptions of the situation.
3. If appropriate, replace your initial perception with the perception that represents the best-fit perception in relation to the facts.

Mind skill 5:   Creating explanations

1. If relevant, what do you consider to be the explanations for how you became insufficiently outgoing in the first place?
2. What do you consider to be the explanations for how your still being insufficiently outgoing is maintained?
3. Challenge any possibly inaccurate explanations that maintain your being insufficiently outgoing now and, if appropriate, either discard them or restate them more accurately.
4. Put your more realistic explanations on to a reminder card or a cassette and rehearse them daily for as long as necessary to learn them properly.

Mind skill 6:   Creating expectations

1. Think of a particular person whom you would like either to initiate contact with or to get to know better and concerning whom you have been insufficiently outgoing until now to do this.

2. Make up an activity sheet with the following headings:

Gains of being more outgoing (pluses)	Risks of being more outgoing (minuses)

3. On the activity sheet first list your current expectations of gain and risk. These are the ones which, on balance, may inhibit you from being more outgoing. Then draw a line under each list.

4. Now create as many extra expectations of gain and risk as you can and list them in the appropriate columns under your lines. Pay particular attention to creating gains.

5. Assess your revised list of gains and risks. If appropriate, set yourself goals and alter how you communicate so that you are more outgoing.

11

Listening Better

Don't walk ahead of me,
I may not follow.
Don't walk behind me,
I may not lead.
Just walk beside me,
And be my friend.

Anon

The couple that listens together, stays together. A characteristic of all successful couple relationships I know is that each partner is committed to showing their love and caring by trying to listen well. Partners create a warm and respectful emotional climate in which what each has to say is important to the other.

Being a couple involves an ongoing conversation with your partner, in which you encourage one another to share thoughts, feelings and reminiscences. You experience yourself more fully not just by disclosing, but by having your disclosures sensitively understood. Such listening takes place both on a daily basis and in times of problems and crises, where both of you may need to exercise much greater discipline to stay tuned in to your mate. Below is an example of a happily married couple who tone up their relationship each day by listening and talking to one another.

Trish and David have been married for twenty years and, because one of them is infertile, have no children. They are devoted to one another, highly committed to their relationship and to each other's happiness and personal development. Furthermore, Trish and David are best friends. Within the context of a real relationship that allows for some conflict, they very much enjoy each other's company. Both Trish and David go out to work. However, every evening before dinner they will spend at least an hour having a drink and catching up with one another by asking how their day has been and discussing their thoughts, feelings and experiences concerning their joint and separate lives. Trish and David do not just go through the motions of listening. They genuinely care about what is happening in one another's lives and are prepared to allow themselves to be influenced by it. Their conversations are intermingled with comments, looks and humour that have shared meanings that each knows the other will understand.

Four kinds of listening take place in any person to person conversation. Listening takes place between both of you and within each of you. The quality of your inner listening, or being appropriately sensitive to your own thoughts and feelings, may be vital to the quality of your outer listening. If either you or your partner listen either poorly or too much to yourselves, you listen less well to one another. Conversely, if you listen well to one another, this may help the quality of your inner listening. Following is a saying of Lao-tse that beautifully illustrates the unfolding and healing effect of outer listening on inner listening.

> It is as though he/she listened
> and such listening as his/hers enfolds us in a silence
> in which at last we begin to hear
> what we are meant to be.

DEVELOPING YOUR COMMUNICATION

The reason why we have two ears and only one mouth is that we may listen the more and talk the less.

Zeno of Citium

Active listening

A distinction exists between hearing and listening. *Hearing* involves the capacity to be aware of and to receive sounds. *Listening* involves not only receiving sounds but, as much as possible, accurately understanding their meaning. As such it entails hearing and memorizing words, being sensitive to vocal cues, observing body language, and taking into account the personal and social context of communications. However, you can listen accurately without being a rewarding listener. *Active listening*, a term popularized by Thomas Gordon in his 1970 book *Parent Effectiveness Training*, entails not only accurately understanding speakers' communications, but also showing that you have understood. As such, active listening involves both receiving and sending communication skills.

You can flexibly integrate active listening into your repertoire of communication skills, rather than use it all the time. Active listening is useful when you are trying to understand others and help others to understand themselves. However, personal relationships are two-way processes and sometimes you may gain from not using active listening or using it sparingly: for example, when you consider your partner talks too much or when you feel too tired or hassled to listen properly.

Taking your partner's perspective

A native American proverb says: 'Don't judge any person until you have walked two moons in their moccasins.' If people are to feel you receive them loud and clear, you need to develop the ability to 'walk in their moccasins', 'get inside their skins' and 'see the world through their eyes'. At the heart of active listening is a basic distinction between 'you' and 'me', between 'your view of you' and 'my view of you', and between 'your view of me' and 'my view of me'. Your view of you and my view of me are both inside or internal perspectives, whereas your view of me and my view of you are both outside or external perspectives.

The skill of listening to and understanding your partner is based on your choosing to acknowledge the separateness between 'me' and 'you' by getting inside your partner's internal perspective rather than remaining in your own external perspective. If you respond to what your partner says in ways that show accurate understanding of their perspective, you respond as if inside their internal perspective. Such responses do not mean you agree with them, rather that you acknowledge that what they say is their subjective reality. However, if you choose not to show understanding of your partner's perspective or lack the skills to understand them, you respond from your external perspective.

Following are examples of responses by listeners from their *external* perspectives.

'Don't talk to me like that.'
'Let me tell you about a similar experience I had to yours.'
'You're not still going on about that, are you?'

Following are examples of responses by listeners as if from speakers' *internal* perspectives.

'You feel betrayed by Steve.'
'You have mixed feelings about accepting the job.'
'You're frustrated that Katie does not pull her weight cleaning the flat.'

Showing that you are listening

Here I review some of the main bodily communication skills that demonstrate interest and attention (Argyle, 1992; Egan, 1998). In varying degrees, they provide nonverbal rewards for talking.

Important aspects of your *body posture* include physical openness, being relaxed and your degree of trunk lean. Physical openness means facing the speaker not only with your face but with your body. You need to be sufficiently turned towards your partner so that you can receive all their significant facial and bodily messages. A relaxed body posture, provided you do not sprawl, conveys the message that you are emotionally accessible. If you do sit in a tense and uptight fashion, your partner may either consciously consider or intuitively feel that you are too bound up with your personal agendas and unfinished business to be fully accessible to them.

Your *trunk lean* may be forwards, backwards or sideways. If you lean too far forward you look odd and your partner may consider that you invade their personal space. If you lean far back, your partner may find this distancing. A slight forward trunk lean can both encourage talkers and avoid threat, especially at the start of relationships.

A friendly relaxed *facial expression*, including a smile, initially demonstrates interest. However, as your partner talks, your facial expressions need to show that you are tuned into what they say. For instance, if your partner is serious, weeping or angry, adjust your facial expression to indicate that you observe and hear what they communicate.

When listening, *gaze* means looking in the direction of the speaker's face; eye contact means looking at the speaker's eyes. Good gaze skills indicate your interest and enable you to receive important facial messages. In addition, gaze can give you cues about when to stop listening and start responding. However, the main cues used in synchronizing conversations are verbal and vocal messages rather than bodily messages.

Good *eye contact* skills involve looking in the speaker's direction so that you allow the possibility of your eyes meeting reasonably often. Too much eye contact, including staring at your partner, threatens. Looking down or away too often may indicate that you are tense or uninterested.

The head nod is perhaps the most common *gesture* in listening – 'small ones to show continued attention, larger and repeated ones to indicate agreement' (Argyle, 1992, p. 11). Head nods are rewards for talking. On the negative side, head nods can also be powerful ways of controlling what your partner says and does not say. Then unconditional acceptance becomes conditional acceptance. Arm and hand gestures can also be used to show responsiveness to your partner. However, listeners who gesture either too little or too much with their heads and arms can discourage.

In Chapter 2 I mentioned the various *spatial zones* for different kinds of conversations. Active listening entails respecting these zones. If you move too quickly into someone else's personal space, they may both feel uncomfortable and move away.

When you date there may be high levels of *touch* as you listen to and get to know one another. Your body contact may include holding hands, a semi-embrace, and sitting close so that your legs touch. In many relationships, touch can be an effective way of showing you are closely listening and concerned for someone who is hurting and in pain. Demonstrations of concern include touching another's hands, arms, shoulders and upper back or hugging them. The intensity and duration of touch should be sufficient to establish contact and yet avoid creating discomfort. Part of being a rewarding listener includes picking up messages about the limits and desirability of your use of touch.

Both *within* your bodily communication and also *between* your bodily communication and your vocal and verbal communication, consistency increases the chances of your being perceived as genuinely listening. For instance, you may be smiling and at the same time either fidgeting or tapping your fist. Your smile may indicate interest, your foot tapping impatience, and overall your message may appear insincere.

Good vocal communication counts

The emotional atmosphere you provide when you listen can be greatly enhanced by your vocal communication. Speakers need to feel that you are responsive to their feelings. One of the main ways you can do this is by using vocal communication that neither adds nor subtracts emotional meaning and emphasis. Respond with a comfortable and easy to hear voice level. If you talk too loudly, your partner may feel dominated. If you talk too softly, not only may you be difficult to hear but you may convey weakness and underconfidence. Articulate your words clearly, since poor enunciation can interrupt the speaker's train of thought. Also, speak at a medium level of pitch, since high pitched and shrill voices can be disconcerting and harsh tones can be threatening.

Communicate with appropriate emphasis and avoid being monotonous. Allow your voice to be expressive in accurately picking up your partner's major feelings and feeling nuances. Also, you create a more relaxed atmosphere if you do not talk too fast when you respond. However, be careful not to come across as ponderous through speaking too slowly. Your use of pauses and silences can enhance your capacity to be a rewarding listener. To make it easy for speakers to tell their stories, you can pause after each utterance to see if they wish to continue. Also, good use of silences can allow your partner more psychological space to think things through before speaking and to get in touch with her or his deeper feelings.

Permission to talk and small rewards

Opening remarks, openers or permission to talk are brief statements indicating that you are prepared to listen. Such remarks can occur at any time in a relationship. The message contained in all opening remarks is 'I'm interested and prepared to listen. I'm giving you the opportunity to share what you think and feel.' A good time to use an opening remark can be when you sense something is bothering your partner and she or he requires encouragement to share it. Such an opener may be a response to your partner's bodily communication.

Examples of opening remarks include 'How are you?', 'How was your day?', 'You seem tense today', and 'What's the matter?' Sometimes you rightly sense that your date or partner wants to talk, but has difficulty doing so. In such situations follow-up remarks – for instance, 'It's pretty hard to get started' or 'Take your time' – may further help the speaker open up. Poor bodily communication can totally destroy the impact of an opening remark. For example, a husband who looks up and says 'What's on your mind dear?' and then continues reading the newspaper discourages his wife from telling him.

Small rewards are brief verbal expressions of interest designed to encourage speakers. The message they convey is 'I am with you. Please go on.' Small rewards can be used for good or ill. On the one hand they can reward your partner for helping you understand their perspective. On the other hand, they may range from crude to subtle attempts to shape what another says. Of verbal small rewards, perhaps the most frequently used, 'Uh-hum', is more vocal than verbal. Other small rewards include 'tell me more', 'go on', 'I see', 'and ...', 'so', 'really', 'then', 'yes' and 'I hear you'. Another kind of small reward is to repeat the last word someone has said:

Eleanor:	I'm feeling nervous.
Josh:	Nervous.

Reflecting feelings

Reflecting or mirroring feelings is the main skill of active listening. Reflecting feelings entails responding to speakers' music and not just to their words. It involves feeling and accurately understanding a speaker's flow of emotions and experiencing and sensitively communicating your understanding back. When you reflect feelings, you give your partner the opportunity to listen more deeply to their own feelings.

There is a risk that if you constantly reflect speakers' feelings, you can just encourage self-pity. For instance, Mark may persist in feeling sorry for himself when discussing his relationship with Maria, which is not going well. You need to use your judgement in how much and when to reflect feelings. For example, you might use reflecting feelings responses to allow Mark to express his feelings and to show that you understand them. Then, possibly, you could ask a question like 'Well, is there anything you can do to improve the situation?'

Let's start with the obvious. A good but not infallible way to discuss what another feels is to listen to their feelings words and phrases. Sometimes people ask: 'Well, what did you feel?' just after they have already been told. Sometimes feelings words are not the central message. For instance, Vanessa may say 'It's just great' that, after the break-up of a relationship, she is living on her own again, at the same time as her voice chokes, her face looks sad and the corners of her mouth are turned down. Also, sometimes people say 'I feel' when they mean 'I think'. For example, 'I feel that equality between the sexes is essential' describes a thought rather than a feeling. On the other hand, 'I feel angry about sex discrimination' describes a feeling. It is important that you distinguish between speakers' thoughts and feelings, if you wish to be skilful at picking up feelings accurately.

A simple tip for reflecting feelings is to start your responses with the personal pronoun 'you' to indicate that you are taking your partner's perspective. You can reflect feelings using feelings words like angry, anxious, sad or happy: for example, 'You feel sad ...'. Feelings phrases are colloquial expressions used to describe feelings words. For instance, 'I'm over the moon' is a feelings phrase describing the emotion of joy. The following is an example of someone using feelings words and phrases that communicate clearly what he means. Randy says to Georgia: 'I really enjoyed our date last night. It was just great. Even after so little time I feel there is something special between us. When can we meet again?' Randy's feelings words and phrases are 'really enjoyed', 'just great', 'something special between us', and 'can we meet again?'

When reflecting feelings it is cumbersome always to put 'You feel' before feelings words and phrases. Sometimes 'You're' is sufficient: for example, 'You're delighted' instead of 'You feel delighted'. Even better is to paraphrase or find different words to describe another's feelings because you can drive speakers crazy if you keep parroting them. Nevertheless, sometimes it is best to use a speaker's words, but do so sparingly. Here are a couple of basic paraphrasing examples.

Kirsty paraphrasing Nick's feelings
Nick: I feel really delighted ...
Kirsty: You're over the moon ...

> *Sam paraphrasing Barry's feelings*
> **Barry**:   I've got the blues.
> **Sam**:   You feel really down.

Try to understand the strength of the speaker's feelings. For instance, after a row, the speaker may feel 'devastated' (strong feeling), 'upset' (moderate feeling), or 'slightly upset' (weak feeling). Sometimes people use many words to describe their feelings. The words may cluster around the same theme, in which case you may choose to reflect the crux of the feeling. Alternatively, speakers may verbalize varying degrees of mixed feelings ranging from simple opposites, for instance 'happy/sad', to more complex combinations, such as 'hurt/anger/guilt'. Good reflections pick up all key elements of feelings messages, as in the following example.

> **Emily**:   It's great when Bob and I are together, but I don't want to be around him all the time.
> **Diana**:   You enjoy Bob's company, but want your own space too.

Sometimes you can assist speakers to find the right way to express their feelings. Here reflecting feelings involves helping others choose feelings words that resonate for them.

> **Andy**:   I don't know how to express my reaction to the way my father treated me ... possibly angry ... upset, no that's not quite it ... bewildered ...
> **Louise**:   Hurt, anxious, confused ... do any of these words strike a chord?

Much information about your partner's feelings comes from their vocal and bodily communication. Frequently, people's vocal and bodily communication is inconsistent with their verbal communication. Speakers may struggle to express what they truly feel in face of their conditioning about what they should feel. Also, in relationships, it takes time to develop the trust that leads to greater transparency.

If you are unclear about your partner's real or underlying feelings, you can check with them. For instance, you may make comments like 'I think I hear you saying ...' (state feelings tentatively) or 'I want to understand what you're feeling, but I'm still not altogether clear'. Another option is to reflect back the mixed message: for instance, 'On the one hand you are saying you don't mind. On the other hand, you seem tearful.' After a pause you might add 'I'm wondering if you are putting on a brave face?' A further consideration in picking up feelings is to understand whether and to what extent your partner possesses insight into their feelings: for example, being able to acknowledge to themselves that they feel angry or hurt.

Whenever you can, try to communicate back your partner's main feeling. Even though speakers may not start with their main feeling, they may feel better understood by you if you reflect their main feeling at the front of your response.

Damien:	We just argue and argue and don't seem to get anywhere. I don't know what to do. It's so frustrating. I wish I knew the answer.
Laura:	You're extremely frustrated with our constant unproductive arguments and not knowing how to improve matters.

Sometimes you can reflect your partner's feelings and the reasons they offer for them. A simple way of doing this is to make a 'You feel ... because ...' statement that mirrors their internal viewpoint. Reflecting back reasons does not mean that you make an interpretation or offer an explanation from your own perspective.

Sanjay:	I'm really delighted that I finally seem to be working with a group of people who think the same way as I do about running a company.
Dina:	You feel thrilled because you are now working with like minded colleagues.

You respond to your partner's utterances with differing degrees of tentativeness depending on how clearly they have communicated and how confident you are about receiving their messages accurately. However, all your reflections of feelings should contain an element of checking the accuracy of your understanding. Sometimes you check by slight voice inflections. On other occasions, you check by asking directly: for instance, 'Do I understand you properly?'

Interspersing active listening with questions

Questions can show your partner you are interested in what they say. Questions can also help or hinder another in managing problems. Let's take the example of Jack who has a problem at work that he wishes to discuss with his partner Becky. There are two extremes to how Becky might question Jack. Becky could use questions to take control of Jack's problem and come up with solutions for him. Alternatively, Becky could use questions to help Jack come to his own solutions. Underlying these two ways of questioning is the issue of who owns the problem, Becky or Jack. When Becky asks controlling questions for her purposes, she owns Jack's problem. However, if Becky asks questions that help Jack to cope with the problem on his terms, she allows the ownership of the problem to remain with him (Gordon, 1970). If Becky uses good questioning skills she can help Jack to explore, clarify and enlarge his own perspective.

Speakers feel interrogated if you ask a series of questions in quick succession. You can soften your questioning if you pause to see if another wants to continue responding and then reflect each response before asking another question. Following are two brief conversations between Becky and Jack about his work problem.

Becky owning the problem

Jack: I'm having difficulty getting on with my boss.

Becky: Why do you always have problems with people at work?

Jack: I have this large project to finish and he refuses to let me have more help.

Becky: Why aren't you being more assertive with him?

Jack: I've tried to talk to him, but I don't seem to make any impression.

Becky: If I were you, I'd tell him to stop making unrealistic demands and realize how hard you work.

Becky allowing Jack to own the problem

Jack: I'm having difficulty getting on with my boss.

Becky: You're worried about this conflict. What do you think is going on?

Jack: I have this large project to finish and he refuses to let me have more help.

Becky: You feel stressed because he's not backing you up. Is there anything you think you can do about it?

Jack: Last time I talked with him, I didn't explain clearly how many different angles there are to the project. Perhaps I could sit down with him and try to negotiate some limits on it.

Though these are only short excerpts, in the first one Becky dominates Jack, whereas in the second Becky uses questions to help Jack enlarge his own perspective and do his own work. Also, in the second excerpt Becky shows understanding of Jack's feelings.

Four common listening mistakes

If people are going to give you the gift of revealing themselves, they need psychological safety and space. Such safety and space is both quantitative and qualitative. A tragedy in many couple relationships is that often, unintentionally through using poor skills, partners block one another when attempting to listen. You may wish to express caring by helping your partner. However, instead you may communicate that they are not absolutely free to talk about and to be themselves. Though there are many other mistakes, following are four major ones that you can make when you listen.

The first common mistake is to keep interrupting. Here you do not allow your partner to finish what they are saying. Sometimes, in heated arguments, both partners cease listening because each is so busy trying to prove their points. Frequently, even in normal conversations, partners interrupt one another. Beck observes that interruptions can evoke many negative thoughts in partners who are cut off such as ' "*He's not listening to me*", "*She doesn't think much of what I have to say*", "*He's only interested in hearing himself talk*" ' (Beck, 1988, p. 289).

The second common mistake is to talk too much. When you monopolize the conversation, you are so busy talking about your own agendas that your partner has little chance to speak. Also, you may dominate by switching the focus of the conversation back onto yourself. If you talk too much, you have little opportunity to listen. Furthermore, you can be impervious to the effect you have on your partner as you hold forth at great length.

The third common mistake is to be too judgemental. Listening well requires you to possess an accepting attitude that respects others as separate and unique human beings. Be careful about making judgemental statements concerning your partner's thoughts, feelings and actions indicating that she or he falls short of your standards: for example, 'You shouldn't be so depressed', 'You should respect your parents', and 'You shouldn't have done that'.

The fourth common mistake is to give gratuitous advice. As illustrated in the earlier example of Becky and Jack, you can be controlling and take over the ownership of your partner's problems and life. You may barely listen to what your partner says before you come up with what she or he should be doing. Your style of responding implies 'I know what's best for you'.

EMPOWERING YOUR MIND

The more faithfully you listen to the voice within you the better you will hear what is sounding outside.

Dag Hammarskjöld

How many people do you know with whom you can share the secrets of your heart? My guess is very few indeed. Unfortunately, all too many partners' minds interfere with their listening. However, you can use your mind to guide you in listening well. Here I briefly illustrate how each of the mind skills targeted in this book can be used to support rather than sabotage creating happiness by using good listening skills.

Creating self-talk

You can create goal-clarifying self-talk that disciplines you to focus on listening: for example, 'STOP ... THINK ... I can show my love for my partner by listening well to her/him'. When you feel yourself getting emotionally aroused, for instance anxious or angry, you can create cooling and calming self-talk statements such as 'Calm down ... my anxiety is a signal that I need to listen carefully'. You can also create coaching self-talk statements for the skills of listening well: for instance, 'Let's make the effort to understand her/his perspective'. Furthermore, as shown below, you can create corrective self-talk once you realize you are prone to making common mistakes that block your listening.

Examples of corrective self-talk:

For interrupting: 'Remember to hear her/him out.'

For talking too much: 'Conversation is a two-way process. I can use my
                          skills of allowing her/him to take her/his turn to talk.'

| *For being too judgemental:* | 'When I listen, I can learn to live and let live more.' |
| *For giving too much advice:* | 'I am more helpful if I let other people own their problems.' |

Creating visual images

You can use visual images to enter into your partner's perspective. For instance, you can picture how you come across to your partner when you listen. In addition, when your partner describes past or current experiences, you can create imaginary pictures that may help you understand these experiences. Furthermore, when your partner describes fantasies to you, you can try to visually picture them too. However, be careful to remember that your visual images may contain errors. Your imagination may be heavily coloured with your own personal experiences, developmental history and current social and cultural environment (McMillan, 1997). Asking your partner to describe their experiences and visual images more graphically is one skill for guarding against your potential to distort images.

Creating rules

Since poor listening contributes so much to causing and sustaining relationship distress, a good idea is for partners to establish a relationship rule that 'We strongly prefer to listen to one another carefully, especially at times when one or both of us experiences pain in the relationship'. Already I have mentioned the common listening mistakes of being too judgemental and giving gratuitous advice. Here your rules and personal agendas may intrude on your capacity to care for and nurture the growth and happiness of your partner. For instance, if you are highly critical of your partner and express your views in rigid and dogmatic fashion, there is a good chance that you possess one or more unrealistic rules that 'drive' this unhelpful communication. If this is the case, you can detect, challenge and restate the unrealistic rules so that they become realistic rules that enhance rather than erode your ability to listen.

Creating perceptions

Humility is always in order when contemplating how good a listener you are. Without knowing it, you can easily distort your partner's experience by passing it through a filter of your own experiencing and life history. Furthermore, when anxious, your mind tricks and self-protective habits can interfere with the accuracy of your perceptions. For instance, when given feedback that differs from your picture of yourself, you may become critical and defensive. Also, you may react strongly to trigger or 'red flag' words and phrases that you perceive to be emotionally charged 'put-downs'. Furthermore, there may be certain topics and situations where your anxiety interferes with your ability to perceive your partner's communications accurately. You can use skills of testing the reality of your perceptions so that your own experiencing, defensiveness and agendas do not distort how you perceive your partner and others.

Creating explanations

Each of you needs to assume responsibility for how well you listen. Even if you consider that your partner or another person is behaving unreasonably, you still need to assume responsibility for listening to their pain, so that you may address the situation as constructively as possible. Being critical/defensive, dominant/controlling, and withdrawn/submissive are three styles of interacting that may interfere with your listening and with your own and others' happiness (Epstein, Pretzer and Fleming, 1987). Though not universally, perhaps men are more inclined to be dominant and controlling and women more inclined to be withdrawn and submissive.

If you possess any of these three styles, you need to assume more responsibility for your contribution to creating unhappiness through not listening properly. If you are critical/defensive or dominant/controlling, your outward communication shows that you do not listen properly. However, outwardly the effects of being withdrawn/submissive on your listening may be less obvious. If you allow others to interrupt, monopolize, judge and give advice, then your irritation with them may cause you inwardly to tune out from them. Here, if you are to tune in again, you can create explanations that allow you to be more assertive and set limits on their overbearing behaviour.

Creating expectations

I urge you to create realistic expectations about the consequences for creating happiness of both listening well and of not listening well. The road to relationship alienation and distress is paved with poor listening. When your partner perceives that you genuinely attempt to hear and understand them, even though you may not necessarily agree, chances are that they will become more reasonable than otherwise would have been the case.

An important skill is to avoid mindreading or responding on the basis of unnecessary expectations concerning what your partner thinks or is about to say. For example, if you rush in to finish off your partner's sentences, your responses can get their train of thought wrong. Furthermore, even when your partner corrects you, you may still erroneously think that your version is best. An important skill of creating accurate expectations of what your partner may say next is to listen carefully to what has already been said. Ways of testing the reality of your expectations about what your partner thinks or will say include either holding back and waiting for them to say it or tactfully asking them what their views are on the topic under consideration.

ACTIVITIES

As you see fit, do the activities either on your own, or with your partner, or with some other suitable person, such as a relationship counsellor or trainer.

Activity 11.1   Taking another's perspective

Part A   Identifying another's internal perspective

Part A of this exercise asks you to identify whether the listener has responded as if from the speaker's internal perspective. Some responses may seem artificial since they have been devised to make the point of the activity clear. Answers for this activity are provided at the end of the chapter. Below are some statement-response excerpts from different relationships. Three responses have been provided for each statement. Write IN or EX by each response according to whether it represents the speaker's internal viewpoint or comes from an external viewpoint.

Example

William and Sonia

William:	'I'm worried about the kids. They always seem to be out late these days and I'm beginning to feel that I scarcely know them.'
Sonia:	
EX	(a) 'If you took a bit more interest you would know them better.'
IN	(b) 'You're concerned that you're becoming distant from the kids because you see so little of them.'
EX	(c) 'You're a good dad and deserve better than this.'

Statements and responses

Joanna and Lesley

Joanna:	'My husband is overly critical of me.'
Lesley:	
_____	(a) 'Mine is too.'
_____	(b) 'Why don't you tell him he's not so great either!'
_____	(c) 'You feel unfairly attacked by your husband.'

Mohammed and Kylie

Mohammed:	'I'm finding it difficult to stay interested in my studies.'
Kylie:	
_____	(a) 'You're struggling to stay motivated to study.'
_____	(b) 'What are you going to do if you drop out?'
_____	(c) 'Your course sounds pretty boring to me.'

Part B   Practice – summarizing one another's internal perspective

Work with your partner.

1. Talking in the first person singular – 'I' messages – partner A talks for at least two minutes about what he/she considers important in a close relationship (Partner A's internal perspective). Partner B responds with small rewards and encouraging vocal and bodily communication, but does not interrupt.
2. When Partner A finishes, Partner B, talking in the second person singular – 'You' messages – summarizes the main points of what Partner A was saying. Partner A responds with small rewards and encouraging vocal and bodily communication, but does not interrupt.
3. When Partner B finishes summarizing, Partner A comments on how accurate Partner B was in understanding his/her internal perspective. Partner B can respond to this feedback.
4. Then reverse roles and repeat 1, 2 and 3 above.

Activity 11.2   Developing bodily communication skills

Part A   Assessing bodily communication

In each of the following areas, assess how good or poor your bodily communication is when you listen.

(a) posture
(b) facial expression
(c) gaze
(d) eye contact
(e) gesture
(f) proximity
(g) touch

   Once you have identified specific poor bodily communication skills when listening, set your goals for change.

Part B   Practice – using terrible and good bodily communication skills when listening

Work with your partner and hold a conversation on a topic of mutual interest.

1. First two minutes: both of you converse normally.
2. Second two minutes: remaining silent, use terrible bodily communication skills when listening as your partner talks.
3. Third two minutes: still remaining silent, use good bodily communication skills when listening as your partner talks.
4. Evaluation period: discuss what it felt like receiving and sending terrible and good bodily communication messages. Your evaluation session may be more educational and fun if you play back a video of your six-minute conversation.
5. Then reverse roles and repeat 2, 3 and 4 above.

Activity 11.3   Developing vocal communication skills

Part A   Assessing vocal communication

In each of the following areas, assess how good or poor is your vocal communication when you listen.

(a) volume
(b) articulation
(c) pitch
(d) emphasis
(e) speech rate and use of silences

   Once you have identified specific poor vocal communication skills when listening, set your goals for change.

Part B   Practice – using terrible and good vocal communication skills when listening

Work with your partner and hold a conversation on a topic of mutual interest.

1. First two minutes: both of you converse normally.
2. Second two minutes: use terrible vocal communication skills as you show your partner you are listening to what s/he says.
3. Third two minutes: use good vocal skills to show your partner you are listening to what s/he says.
4. Evaluation period: discuss what it felt like receiving and sending terrible and good vocal communication messages. Your evaluation session may be more educational and fun if you play back a cassette of your six-minute conversation.
5. Then reverse roles and repeat 2, 3 and 4 above.

Activity 11.4   Developing skills for reflecting feelings

Part A   Identifying and paraphrasing feelings words and phrases

For each of the following statements, (a) identify the words and phrases the speaker has used to describe how he or she feels; and (b) paraphrase these words and phrases to accurately reflect how the speaker feels. At the end of the chapter, possible answers are provided.

1. **Ryan to Jordan**: 'I find being without a job depressing. I'm young and want to get ahead. Right now my prospects look bleak.'

Ryan's feelings words and phrases: _____

_____

Paraphrases of feelings words and phrases: _____

2. Christine to Pat: 'I'm determined to be my own woman. It's exciting to think I could have a successful career.'

Christine's feelings words and phrases: _____

_____

Paraphrases of feelings words and phrases: _____

_____

Part B   Reflecting feelings and reasons

For each of the following statements formulate a 'You feel ... because ...' response that reflects the speaker's main feeling or feelings and states their explanation for it/ them. At the end of the chapter, possible answers are provided.

1. Maureen to Vince: 'I hate being teased. I just hate it. I'm no different from the other girls and yet they seem to enjoy ganging up on me. It makes me feel so angry and lonely.'

You feel _____

because _____

_____

2. Ian to Sally: 'I get annoyed when people don't understand my relationship with Tom. Sure we are emotionally very close, but what's wrong with that? Some people can't understand intimate friendships between guys.'

You feel _____

because _____

Part C   Practice with your partner

1. Each partner takes three-minute turns to be speaker and listener. When listening, help your speaker to talk about his/her feelings about a topic that s/he nominates by reflecting them accurately. Pay attention to vocal and bodily as well as verbal messages.

2. Again each partner takes three-minute turns to be speaker and listener. When listening, help your speaker to talk about his/her feelings about a topic that s/he nominates by reflecting them accurately. However, this time you may intersperse a few questions with your active listening.

Part D   Practice in your relationship

1. State as specifically as possible the changes you wish to make in your active listening skills in your relationship with your partner: for instance, 'Reflecting all his/her feelings more accurately not only with my words, but with my vocal and bodily communication'.
2. Plan how to implement the change(s) in your active listening skills, for instance when and in what situations.
3. Indicate the specific consequences for yourself and for your partner that you predict will follow from your improved active listening skills.
4. Implement your plan to show improved active listening skills.
5. Assess the positive and negative consequences for yourself and for your partner of using better active listening skills. Have your predictions been confirmed or negated? Has this activity taught you something about how you can strengthen your active listening skills? If so, what?

Activity 11.5   Developing mind skills for listening better

Address the mind skills that you identify as most important to helping you to improve your listening. Consult the text if in doubt about any of the mind skills.

Mind skill 1:   Creating self-talk

1. Think of a situation in which you might listen less well than you would like.
2. Identify any negative self-talk that contributes to your listening less well.
3. Specify a clarifying-goals statement for the situation and create two each of calming and/or cooling, coaching and affirming statements. Then, if appropriate, develop self-talk that puts together goals, calming and/or cooling, coaching and affirming statements.
4. Put your statements on cue cards or on a cassette and rehearse them daily for as long as you need to learn them properly.
5. Try out your self-talk in real life and assess its consequences.

Mind skill 2:   Creating visual images

1. Think of a situation in which you might listen less well than you would like.
2. Think of the verbal, vocal and bodily communication skills you require that will help you to perform competently in the situation.
3. Visually rehearse yourself communicating competently in the situation, including coping with any difficulties and set-backs that occur.
4. Accompany your visual rehearsal with appropriate coping self-talk.
5. Practise your visual rehearsal plus coping self-talk skills daily for as long as you find it helpful, then also practise communicating effectively in the real-life situation.

Mind skill 3:   Creating rules

1. Detect any unrealistic rules that contribute to your listening less well than you would

like to.

2. Use disputing and challenging skills to question the most important unrealistic rule that you detected above.

3. Restate the unrealistic rule you disputed above into a more realistic rule.

4. Put your realistic rule on to a reminder card or cassette and rehearse it daily for as long as necessary to learn it properly.

Mind skill 4:　Creating perceptions

Part A:　*Creating more accurate perceptions of yourself*

If you think that your listening less well than you would like to your partner is partly maintained by inaccurate perceptions of yourself,

1. Identify your inaccurate perceptions of yourself and of how you communicate.
2. Use questioning skills to challenge your inaccurate perceptions.
3. Restate your inaccurate perceptions with more realistic perceptions.
4. Put your more realistic perceptions on to a reminder card or a cassette and rehearse them daily for as long as you need to learn them properly.

Part B:　*Creating more accurate perceptions of your partner*

If you think that your listening less well than you would like is partly maintained by inaccurate perceptions of your partner,

1. Identify your inaccurate perceptions of her/him and of how s/he communicates.
2. Use questioning skills to challenge your inaccurate perceptions.
3. Restate your inaccurate perceptions with more realistic perceptions.
4. Put your more realistic perceptions on to a reminder card or a cassette and rehearse them daily for as long as necessary to learn them properly.

Mind skill 5:　Creating explanations

1. If relevant, what do you consider to be the explanations for how you learned to listen insufficiently well in the first place?

2. What do you consider to be the explanations for how your still listening insufficiently well is maintained?

3. Challenge any possibly inaccurate explanations that maintain your listening insufficiently well now and, if appropriate, either discard them or restate them more accurately.

4. Put your more realistic explanations on to a reminder card or a cassette and rehearse them daily for as long as necessary to learn them properly.

Mind skill 6:　Creating expectations

1. Make up an activity sheet with the following headings, then assess the risks and gains of your improving your listening skills in your relationship with your partner.

Gains of listening better (pluses)	Risks of listening better (minuses)

2. To what extent do you engage in mindreading or responding on the basis of unnecessary expectations about what your partner thinks or is about to say? If so, set yourself specific verbal, vocal and bodily communication goals to correct how you listen.

ANSWERS TO ACTIVITIES

Activity 11.1   Taking another's perspective

Part A   Identifying another's internal perspective

1. (a) EX   (b) EX   (c) IN
2. (a) IN   (b) EX   (c) EX

Activity 11.4   Developing skills for reflecting feelings

Part A   Identifying and paraphrasing feelings words and phrases

Other paraphrases than those suggested below may also be appropriate.

1. Ryan's feelings words and phrases: 'depressing', 'want to get ahead', 'bleak.'
Paraphrases of feelings words and phrases: 'a downer', 'wish to be successful', 'unpromising'.
2. Christine's feelings words and phrases: 'determined', 'exciting', 'successful'.
Paraphrases of feelings words and phrases: 'resolved', 'thrilling', 'good.'

Part B   Reflecting feelings and reasons

Other responses than those suggested below may also be appropriate.

1. 'You feel mad and isolated because you loathe being treated and picked on as though you're different.'
2. 'You're angry because people think your feelings for Tom are gay.'

12

Showing You Care

Love seeketh not itself to please,
Nor for itself hath any care,
But for another gives its ease,
And builds a Heaven in Hell's despair.

William Blake

Showing you care is a fundamental way partners can create happiness in relationships. Humans are capable of reaching for the stars. Humankind is defined not just by its weaknesses and frailties, but by its better qualities and the heights it can attain. Already, in couple relationships, many of you transcend yourselves by cherishing the security, happiness and unfolding of potential of your partners. Furthermore, most parents make huge sacrifices for their children. Selflessly creating happiness for another creates happiness in givers too. Caring can be generous and benevolent rather than selfish and possessive. At its best, showing you care represents what the late Martin Luther King called 'strength to love' (King, 1963) rather than compensating for inner weakness and insufficient self-love.

DEFINING CARING

With dictionary definitions, the verb 'care' consists of two interrelated components: caring for and taking care of. Caring for someone represents the feeling component of caring. If you care for someone, you love or like them and feel concern for and interest in them. Taking care of someone in some way, however large or small, represents the communication component of caring. In various ways, you attend to their welfare, look after their interests, and provide for them. Caring for another also involves consideration: being thoughtful for others and having regard for their feelings. Consequently, caring can encompass not just positive communication, but avoiding negative communication. For example, when receiving care from your partner, you can use good communication skills and avoid using poor skills.

Appropriate self-care, as contrasted with selfishness, is an important dimension of caring. Nevertheless, caring is most commonly viewed in terms of providing care for another rather than for yourself. Just as caring for yourself should be based on respecting your own uniqueness and potential, so caring for your partner involves respecting their difference and potential. A possible distinction exists between ordinary caring and tough caring. In ordinary caring, you send caring messages with the probability that they will please your partner. In tough caring, you send messages that may challenge your partner's view of him/herself. You care for your partner so much that you are not willing to let them be less than they could be. Hopefully, such caring leads to constructive dialogue and possibly change.

The way two people care in a relationship can be viewed as a pattern of communication or system in which both partners' experiences of giving and receiving care influence one another. In any close relationship, there is a tension between autonomy and dependence. The ideal relationship mixes interdependence with autonomy. Here both partners exist as separate selves and there is a fluid state between being individuals and sharing dependencies.

Prominent among the less stable communication patterns for care is one reflecting a difference between each partner's wishes for emotional closeness and emotional distance. Such patterns can take various forms. For instance, the more one partner exhibits caring behaviour, the more the other may withdraw. Alternatively, the more one partner demands to receive care, the more the other partner may avoid providing it. A third variation is for one partner both to exhibit much caring behaviour and demand care in return, only to find little, if any, care coming back.

Another potentially unstable caring pattern in today's world is that between the care-taking woman and the cared-for man. A variation of this pattern is that between the protecting man and the dependent woman. The rise of feminism challenges such patterns. The repercussions of the changing power relationships between the sexes are still being worked out. Not only are men increasingly performing traditionally female caring activities, such as cooking, but women are increasingly performing traditionally male caring activities, such as earning income.

DEVELOPING YOUR COMMUNICATION

Good, the more
Communicated, more abundant grows.

John Milton

Happy couples regularly 'tone up' their relationship through exchanging caring communications. Paraphrasing Shakespeare's statement 'They do not love that do not show their love', they do not care that do not show their care. If you think caring thoughts but do not show them, as far as your partner is concerned you may as well forget them. Prominent themes in caring communications include: your partner's happiness is important to you, you are willing to support them emotionally, you are concerned for their welfare, you desire to give happiness and to avoid hurt, and you respect your partner's difference from you and their unique potential for growth.

A number of analogies highlight the role in relationships of communicating that you care. A construction or engineering analogy is that continuing to show you care reinforces a relationship's foundations. Litvinoff (1992) uses a banking analogy. Loving or caring communications when things are going well in relationships are bank account 'deposits' that partners can draw on in difficult times. Even during bad times, partners may make loving gestures that build up the credit side of their account. A legal analogy is that partners fulfil their contractual duty of care to each other by showing caring. Negligence in showing you care breaches the relationship contract and can lead to serious repercussions, including divorce.

Following are some communication skills for caring. Here I mainly emphasize sending positive caring messages. However, you can also show caring in how you deal with anger and how you solve problems in your relationship. Such skills are covered in later chapters.

Showing care to your partner

Verbal communications that show you care include statements such as 'I love you', 'I care for you', 'Your happiness is important to me', and 'I want to help you'. Vocal communication messages are extremely important in expressing caring. Frequently vocal messages for caring express tenderness: for instance, a soft yet easily audible voice, clear articulation, an emphasis on words like care and love, and a comfortable speech rate. Your voice conveys kindness and concern rather than harshness and disinterest.

Bodily communication can support or negate caring words. Your gaze, eye contact, body orientation and facial expression can each demonstrate your interest and concern for your partner. Similarly, when your partner shares a problem, be careful to use good attending and listening skills. Touch or physical affection can be a wonderful way to show you care. As with all touch messages, you are in your partner's close intimate zone and consequently require sensitivity about their willingness to be touched.

Your actions can speak louder than your words regarding how much you really care. In the following review of caring communications, I mention numerous ways of showing you care through your actions.

Some caring communications

In the mid 1990s, I asked 41 Relate (marriage guidance) counsellors in Britain and 15 Australian postgraduate counselling psychology students to list ways that they show that they care to their partner (or a hypothetical partner) and how their partner (or a hypothetical partner) shows that they care to them. Below are some suggestions based on their responses.

Displays of physical affection are important. Illustrative ways of showing you care include cuddles, loving glances, kisses, holding and being held, massaging shoulders, holding hands, and being physically close.

You can show you care by giving positive verbal feedback. In addition to obvious messages, such as 'I love you', other kinds of positive feedback include paying compliments — for instance 'You look nice', expressing appreciation for your partner's actions, offering congratulations for achievements, and leaving notes with caring messages.

When you care for your partner you show interest in and concern for them. Questions you can ask include 'How has your day been?', 'How are you feeling?', 'How did a particular event (specify) go?' Also you can show concern over your partner's health and the safety of their travel. Furthermore, you can phone both when you are away and before special or difficult events in your partner's life.

Offering support and understanding is another way to show you care. Here your listening skills are important for understanding your partner's worries and stresses, responding to what is said and left unsaid, offering emotional support and genuine reassurance, and being emotionally present in crises and at growth points. In addition you can show understanding by laughing or crying with your partner or, if necessary, challenging them.

Giving gifts is another way to show you care. You can give presents and cards on birthdays, anniversaries and other special days. You can bring flowers and small special presents; you can arrange little surprises and treats. In addition, you can take and share photographs of 'our' memories of good times you and your partner have shared together.

Offering practical help at home is a good way to show you care. Such help can include making cuppas – for instance, morning tea; cooking meals, including special meals; bringing breakfast in bed; washing up; and making the home cosy. In addition, you can do your share of caring for children and of looking after one another when ill. Other practical ways of showing caring include paying bills, checking you are properly insured and opening the garage door.

Couples can show they care for one another by spending time together. You can set aside regular times for conversation and support. You can share everyday tasks. Also, you can share leisure time: for instance, walking the dog, doing the crossword together, going out on special occasions, and arranging, booking and enjoying holidays. To spend quality time together, partners may also need to show caring by coordinating time schedules with one another.

Respecting your partner as different from you is fundamental to showing that you care for them. You can free your partner to be themselves and not your image of them. You can accept your partner emotionally and physically. Also, you can take care to respect one another's need for psychological and physical space. Furthermore, you can encourage your partner when developing her or his personal interests, talents and potentials.

Checking what care your partner prefers

You can ask your partner how they like to be cared for, what you do that they like or dislike, or what you are not doing that they would like. Such checking does not oblige you to show you care in ways that you do not want. However, it enables you to know more about your partner's preferences and wishes and so avoid unnecessary mistakes.

During and after specific caring communications, you can assist your partner to feel safe about providing feedback concerning the direction, quantity and quality of your care. If you genuinely want to please your partner, you do not want her or him putting on false shows of appreciation. You can use your skills of listening and showing understanding to establish an emotional climate conducive to honest feedback.

Receiving care from your partner

Make it easy for your partner to care for you appropriately. For example, your partner is more likely to continue to give care to you if you show gratitude. If you fail to appreciate openly your partner's caring behaviours, you lower the chances of these behaviours being repeated. Without necessarily meaning it, you may give your partner the impression you take for granted what they do. Thus your neutral message of not openly appreciating their care can easily turn into a negative message.

You can show gratitude by verbal, vocal, bodily, touch and action communications. Choose the ways of communicating appropriate for each situation. Simple verbal messages are 'Thank-you' and 'I appreciate that'. Your vocal communication can emphasize words like 'thank' and 'appreciate'. Your bodily communication might include a smile and good eye contact. Your touch communication could be a hug or a kiss. Your action-taking communication could be doing a favour for the care-giver in return.

Expressing appreciation is a form of feedback. However, even when pleased with how your partner cares, you may still wish to let them know how to please you more. Where possible, accentuate the positive rather than seeming negative and critical. You can acknowledge the pleasure your partner gives you and emphasize that you would like even more of something that you already like.

If you are dissatisfied with some aspect of your partner's care, for instance with a present that you do not like, you can provide some tactful, but honest feedback. Providing such feedback can be difficult since you do not wish to cause hurt or offence. Nevertheless, in the interests of the integrity of your relationship, sometimes you may be wise to do so. You can send an 'I' message that acknowledges your partner's effort, but then gently lets them know how you feel. If your partner persists in caring for you in inappropriate ways, use stronger verbal, vocal and bodily communication.

You can also create happiness by developing good skills at requesting care. Some partners get angry when they do not receive the care they want. It is preferable to assume responsibility for obtaining it. So long as you are not too demanding, one way to get the care you want is to ask for it. Partners in successful relationships want to please one another and to see one another as caring persons. Requests for care symbolize a commitment to the continuing health of the relationship. On the other hand, failure to request care can create undercurrents of dissatisfaction that may later surface as open hostility. Below is a brief vignette, showing good skills in communicating a request to receive care.

Jen and Walt have lived together for five years and been married for one year. If necessary, Jen lets Walt know that she wants to receive care by saying 'I really need you to care for me at this moment.' Also sometimes, without being at all demanding, Jen gently tells Walt what she would like him to do and say.

Caring for yourself

You can also create happiness by developing skills at caring for yourself so that you possess the energy and motivation to keep caring for your partner. Self-care can be distinguished from selfishness. Caring for yourself means that you prize yourself sufficiently to consider that you are worthy of care. You are a person in your own right and not just an extension of another, for instance someone else's partner or parent. If you allow yourself to become a caring doormat, for instance 'superwoman' or 'superman', your resentment is likely to interfere with your ability to care.

Instead of assuming that your partner will know your self-care needs, you can request physical and psychological space. In addition, you can either negotiate or, if necessary, unilaterally set limits on the amount of care you offer your partner. Often you require assertion skills to do this, the topic of a later chapter. Also, you can help your partner to care for themselves. Without intending it, you may be encouraging dependency in your partner. For instance, Hilary is very protective about 'her' kitchen and so makes it harder for her partner, Jason, to develop his cooking skills. You may need to help your partner to develop skills of taking care of themselves: for instance, doing the laundry, ironing, cooking, gardening, car maintenance, and looking after finances. Also, you may require better skills at sharing tasks together with your partner rather than doing them on your own.

Caring for yourself may entail learning to be more self-reliant. You may require better skills of coping with your own problems. Some partners easily slip into the trap of dependency. Before seeking help from your partner, think whether you might be better off looking after yourself.

A good way to care for yourself is to identify and engage in pleasant activities. Since a major purpose of self-care is to nourish yourself, try to discover ways of doing this. Below is a vignette that illustrates caring for yourself.

> A month ago Sara's husband Dan was made redundant after eighteen years of working for the same accounting firm. Sara wants to offer emotional and practical support to her husband and three children. However, increasingly Sara becomes aware that she also needs to care for herself. To achieve this end, Sara lists some things she can do to nourish herself, including going for walks on her own with the dog, eating properly, keeping in touch with nurturing friends, taking baths, and playing the clarinet. Sara then follows through by implementing the items on her list.

EMPOWERING YOUR MIND

No act of kindness, however small, is ever wasted.

Aesop

Communicating in caring ways is easier if you can also think in caring ways. How can you create your mind to release the kind and loving part of your human nature? Benevolence, compassion, affection, goodness and altruism are all attributes for which you can train your mind so that you can create more happiness in your own and your partner's lives. You can empower your mind so that you develop a give-give rather than a take-take mentality. Such a mentality does not preclude your gratefully receiving the gifts of your partner's caring. Nor does it preclude looking after your own needs and preferences.

Creating self-talk

You can influence how you care by how you talk to yourself. Many happy people start their day by counting their blessings. If religiously inclined, you may give thanks to God, or to a spiritual mentor, for the blessings you receive on this earth, and ask for strength to be a loving and compassionate person in the coming day. Either at the start of the day or in specific situations, questions to strengthen your altruistic intentions include 'How can I help create happiness for my partner?', 'How can I help relieve my partner's suffering?', and 'How can I show my partner that I care?'

The Buddhists have the idea of making merit through giving. You are the gainer through giving. Your generous actions allow you to become a better person in this life and possibly benefit you in future lives. Another question you can ask yourself is 'How can I become a better and more spiritually developed human being through giving?'

Sometimes providing care is associated with anxiety about whether it will be accepted or rejected. In fact, partners can inhibit caring gestures for fear of rejection. Calming and coaching self-statements are two important ways to deal with anxiety about the consequences of caring. You can calm yourself down and then coach yourself in how to communicate caring skilfully: for example, 'Rather than give my present as soon as I can, I will wait to give my present until s/he is relaxed'. Receiving care, especially when unwanted, can also trigger anxiety. Again, you can use both calming and coaching self-statements to help you cope with firmness and consideration in current and future situations.

If you genuinely feel happier when you give your partner pleasure, you can strengthen your motivation by reminding yourself that this is the case: for example, 'Showing I care enriches us both'. On other occasions, you may have to use self-talk to calm your anger and cleanse your mind before you can communicate to your partner in a caring way.

If you think that you can care better for your partner if you care better for yourself, possible statements that you might make include 'I am worthy of care', 'I am more effective when I care for myself as well as for my partner', and 'I can develop a plan to care for myself'.

Creating visual images

You can use visual images both to overcome inhibitions to showing you care and to assist you in how to care more effectively for your partner. In Chapter 5 I mentioned how you can use cooling visual imagery to think of your partner more kindly: for instance, creating images of good times past, of your partner's strengths, and of good things happening to your partner even though you feel hurt.

A method of using visual imagery to care more effectively is to imagine what might make your partner happy. Then, you can use visualizing to plan and rehearse the verbal, vocal, bodily touch and action communications of competently showing that you care. In addition, if you are prone to unnecessarily negative images about the consequences of caring, you can generate more positive images to replace the negative ones. Overall, you can try to create and implement a picture of yourself as a caring person. One way to do this is to observe and replicate the communications of caring people that you admire, including your partner.

If necessary, you can use visualizing skills to help you care for yourself more effectively. You can draw up a balance sheet in which you imagine both positive and negative consequences of caring for yourself. In addition, you may be more likely to engage in self-care activities if you imagine the pleasures of participating in them.

Creating rules

You may possess unrealistic rules that restrict your freedom of choice and engender negative emotions. Your unrealistic rules can have some truth in them, but they are insufficiently flexible. For instance, you and your partner may possess relationship rules based on rigid notions of reciprocity like 'We must give and take the same amount of care', or 'We must have the same needs for giving care' and 'We must have the same needs for receiving care'.

As an individual you may have unrealistic rules that interfere with your capacity to genuinely care for your partner. Illustrative rules include 'I must always look after number one first', 'I must always get it right', 'I must always be appreciated', and 'I must not ask my partner what s/he wants'. Also, you may possess rules reflecting traditional sex roles, such as 'Women must always look after men', and 'Men must always provide for women'. In addition, some rules can interfere with your capacity to receive the kind of care you would like: for instance, 'I must never refuse care from my partner', 'My partner must know what I want', and 'I must never ask for care from my partner.'

What can you do about unrealistic rules? In Chapter 6 I provided the example of Martyr Toni/Tony who allowed herself/himself to be used as a doormat because of the rule 'I must always take responsibility for keeping the home tidy'. There I provided questions that allowed Toni/Tony to challenge her/his rule, followed by a statement of a more realistic rule that s/he could remember easily. You too can identify, challenge and restate any rule interfering with your capacity to give and receive care in your relationship.

Creating perceptions

Perceiving yourself accurately

Inaccurate perceptions about your own needs and responsibilities to your partner can interfere with your taking adequate care of yourself. On the other hand, you may possess a self-serving bias in which you perceive yourself as better at giving and receiving care than you really are.

> Lily, age 24, fails to see how she controls with caring her partner, Alicia, age 25. Alicia increasingly feels suffocated with Lily's demands for approval for everything she does: for example, she expects praise whenever she cooks. Lily is insufficiently sensitive to Alicia's messages that she is too possessive and demanding.

Both as a giver and receiver of care, you can place unnecessarily negative labels on yourself. Negative labels you can attach to providing care for your partner include 'weak', 'unmanly', and 'sucking up'. Negative labels for receiving care from your partner include 'vulnerable', 'dependent', and 'unable to stand on my own two feet'.

Perceiving your partner accurately

People whose anxieties motivate them to be very controlling insufficiently perceive the separateness and uniqueness of their partners. You may fail to see the kind of care your partner wants. In some instances, partners do not communicate their preferences clearly. In other instances, clear messages about preferences remain unheeded. If you received little care when growing up you may require counselling to heal your hurt and deprivation before you can truly perceive your partner's preferences for care independent of your own.

You can strengthen your altruistic feelings and perceptions by consciously acknowledging that part of your mission in life is to become a loving and compassionate human being. In addition, you can develop your capacity for taking your partner's perspective. Sometimes this requires a big effort to switch off your self-preoccupation and switch into imagining how life is for them – or you can even ask them. Also, you can feel more kindly towards your partner if you perceive them as similar to you, with the same human wants and fears, rather than as different. On some occasions, perceiving your partner more compassionately may require you either to nurture yourself more or to manage feelings – like anger and self-pity – that block caring.

Other ways to help you to look at your partner through kinder eyes include mixing with compassionate people, consciously making an effort to look at your partner's strengths, acknowledging your feelings of gratitude for what your partner has done and still does for you, and practising being a more loving person by doing good deeds on a daily basis.

Creating explanations

You can inaccurately explain your reasons for caring both to yourself and to your partner. If you are honest to yourself in explaining your reasons for providing care, you are better placed to guard against negative reasons, for instance possessiveness, which might adversely affect your relationship. Be careful to avoid explanations that make you out to be a saint or a martyr.

You can inaccurately explain your reasons for showing insufficient care to your partner. As relationships deteriorate, partners tend to become prone to Beck's 'negative cognitive set' (Beck, 1988). Each of you explains that you are victims of one another's persecution. Together you both become less willing to assess the evidence for your 'If it weren't for you ...' explanations. Also, you may fail to give one another the benefit of the doubt for having either positive caring intentions or intentions that mix both good and ill will.

Be careful about how you explain your partner's not caring for you sufficiently. Some of the explanations may lie in your own communication: for instance, insufficiently showing you care, insufficiently showing appreciation for your partner's attempts to care, and not being prepared to ask tactfully for the care you want.

You can also explain your partner's reasons for caring too positively. For example, you may protect yourself against the implications of your partner's lack of care by explaining that 'underneath he/she really does care for me'. It may be preferable to raise the issue with your partner to find out whether or not what is underneath is the same lack of caring you perceive on the surface.

Partners can inaccurately explain the communication pattern between you in the area of care. For example, you and your partner may engage in an emotional closeness-withdrawal pattern in which as one partner demands care, the other partner backs off from caring. If so, probably each partner possesses insufficient insight into how you sustain one another's communication by your own.

If you are poor at caring for yourself you may explain this by your upbringing, religious teaching, biological sex, or your partner's lack of concern for you. Something that is often missing is an adequate acknowledgement of your own contribution to sustaining your insufficient self-care. Your upbringing, religious teaching, biological sex and your partner's behaviours may each influence you. However, by assuming the responsibility for caring for yourself, you reclaim the power to improve your situation.

Creating expectations

You may be poor at creating accurate expectations about the consequences of how you give and receive care. There are numerous risks and gains attached to caring for your partner. You may make mistakes because you try to read your partner's mind, instead of inquiring about the kind of care wanted. You may unnecessarily inhibit showing you care to your partner because of unrealistic expectations about rejection or getting it wrong. Also, you may fail to see the gains to yourself, your partner and your relationship if you show care in appropriate ways. In addition, you may fail to predict the negative consequences of not maintaining caring communications: for instance, your partner may feel hostile and think you take her or him for granted.

You may also require more realism when you create expectations about the consequences of how you receive care from your partner. For instance, if you are poor at showing appreciation, the likely consequences are that your partner will be less ready to care for you. However, if you show appreciation when you do not mean it, you may continue to receive the care you do not want.

Patterns of caring between partners have predictable expectations built into them. However, partners can inaccurately expect their patterns of caring to be more durable than in reality. For instance, men who expect their wives to be the predominant home-makers and women who expect their husbands to be the predominant bread-winners are each vulnerable if their partner wants to modify or change roles.

ACTIVITIES

As you see fit, do the activities either on your own, or with your partner, or with some other suitable person, such as a relationship counsellor or trainer.

Activity 12.1   Developing communication skills for showing care

Part A   Assessing skills of showing care

For each of the following areas, identify what are your good skills and what are your poor skills for showing your partner that you care.

Showing physical affection
my good skills
my poor skills
Giving positive verbal feedback
my good skills
my poor skills
Showing interest and concern
my good skills
my poor skills
Offering support and understanding
my good skills
my poor skills
Giving gifts
my good skills
my poor skills
Practical help at home
my good skills
my poor skills
Spending time together
my good skills
my poor skills
Respecting another's difference
my good skills
my poor skills
Checking what care your partner prefers
my good skills
my poor skills

Part B Improving skills of showing care

1. Summarize your main good and poor communication skills for showing your partner that you care.

2. If appropriate, identify one or more of your poor communication skills and develop a plan to improve how you show your partner that you care. In your plan, specify

(a) your goals, including a time frame,
(b) the steps you intend taking to attain each of your goals, and
(c) how you will monitor your progress.

Activity 12.2 Developing communication skills for receiving care

Part A Assessing skills of receiving care

For each of the following areas, identify what are your good skills and what are your poor skills at receiving care from your partner.

Expressing appreciation
my good skills
my poor skills
Providing honest feedback
my good skills
my poor skills
Requesting care
my good skills
my poor skills

Part B Improving skills of receiving care

1. Summarize your main good and poor communication skills for receiving care from your partner.
2. If appropriate, identify one or more of your poor communication skills and develop a plan to improve how you receive care from your partner. In your plan, specify

(a) your goals, including a time frame,
(b) the steps you intend taking to attain each of your goals, and
(c) how you will monitor your progress.

Activity 12.3   Developing mind skills for showing care

Address the mind skills deficiencies that you identify as most important to helping you to show that you care. Consult the text if in doubt about any of the mind skills.

Mind skill 1:   Creating self-talk

1. Think of a situation in which you might show care to your partner less well than you would like.
2. Identify any negative self-talk that contributes to your showing care less well.
3. Specify a clarifying-goals statement for the situation and create two each of calming and/or cooling, coaching and affirming statements. Then, if appropriate, develop self-talk that puts together goals, calming and/or cooling, coaching and affirming statements.
4. Put your statements on cue cards or on a cassette and rehearse them daily for as long as necessary to learn them properly.
5. Try out your self-talk in real life and assess its consequences.

Mind skill 2:   Creating visual images

1. Think of a situation in which you might show your partner care less well than you would like.
2. Think of the verbal, vocal, bodily, touch and taking action communication skills you require that will help you to show care competently in the situation.
3. Visually rehearse yourself communicating competently in the situation, including coping with any difficulties and set-backs that occur.
4. Accompany your visual rehearsal with appropriate coping self-talk.
5. Practise your visual rehearsal plus coping self-talk skills daily for as long as you find it helpful, then practise communicating competently in the real-life situation.

Mind skill 3:   Creating rules

1. Detect any unrealistic rules that contribute to your showing care to your partner less well than you would like.
2. Use disputing and challenging skills to question the most important unrealistic rule that you detected above.
3. Restate the unrealistic rule you disputed above into a more realistic rule.
4. Put your realistic rule on to a reminder card or cassette and rehearse it daily for as long as necessary to learn it properly.

Mind skill 4:   Creating perceptions

Part A: Creating more accurate perceptions of yourself

If you think that in your relationship with your partner your showing care less well than you would like to is partly because of inaccurate perceptions of yourself,

1. Identify your inaccurate perceptions of yourself and of how you communicate.
2. Use questioning skills to challenge your inaccurate perceptions.
3. Replace your inaccurate perceptions with more realistic perceptions.

4. Put your more realistic perceptions on to a reminder card or a cassette and rehearse them daily for as long as necessary to learn them properly.

Part B: *Creating more accurate perceptions of your partner*

If you think that your showing your partner care less well than you would like to is partly because of inaccurate, and possibly unkind, perceptions of her/him,

1. Identify your inaccurate perceptions of her/him and of how s/he communicates.
2. Use questioning skills to challenge your inaccurate perceptions.
3. Restate your inaccurate perceptions with more realistic perceptions.
4. Put your more realistic perceptions on to a reminder card or a cassette and rehearse them daily for as long as necessary to learn them properly.

Mind skill 5:   Creating explanations

1. If relevant, what do you consider to be the explanations for how you learned to show care to your partner insufficiently well in the first place?

2. What do you consider to be the explanations for how your still showing care insufficiently well is maintained?

3. Challenge any possibly inaccurate explanations that maintain your showing care to your partner insufficiently well now and, if appropriate, either discard them or restate them more accurately.

4. Put your more realistic explanations on to a reminder card or a cassette and rehearse them daily for as long as necessary to learn them properly.

Mind skill 6:   Creating expectations

1. Make up an activity sheet with the following headings, then assess the risks and gains of improving your skills of showing your partner that you care.

Gains of showing care better (pluses)	Risks of showing care better (minuses)

2. To what extent do you engage in reading your partner's mind about her/his preferences for care? If so, set yourself specific verbal, vocal and bodily communication goals to check what kind of care from you your partner really prefers.

13

Sharing Intimacy

I love you ever and ever and without reserve.
The more I have known you, the more I have lov'd.

John Keats

Happy couples create and cultivate intimacy. You express your love by wanting to know and be known by one another at a deep level. However, at the heart of intimacy exists a tension between partners as separate individuals and your being connected together. Such a tension has the potential to be both a strength and a weakness. Ideally as partners you cherish your own and one another's development as separate selves who then make the whole of your relationship greater than the sum of its parts. Rather than being threatened by one another's separate identity, you see this as the foundation for a stronger and more stimulating sense of togetherness.

Nevertheless, intimacy does not always come with the territory in relationships that possess the outward form of closeness, for instance marriage. Rather, partners struggle to attain, maintain and develop differing degrees of intimacy. Problems can arise if partners have different preferences concerning how intimate to be with one another and are unable to negotiate their differences successfully. By about two to one, women want more closeness than men. If you are not careful as a couple, you can establish a demand-withdraw communication pattern. The partner with the greater preference for closeness demands and, in turn, their partner withdraws. Such holding back is more likely to be ongoing if your relationship deteriorates.

DEFINING INTIMACY

The Latin word *intus*, meaning within, is the basis of the word intimacy. Non-sexual intimacy entails each partner getting in touch with their own internal world and sharing it with one another. Furthermore, you are sufficiently open to allow your own internal world to be changed by your partner's.

Here I suggest a simple fivefold classification of intimacy. First, there is *personal information* intimacy. For instance, partners may reveal risky information involving perceived weaknesses, shameful acts, taboo behaviours or family secrets as well as information about their achievements and matters of pride. Second, there is *emotional* intimacy involving the willingness to experience and share feelings with one another. Third, *intellectual* intimacy entails sharing your ideas and opinions. Fourth, *spiritual* intimacy involves sharing your philosophies of life and religious beliefs. Fifth, there is *relationship* intimacy that entails sharing your thoughts and feelings about what is going on in your relationship. Such 'you-me' talk may range from expressions about the closeness and value of the relationship to discussing differences between you openly.

Being honest with yourself and your partner is the central theme that runs throughout all five of these categories of intimacy. In an Australian relationship and intimacy survey, people were asked: 'Please select five qualities in a partner you consider to be most important to you.' Far more respondents selected honesty than any other quality in a partner. Qualities like physical attractiveness and being a considerate lover were each selected by well under half as many respondents (Market Research Section, 1997).

Dimensions of intimacy

Following are some important dimensions of intimacy with your partner. Simply stated, *intimacy with yourself* is knowing your internal world; *reaching out* is sharing your internal world with your partner; *receiving intimacy* is sharing your partner's internal world; and your *communication pattern* is how you and your partner coordinate the sharing of your internal worlds.

Intimacy with yourself provides the foundation for intimacy with your partner. The process of intimacy is best served by partners developing a secure sense of themselves as separate persons. Intimacy with yourself involves knowing and exploring your internal world. You possess sufficient emotional literacy to experience, identify and accurately label your feelings and thoughts. You possess a basic acceptance of yourself as a person that allows you to be open to your contrasting emotions. You can experience happiness, joy and strength as well as sadness, psychological pain and vulnerability. Where appropriate, you can explore your feelings further and, as a result, either accept, strengthen, refine or discard them.

Another way of viewing intimacy with yourself is that you are capable of solitude (Dowrick, 1991, 1993). You have sufficient comfort with yourself that, if necessary, you can live without a relationship. You can choose whether or not to be alone or with other people. You do not need to compulsively enter relationships to escape from the pain of loneliness.

Intimacy with your partner involves *reaching out* and sharing your internal world with her or him. Authenticity, genuineness, honesty and realness are nouns that describe the process of reaching out intimately. If your relationship develops, you increasingly drop your social masks, facades and defences. You are willing to be known and to share vulnerable and childlike parts of yourself as well as your strengths. Frequently, the notion of encounter is used to describe special moments of intimacy. Partners experience and communicate thoughts and feelings in a way that transcends the boundaries of existential isolation and is deeply enriching.

Receiving intimacy entails allowing yourself to become open to the internal world of your partner and to be influenced by it. Openness to your partner's internal world requires you to accept and respect her/him as different. You strive to create an emotional climate whereby your partner feels safe to risk revealing him/herself to you authentically. Receiving intimacy means that you are concerned enough about your partner to want to know them fully. Such knowledge includes their thoughts and feelings about their childhood, their subsequent background, their present lives, and their relationship with you.

What are some *communication patterns* for partners influencing one another? One of the most consistent findings of the self-disclosure research (for example, Cozby, 1973; Berg and Derlega, 1987) is that people tend to match the intimacy level of one another's disclosures.

> Kevin and Leanne have been dating for three months. At first, Leanne thought that Kevin was the strong, silent type. As Kevin disclosed more of himself, Leanne was surprised to find out how sensitive and emotional he was, how much he valued close friendships, and how willing he was to listen to her talk about her goals in life. Kevin, on the other hand, was learning that Leanne was a very determined person who wanted to combine having her own business with raising a family. He admired her openness and willingness to share her doubts about her femininity. Leanne's openness made it easier for Kevin to share his doubts about not being the typical male and his feelings of hurt at the ridicule he had received because of this. Both Leanne and Kevin were also able to share what they liked and disliked about their bodies.

In choosing whether to deepen the intimacy level of a relationship, one of the main ways you psychologically feel each other out is by making progressively more intimate disclosures. Simply stated, the process of deepening a relationship involves matching the intimacy level of another's disclosures prior to disclosing at a still more intimate level. If you both wish to develop your relationship, you are likely to coordinate the deepening of the intimacy level of your disclosures. More often than not, relationships do not make a smooth progression to more intimate disclosures, but instead trace a jagged line in that direction.

The progressive matching of the intimacy level of disclosures can deepen relationships for a number of reasons. One explanation is that your disclosure is a reward to another, indicating liking. The disclosure is to be matched if the relationship is to remain in balance. Another explanation emphasizes how disclosures are received. If your disclosure is met with acceptance by another, this acceptance not only establishes the other as less threatening and more like you, but also gives the other permission to make a similar disclosure. Consequently, by accepting disclosures as well as by disclosing, you develop trust in your relationship.

The matching of disclosures may be more important when developing relationships than when they are mature. Partners may not feel under such a great obligation to establish trust since the trust is already there (Duck, 1998). However, honesty is extremely important to maintaining mature relationships. Though the matching of disclosures may be less obvious, it is still likely to be present. When each partner stays honest, this encourages and maintains mutual honesty.

Problematic communication patterns for intimacy include being too distant, too enmeshed, or in imbalance. Matching shallow levels of disclosure exemplifies a pattern of being too distant. Possibly both partners fear intimacy and, hence, relinquish some of their capacity to reap its rewards.

The word enmeshment means entanglement as in the meshes of a net. Either or both partners lose some of their individual sense of self if they become too fused. When enmeshment occurs both partners settle for a less than genuine intimacy by developing an emotionally constricting 'we-self' at the expense of their individual selves. Spending almost all your time with your partner can contribute to becoming enmeshed.

An example of an unbalanced communication pattern is that mentioned earlier where one partner, frequently the woman, strives for greater emotional closeness, with the other partner, usually the man, preferring to keep more emotionally distant. Another unbalanced intimacy pattern is where one partner plays more the parent role and the other partner more the dependent child role. Children have a habit of growing up!

Respecting privacy

All partners are different and you will vary in how you wish to give and receive intimacy. Also, your wishes for privacy vary. Imagine each of you as a large house. Each partner may want the other partner to enter most rooms in your house, but not necessarily all rooms all of the time. Also, each of you may have more interest in entering some rooms than others. To expect a perfect situation of total openness to one another and total interest from one another is unrealistic. You can respect one another's wishes for privacy, though as the level of mutual trust in your relationship develops your private areas are likely to become fewer. Also, acknowledge that you cannot always expect to receive from one another total interest in what you reveal.

DEVELOPING YOUR COMMUNICATION

It is in our faults and failings, not in our virtues,
that we touch one another and find sympathy.

J. K. Jerome

Below I describe some skills for creating happiness by reaching out, receiving your partner's internal world, and maintaining a pattern of intimate communication. Needless to say, such skills entail vocal and bodily as well as verbal communication.

Reaching out to your partner

Intimacy requires letting yourself be known. You need to reveal personal information as well as your feelings. Be worth knowing. You can develop as a person by keeping engaged in life. If you allow your internal world to become impoverished and have few interests and activities, you will have little stimulating to disclose.

Instead of waiting to be asked questions about yourself, you can take the initiative in talking about yourself. You can help your partner gain knowledge of your past, present and future. Furthermore, you can develop skills of requesting air time and letting your partner know that you want their attention. For example, if you want to share a sensitive disclosure, you can either choose or arrange a time when you can talk the matter through. If necessary, you can back this up by signalling the importance of such a discussion to you.

You may require assertion skills to ensure that your partner listens to you. A problem is that some partners talk too much about themselves. Communication patterns can become established early in relationships, so from the beginning you may need to be firm about giving feedback that yours is to be a two-way relationship. For example, when you are disclosing and your partner switches the focus back to him/herself, you can let it be known that you wish to continue. S/he can have a turn either later or another time.

You can attempt to attain greater intimacy by taking calculated risks. Revealing negative aspects of yourself can deepen relationships. If you have never tried, you have not collected the evidence that you will worsen rather than improve your relationship by risking specific disclosures. You need not 'let it all hang out'. Also, where appropriate, you can match the risk taken by another's disclosures by self-disclosing in the same or another area.

Tune into how your partner reacts to your disclosures. If you have revealed something which changes their picture of you, they may require your help in dealing with this change. You also need to learn what interests your partner about you and how not to bore them.

Expressing your feelings involves revealing to the external world the emotions of your internal world. Thus expressing feelings entails a translation of your inner sensations into outer expressions. Sometimes the process of translation is immediate – for instance your startled reactions to a loud noise. On most occasions, expressing feelings involves conscious choices regarding both how you label feelings and whether and how you reveal them.

Identifying and labelling your feelings accurately requires intimacy with yourself. For instance, Rob asks his partner Amy if she will go out to dinner with him that evening, and she politely but firmly refuses. Rob might have a range of possible feelings including hurt, anger, anxiety, relief, resignation, cheerfulness and concern. If Rob thinks about his feelings or wants to talk about them to Amy, he needs to put them into words. Some slippage may occur between Rob's feelings and their verbal description. For instance, he may find it difficult to admit that he is hurt, finding it more comfortable to label his feeling as anger. He may experience difficulty acknowledging his ambivalence and the nuances in the intensity of his feelings. In addition, he may lack the vocabulary to identify and express his feelings adequately. To send good feelings messages, it is useful to build up a repertoire of words to describe and to catch the nuances of your own and your partner's feelings.

Apart from identifying and labelling your feelings accurately, other skills for expressing feelings include sending 'I' messages and sending consistent verbal, vocal and bodily messages. Also, with feelings you find difficult to express, you can think through and rehearse how best to communicate them to your partner prior to taking the risk of doing so.

The communication skills for intellectual intimacy and spiritual intimacy with your partner are similar to those for disclosing personal information and for emotional intimacy. For example, be prepared to take the initiative, request disclosure time, assert your right to air time, take calculated risks, send 'I' messages and, if necessary, rehearse how best to communicate your opinions and beliefs.

De Angelis (1997) advises women that their minds are their most attractive feature and that they should never edit their opinions or values to be liked by a man. In reality, for both sexes, caution and attention to timing is sometimes advisable. For example, if you have a highly jealous spouse, it may be judicious not to talk about innocent encounters with the opposite sex.

Receiving intimacy from your partner

This section focuses in particular on communication skills for assisting your partner to share very private information. Each of us has imperfections that we fear to reveal to others. Words and phrases to describe such information include negative or risky self-disclosure, taboo subjects, secrets, skeletons in the cupboard, or stigmas. Following are some skills of assisting your partner to share negative aspects of her or his internal world.

If your partner struggles to tell you something of which they are ashamed, be careful not to be judgemental. You can show unconditional acceptance of your partner as a valuable person independent of their specific behaviours. The fact that your partner fears telling you means that they already judge the information negatively, but trust you sufficiently not to make matters worse. Use skills of active listening and showing understanding to help your partner experience the feelings attached to the disclosure, for instance, anxiety, relief or tears. Assist them to reveal as much of the story as they are comfortable with at this stage. Give your partner space to explore their thoughts and feelings about what they are telling you. Where appropriate, ask questions that encourage them to continue and elaborate their story.

You can show that you care for your partner not only by listening, but by actively showing your support. If your partner appears hesitant, you can tell them of your concern and willingness to be there for them. Also, you can respond to specific parts of their story with comments like 'That must have been awful for you'. In addition, you can express appreciation for their trust in you as well as admiration for their courage. Furthermore, you can show that you understand the intensity of their feelings by varying the emphasis of your voice. Also, you can show your compassion by speaking gently. Bodily communication, such as interested and responsive facial expressions and good use of gaze and eye contact, can encourage intimate disclosures. Also, consider using touch messages: for instance, hugging or holding hands.

What your partner says may trigger something that you would like to reveal about yourself. Be sensitive that this may not be the best time to switch the agenda from your partner's concerns. Nevertheless, on some occasions, sharing something shameful about yourself may ease your partner's burden of self-devaluation as well as yours.

Above, I have focused on skills of helping another to reveal negative information. However, intimacy also entails sharing and receiving positive information. You may help your partner to feel more positively by accepting aspects of them that they find unacceptable. In addition, you may need to use good skills of receiving intimacy to assist your partner to reveal what s/he likes about him/herself. Many people require loving assistance in owning and revealing their strengths, opinions and spiritual yearnings.

Cultivating intimate communication between partners

An important skill in maintaining an effective relationship is to talk to each other about how you relate. Egan calls this skill 'immediacy', or 'you-me' talk. He distinguishes between relationship immediacy ('Let's talk about how we've been relating to each other recently') and here-and-now immediacy ('Let's talk about what's going on between you and me right now as we're talking to each other') (Egan, 1977, p. 235). Thus Egan's 'you-me' talk can either have a recent past or a present focus. Another focus for 'you-me' talk sessions is how you want your relationship to develop in future.

When talking about how you relate, partners require skills of giving and receiving feedback. Partners can share positive and negative feelings about how each other relates. Other areas for feedback include 'How committed we are to the relationship', 'What issues we have avoided in the past', 'What issues we are not bringing up at this moment', 'What we want from our relationship', 'What the strengths are in our relationship', 'What is missing in our relationship', 'Other relationships that significantly impact on our relationship', and 'How we might improve our relationship'. Skills for 'you-me' talk sessions include getting in touch with what you think and feel, sending 'I' messages, being specific, and inviting rather than cutting off discussion of the points you make. In addition, tact and diplomacy can help soften painful communication.

A host of practical considerations can make it difficult for partners to cultivate intimacy and stay connected. Such considerations include cramped living space, noise, shortage of money, fatigue, dependent children, caring for in-laws, work pressures and health problems. These stresses interfere with couples spending quality time together. There is no magic wand to wave for maintaining intimacy in your relationship. Where possible, use good time management skills: for instance, deliberately allocating time, space and energy for conversing and enjoying one another's company. Then, at least, you give yourselves a chance of maintaining intimacy. Also, become aware when you start spending less time together and try to repair your intimacy pattern before it is too late.

Mick and Shannon, a couple in their late thirties, had been married for fifteen years and had two girls, aged 12 and 10. Until recently Mick had been a company lawyer who worked long hours, including taking work home evenings and weekends. Shannon was a school teacher. Not seeing much of Mick, she adjusted her schedule to include numerous committees and outside activities. When Mick's company was unexpectedly taken over, he lost his job. As part of his soul-searching on being made redundant, Mick decided to seek a less demanding job so he could spend more time with his wife and family. This prompted a series of discussions with Shannon about how they wished to relate in future. Shannon was sceptical about whether Mick would change his ways. Nevertheless, they agreed to set aside an evening a fortnight to have a social evening together, to do the shopping together on Saturday mornings and to have coffee out afterwards. They also agreed to go camping more. To Shannon's delight, Mick turned down some job offers that would have left them little time to have a relaxed intimate relationship. Eventually Mick took a job where he could restrict his work. Also, Shannon relinquished some of her outside activities to spend more time at home.

Mick and Shannon discussed early warning signals for their relationship becoming distant again, for instance Mick's irritability, Shannon experiencing difficulty getting through to him, and Shannon looking for satisfaction outside the home. Mick and Shannon agreed in future to confront earlier on any problems of losing intimacy in their relationship.

EMPOWERING YOUR MIND

All of us over time have difficulty with intimacy, and over time, we will either move forward or backward in this dimension.

Harriet Goldhor Lerner

This section illustrates mind skills that you can use to increase your chances of skilfully communicating and sharing intimacy. Where appropriate, refer back to Part Two of this book for further details of how to develop and use specific mind skills.

Become aware and try to deal with any thoughts that lead you to become anxious about intimacy, trust and commitment. Anxiety can motivate you not to risk disclosing at all or to say only part of what you think and feel. A common conflict is that between wanting intimacy and viewing closeness as dangerous – wishing to be known, yet fearing it. Sometimes a degree of intimacy can give rise to fears about greater intimacy and thus prevent further reaching out. In addition, people of both sexes who have experienced relationship break-ups can become very wary of opening up their internal worlds to potential new partners.

Harmful anxiety can motivate you to reach out too much as well as too little. Anxiety-motivated intimacy is a form of pseudo-intimacy. Rather than genuine disclosure, you disclose to manage your partner's impressions of you. In addition, you can play various roles that act as decoys or camouflages for what you truly feel: for instance, acting the clown, acting angry, acting cynical, acting fragile, acting strong, and being dominating (Powell, 1969).

Creating self-talk

Whether you establish roadblocks to intimacy with your partner by economizing on the truth or by putting on a false front, you can create coping self-talk that helps you to manage your anxieties and disclose appropriately. Let's take the example of Becky who decides to reveal to Steve, her partner of a few months, that she had an abortion three years ago in her final year at university. Ever since, Becky has never told anyone new in her life about her abortion. Becky's clarifying-goal self-statement is 'My goal is to have an honest and real relationship in which I can be loved for who I am'; her calming self-statements include 'Calm down' and 'Breathe slowly and regularly'; her coaching self-statements include 'Tell Steve in a calm and unhurried voice that I have something important about my past that I want to share with him'; and her affirming self-statements include 'I'm a valuable person in my own right' and 'I have good skills at sharing sensitive information and handling other people's reactions to it'.

Often partners require coping self-talk when receiving disclosures too. For example, if Steve starts feeling anxious when hearing Becky's disclosure, he can tell himself 'Calm down' and 'Use my skills of active listening and showing understanding'.

Creating visual images

You can use visualizing skills to increase intimacy. For example, by using your imagination, you can develop a better understanding of your partner's life experience, both past and present. In addition, you can visually rehearse how best to reach out to your partner and also how best to receive his/her disclosures. Such imaginal rehearsal can have the twin goals of calming your anxiety and increasing your chances of communicating competently.

You can use visual images to remember your partner when you are parted, be it for a working day or for longer periods. Such visual reminders may stimulate you to contact them and ask how they are going. Also, you can use visualizing skills to strengthen your motivation for positive displays of intimacy by imagining your partner's pleasure in receiving what you say and do. In addition, you can block possible communications that might impair intimacy, for example, criticizing your partner in public, by imagining their negative consequences.

Together you and your partner can develop intimacy by sharing your dreams and fantasies. Also, you can develop visual pictures of the life you want to lead, both now and in future.

Creating rules

You and your partner may possess unrealistic rules concerning intimacy that require identifying, challenging and restating. You may turn your preferences into demands that restrict your freedom to think and act rationally. Rules that may block intimacy with yourself include 'Males must not focus on their feelings', 'Women must not acknowledge being ambitious and liking power', and 'I must not be compassionate'. Unrealistic rules that can inhibit your being completely honest with your partner include 'I must not acknowledge and show my yearning for human closeness', and 'I must always be in an intimate relationship whether or not I truly care for my partner'.

Rules likely to interfere with your capacity to listen well include 'My partner must always be consistent', 'My partner must always live up to my expectations', and 'I must always actively help my partner solve his/her problems'. Your rules can also contribute to your being unhappy with the pattern between you of communicating intimacy: for example, 'We must have the same needs for emotional closeness' or 'We must put career and other daily activities ahead of creating quality time in our personal relationship'.

Creating perceptions

You may perceive yourself insufficiently accurately in ways that interfere with being intimate with your partner. To maintain your self-picture you may edit out significant personal information, both positive and negative. For instance, you can exaggerate either your strengths or deficiencies or a mixture of the two. You may consider yourself so unlovable that you cannot accept your partner's affectionate interest. You may engage in various self-protective habits to contain your anxiety and maintain your current way of viewing yourself. Illustrative self-protective habits that can block or interfere with intimacy include compulsive activity, compulsive sex, and serial relating in which as soon as intimacy and commitment threatens you move on to your next relationship.

The negative effects of partners' self-protective thinking on intimacy can scarcely be overemphasized. In order to protect your own distorted self-pictures, each of you can distort your pictures of one another. Thus intimacy becomes doubly difficult because you see neither yourself nor your partner clearly. However, by striving to overcome your own mind tricks and self-protective habits, you can perceive yourself and your partner more accurately.

Partners can also perceive one another inaccurately through insufficient information. Here you may attain greater intimacy by continuing to collect information about one another – your pasts, presents and hopes for the future. Taking the trouble to know your partner well can also protect you against insufficiently acknowledging how much and in what ways you differ.

In addition, partners can block intimacy through jumping to conclusions about one another's thoughts, feelings, motivations and actions. You may perceive in one another only the thoughts and emotions you are capable of in yourselves. You can protect yourself against misinterpreting your partner if you listen to them carefully and, if necessary, ask them to explain themselves.

Creating explanations

You can offer all sorts of reasons why you are less than successful in developing and maintaining intimacy in your relationship with your partner. Illustrative explanations for insufficiently reaching out to your partner include 'It's my nature', 'It's my upbringing', 'It's my culture', 'It's my sex-role conditioning', and 'I've tried to get through in the past, so it's no use trying again'. Illustrative explanations for inadequately receiving your partner's intimacy include 'S/he is manipulating me', 'S/he is trying to gain power over me', 'S/he never listens to me', 'I don't really care about him/her' (when underneath you really do care), and 'It's up to him/her to make the first move to improve communication in our relationship'.

If any of the above explanations are ways in which you block intimacy, challenge their accuracy. Often what happens is that people convert partial truths into whole truths. For instance, you may have been brought up in a family of under-disclosers. However, that is no reason why you cannot now assume responsibility for developing your intimacy skills.

In addition, you can challenge the accuracy of your explanations for not receiving your partner's disclosures. For instance, you can challenge the explanation 'It's because s/he never listens to me' by asking yourself questions like 'How well do I disclose and listen to him/her?' and 'Can I think of any occasions where s/he has listened to me?' and 'Why should I let my thoughts and communication be controlled by his/her thoughts and communication?'

Creating expectations

You can be poor at creating expectations about the risks and gains of intimacy with yourself, reaching out to your partner, receiving your partner's intimacy, and developing and maintaining the pattern of communicating intimacy between you. Anxieties attached to knowing yourself better include those surrounding acknowledging your vulnerability and weaknesses. Also, you may possess fears about having failed to live up to your parents' expectations and to your own potential. Anxieties attached to intimacy with your partner include those concerning being overwhelmed, losing yourself in the relationship, having your disclosures used against you, having your confidences breached, getting rejected, and losing your partner. Anxieties attached to changing the pattern of communicating intimacy between the two of you include being taken advantage of by your partner and facing either the unwillingness or inability of your partner to change.

You require the ability to be realistic about assessing the gains of seeking greater intimacy with your partner as well as the risks. You can ask yourself such questions as 'What is the up-side as well as the down-side of risking greater intimacy?', 'Where is the evidence to support or negate my expectations?', 'What is the level of trust in our relationship?', 'What are my strengths and who can offer support to me if my efforts at increasing intimacy with my partner get rejected?', 'If my initial efforts at greater intimacy get rejected, what are the pros and cons of trying again?', and 'What communication skills do I — or we — need to deepen or repair the intimacy level of our relationship?'

ACTIVITIES

As you see fit, do the activities either on your own, or with your partner, or with some other suitable person, such as a relationship counsellor or trainer.

Activity 13.1   Developing skills for disclosing and receiving intimate information

Part A: Disclosing intimate personal information

1. Assess your good and poor skills in each of the following areas of disclosing intimate personal information to your partner:

- being worth knowing
- taking the initiative

- requesting air time
- asserting myself
- taking calculated risks
- reciprocating intimacy
- tuning into my partner's reactions

2. If appropriate, identify one or more skills for disclosing intimate personal information to your partner that you would like to improve. Then, develop a plan to change how you communicate. In your plan, specify

(a) your goals, including a time frame,
(b) the steps you intend taking to attain each of your goals – including how you and your partner might work together, and
(c) how you will monitor your progress.

Part B: Receiving intimate personal information

1. Assess your good and poor skills in each of the following areas of receiving intimate personal information from your partner:

- showing unconditional acceptance
- encouraging the experiencing and exploring of feelings
- showing involvement by your verbal communication
- showing involvement by your vocal communication
- showing involvement by your bodily communication
- showing involvement by touching
- choosing whether or not to match your partner's disclosures.

2. If appropriate, identify one or more skills of receiving intimate personal information from your partner that you would like to improve. Then, develop a plan to change how you communicate. In your plan, specify

(a) your goals, including a time frame,
(b) the steps you intend taking to attain each of your goals – including how you and your partner might work together, and
(c) how you will monitor your progress.

Activity 13.2   Developing skills for expressing feelings

Part A   Feelings you find easy and difficult to express

1. Take a piece of paper. At the top write 'Feelings I find easy and difficult to express to my partner'. Underneath draw a line down the middle. At the top of the left-hand column write 'easy', and at the top of the right-hand column write 'difficult'.
2. In the appropriate columns write feelings you find easy and difficult to express to your partner.
3. Do you detect any theme(s) in the feelings you have listed as either easy or difficult to express to your partner? If so, please specify the theme(s).

Part B   Sending feelings messages

1. For each of the following feelings write down (a) verbal messages; (b) vocal messages; and (c) bodily messages that you could use to express the feeling appropriately to your partner.

Love _____   Anger _____

_____   _____

_____   _____

Fear _____   Sadness _____

_____   _____

_____   _____

Happiness _____   Boredom _____

_____   _____

_____   _____

2. Look at the feelings you listed as difficult to express in Part A of this exercise. For each important feeling write down (a) verbal messages; (b) vocal messages; and (c) bodily messages that you could use to express the feeling appropriately to your partner. Rehearse and practise expressing these feelings. Where possible, enlist the participation of your partner in developing your skills of expressing feelings.

Activity 13.3   Developing intellectual and spiritual intimacy skills

Part A   Intellectual intimacy

1. Identify ideas and opinions you find difficult to express to your partner.
2. For each important idea or opinion write down the (a) verbal messages; (b) vocal messages; and (c) bodily messages that you could use to disclose it appropriately to your partner. Rehearse and practise expressing these disclosures. Where possible, enlist the participation of your partner in developing your intellectual intimacy skills.

Part B   Spiritual intimacy

1. If appropriate, identify spiritual and/or philosophy of life ideas, beliefs and yearnings you find difficult to express to your partner.
2. For each important idea, belief or yearning write down the (a) verbal messages; (b) vocal messages; and (c) bodily messages that you could use to disclose it appropriately to your partner. Rehearse and practise expressing these disclosures. Where possible, enlist the participation of your partner in developing your spiritual intimacy skills.

Activity 13.4   Developing 'you-me' talk intimacy skills

Part A: Assessment on your own

1. What positive feelings and thoughts about how your partner relates to you have you left unsaid?
2. What negative feelings and thoughts about how your partner relates to you have you left unsaid?
3. How committed are you and your partner to your relationship?
4. What issues have you and your partner avoided talking about in the past?
5. To what extent do you and your partner avoid talking about what is going on in your relationship in the 'here-and-now'?
6. What are the strengths of your relationship?
7. What is missing in your relationship?
8. How do you and your partner influence one another in how you give and receive intimacy?
9. Are there any other relationships that significantly impact, for good or ill, on your relationship? If so, how?
10. How might you and your partner work together to improve your relationship?

Part B: Communicating together: holding a 'you-me' talk session

1. Set aside a time to hold a 'you-me' talk session with your partner about your relationship.
2. Decide with your partner which of the above questions you wish to address in this session.
3. Conduct a 'you-me' talk session. Remember to send 'I' messages, be specific, invite rather than cut off discussion, and use tact and diplomacy.
4. Evaluate with your partner the benefits, if any, of holding 'you-me' talk sessions about your relationship.
5. Hold further 'you-me' talk sessions as you both see fit.

Activity 13.5   Developing mind skills for sharing intimacy

Address the mind skills that you identify as most important to helping you to share intimacy. Consult the text if in doubt about any of the mind skills.

Mind skill 1: Creating self-talk

1. Think of a situation in which you might make either a personal information, emotional, intellectual, spiritual or relationship disclosure to your partner less well than you would like.
2. Identify any negative self-talk that contributes to your making this disclosure less well.
3. Specify a clarifying-goals statement for the situation and create two each of calming, coaching and affirming statements. Then, if appropriate, develop self-talk that puts together goals, calming, coaching and affirming statements.

4. Put your statements on cue cards or on a cassette and rehearse them daily for as long as necessary to learn them properly.
5. Try out your self-talk in real life and assess its consequences.

Mind skill 2: Creating visual images

1. Think of a situation in which you might make either a personal information, emotional, intellectual, spiritual or relationship disclosure to your partner less well than you would like.
2. Think of the verbal, vocal, bodily, touch and taking action communication skills you require that will help you to disclose competently in the situation.
3. Visually rehearse yourself communicating competently in the situation, including coping with any difficulties and set-backs that occur.
4. Accompany your visual rehearsal with appropriate coping self-talk.
5. Practise your visual rehearsal plus coping self-talk skills daily for as long as you find it helpful, then also practise communicating competently in the real-life situation.

Mind skill 3:   Creating rules

1. Detect any unrealistic rules that contribute to your sharing intimacy with your partner less well than you would like.
2. Use disputing and challenging skills to question the most important unrealistic rule that you detected above.
3. Change the unrealistic rule you disputed above into a more realistic rule.
4. Put your realistic rule on to a reminder card or cassette and rehearse it daily for as long as necessary to learn it properly.

Mind skill 4:   Creating perceptions

Part A: Creating more accurate perceptions of yourself

If you think that your sharing intimacy with your partner less well than you would like is partly because of inaccurate perceptions of yourself,

1. Identify your inaccurate perceptions of yourself and of how you communicate.
2. Use questioning skills to challenge your inaccurate perceptions.
3. Restate your inaccurate perceptions with more realistic perceptions.
4. Put your more realistic perceptions on to a reminder card or a cassette and rehearse them daily for as long as necessary to learn them properly.

Part B: Creating more accurate perceptions of your partner

If you think that your sharing intimacy with your partner less well than you would like is partly due to inaccurate, and possibly exaggeratedly threatening, perceptions of her/him,

1. Identify your inaccurate perceptions of her/him and of how s/he communicates.
2. Use questioning skills to challenge your inaccurate perceptions.
3. Replace your inaccurate perceptions with more realistic perceptions.

4. Put your more realistic perceptions on to a reminder card or a cassette and rehearse them daily for as long as necessary to learn them properly.

Mind skill 5:   Creating explanations

1. If relevant, what do you consider to be the explanations for how you learned to share intimacy with your partner insufficiently well in the first place?
2. What do you consider to be the explanations for how your still sharing intimacy insufficiently well is maintained?
3. Challenge any possibly inaccurate explanations that maintain your sharing intimacy with your partner insufficiently well now and, if appropriate, either discard them or restate them more accurately.
4. Put your more realistic explanations on to a reminder card or a cassette and rehearse them daily for as long as necessary to learn them properly.

Mind skill 6:   Creating expectations

1. Make up an activity sheet with the following headings, then assess the risks and gains of increasing the intimacy level of your relationship with your partner by improving your skills of sharing intimacy.

Gains of better intimacy skills (pluses)	Risks of better intimacy skills (minuses)

If the gains outweigh the risks, refer back to the activities on developing better communication skills for sharing intimacy and change how you communicate.

2. Make up an activity sheet with the following headings, then assess the risks and gains of making to your partner a specific personal information, emotional, intellectual, spiritual or relationship disclosure that you have not shared before.

Gains of making disclosure (pluses)	Risks of making disclosure (minuses)

If the gains outweigh the risks, refer back to the activities on developing better communication skills for sharing intimacy and make your disclosure.

14

Enjoying Sex Together

Too much of a good thing can be wonderful.
Mae West

Each couple is responsible for the ways in which they create happiness by means of their own unique sexual relationship. Sensual and sexual intimacy entail the capacity to be comfortable with your own and one another's bodies. You can enjoy physical stimulation and warmth as well as emotional excitement and contentment. Enjoying sex together can range from passionate abandon to pleasurable companionship. Sex can be especially emotionally fulfilling in a loving and committed relationship.

In heterosexual relationships, sexual relating has three functions: procreation (conceiving children), relationship enhancement and recreation (Masters, Johnson and Kolodny, 1986). The relationship enhancement function has many dimensions. For instance, effective sexual relating can promote family stability and lessen the likelihood of infidelity. With or without children, sex can bring partners closer together through the pleasure bond. Good sex affirms partners physically, psychologically and, some would say, spiritually. Sex can also be adult play in which partners get away from the daily cares and concerns of work and domestic lives. You can be spontaneous and creative; you can cut through social facades. You can laugh and be merry as you release and enjoy your own and each other's 'erotic child'. In Thailand, which is probably more sexually liberated than either Australasia or Britain, 'sanuk', meaning fun, is a commonly used word to describe sex.

It is everybody's birthright to enjoy their sexuality and use it for finding emotional fulfilment. However, unless you are comfortable with yourself as a sexual person, you are unlikely to have a good sexual relationship with another. Feeling comfortable with your own sexuality allows you to explore your own and your partner's sexuality without the constraints of what is 'acceptable' for the different sexes. What feels good for both of you is what you do, not what society tells you to do.

Sexual relating is likely to be stronger if you can develop it in the context of a good sensual relationship. In sensual relating, you relate to each other as physical persons through your five senses of sight, sound, smell, touch and taste. Ideally, you feel comfortable with your body and with sharing its physical and psychological warmth with your partner. You do not confine touching to erotic situations. Instead, daily you express your need for physical contact and tenderness by affectionate kissing, hugging, stroking, touching, hand holding and lying in each other's arms.

SEXUAL EQUALITY

I am happy now that Charles calls on my bedchamber less frequently than of old. As it is, I now endure but two calls a week and when I hear his steps outside my door I lie down on my bed, close my eyes, open my legs, and think of England.

Lady Hillingdon

Times change. The above quotation from the Victorian era reflects what most people now would regard as outrageous sexual inequality between men and women.

Although there are obvious differences, anatomically male and female bodies are very alike. In terms of their sexual functioning, men and women are also 'incredibly and consistently similar' (Masters and Johnson, 1970, p. 38). However, women's capacity to respond to sexual stimulation is far greater than that of men and men are far more fertile than women. Emotionally men and women are also very similar. Both are highly sexual.

In all cultures, men and women have been subject to sex-role conditioning. Sexual knowledge (or lack of it) and attitudes toward sensual and sexual pleasure are two key areas where men and women can have received different sexual socialization. For example, men more than women may be socialized to be sexual rather than sensual. In many places sex-role conditioning has led to many women feeling that they are second-class citizens. Often in the past, women's potential for sexual arousal and pleasure was viewed by both sexes as less than that of men. Also, women's wishes in regard to making love were sometimes viewed as less important.

However, men have not escaped unscathed from their sex-role conditioning. Jokingly, young men have been observed to need four items to measure their sexual prowess: a ruler, for the length of their penis; a piece of string, for its thickness; a clock, for how long they can delay ejaculating; and a counter, for how many times they get 'it'. Many men accept too much responsibility for the success of sexual encounters. Also, men's socialization frequently generates counterproductive expectations and anxieties about sexual performance. Furthermore, many men experience difficulty in expressing vulnerability, affection and tenderness.

Increasingly, there is a trend toward sexual equality. Making love is recognized as something that partners do *with* each other for mutual gratification rather than something that is done *to* or *for* the other partner. Making love takes place in the context of equal power and mutual respect. Both partners accept joint responsibility for the success of lovemaking. Accordingly, you show sensitivity to your own and your partner's unique erotic capabilities and preferences. When making love together, couples cannot attain the heights of mutual erotic stimulation and emotional fulfilment on any other basis than that of sexual equality.

SEXUAL COMPATIBILITY

Sexual compatibility relates to how well-suited partners are to one another. Compatibility not only means presence of similarities, but also how mutually tolerant partners are of their differences and how well they can negotiate them. Compatibility also relates to partners' honesty and tolerance about their past sexual histories. Differences are the norm rather than the exception in sexual relationships. Each of you can differ in the strength of the sexual desire you bring into the relationship. Furthermore, fluctuations of desire are inevitable according to how each of you feels about your relationship and according to what is going on in other areas of your lives. Differences can also exist in what turns partners on before lovemaking, in preferences for activities during lovemaking, and in how partners like to conclude lovemaking sessions.

In general, men want to make love more than women. In an Australian survey, roughly half the survey respondents reported they wanted to have about the same amount of sex as their partners. However, men were four times more likely than women to want more sex than their partners – 39 per cent of men versus 9 per cent of women (Market Research Section, 1997). The sexes can also differ in how they value the relationship context of sexual acts, with women more inclined to look for elements of affection, commitment and security (King, 1997).

Differences in the mind can lead to differences in how partners communicate sexually. For example, each of you can differ in how positively or negatively you think about sex and in how you think about your bodies. The communication resulting from these different thoughts could range from being very inhibited to being spontaneous, playful and happy. In addition, each of you may differ in your attitudes to fidelity by yourself or your partner.

Increasingly, with the greater trend toward cohabitation, partners are unlikely to enter long term committed relationships, such as marriage, without a reasonable appreciation of their sexual compatibility. Nevertheless, all sexual relationships continue to contain differences of varying degrees of magnitude. Couples require the commitment, willingness and skills to accept or, where necessary, negotiate differences rather than blaming one another for them.

DEVELOPING YOUR COMMUNICATION

Are we not formed, as notes of music are,
For one another, though dissimilar?

Percy Bysshe Shelley

Noted American sex researchers William Masters and Virginia Johnson found that human sexual response was a cycle with four phases: excitement, plateau, orgasm and resolution (Masters, Johnson and Kolodny, 1986). The phases are not always separate and can vary considerably between people and with one person at different times. Another version of the sexual response cycle comes from the American Psychiatric Association, with their four phases being desire, excitement, orgasm and resolution (American Psychiatric Association, 1994). Here I use lay language to present a lovemaking cycle again consisting of four phases: turning on, foreplay, intercourse and afterwards. The phases can overlap and, where necessary, accommodate differences between partners. I identify some communication skills for each stage.

THE LOVEMAKING CYCLE

Phase One: Turning on

For sex to occur, at least one partner must start somewhat in the mood. Getting in the mood is best achieved in the context of a tender and sensual relationship outside the bedroom. Humans get aroused through touching and feeling, sexy thoughts and fantasies, hearing romantic music, and smelling body odours. Some partners feel more randy after being out in the fresh air or exercising physically. If the other partner is not initially in the mood, they may still like the process of being aroused. However, this may not always be the case. Partners require sensitivity concerning one another's feelings and moods about both having and not having sex.

Partners build up a repertoire of signals with which they give and receive messages about when they are in the mood for sex. Good lovers become keenly attuned to what turns one another on: for instance, certain forms of eye contact, touching, breathing, clothing, conversation and so on. Partners can also turn each other off sex: for instance, by bad breath, poor hygiene, dirty clothes, coarse language, and being too pushy. Also, tactless criticism can be a big sexual turn-off.

Sex need not always take place in the bedroom at home. Some partners may enjoy making love in front of a blazing fireplace, in the bath, on the stairs, in hotels and motels, or outdoors – for instance, in a field or on a beach. However, to protect your own and other people's sensitivities, privacy is important. If there is a possibility of being interrupted at home, lock the door and take the phone off the hook. The lighting of the surroundings for sex may be bright, dim or non-existent. There may be music in the background or silence.

Partners can choose to have sex at any time – not just between 11 p.m. and midnight on Saturday evenings! For instance, you may enjoy a 'nooner' or a leisurely afternoon of lovemaking. The duration of your lovemaking may range from a 'quickie' to as long as you can maintain your interest and energy.

Communication skills

Sensual relating skills on a daily basis are very important for creating the context in which both partners are likely to be responsive to one another. Keep connected daily by hugs, kisses, cuddles, and loving looks. In addition, keep expressing tenderness and caring, for instance by compliments and loving gestures. If, after a period of ignoring one another, either James were to cook that special dinner or Kate were to bring home flowers, there is no guarantee that this would act as a turn-on. Instead the other partner might feel that they were being manipulated for sex.

Your sexual relationship may be richer if both partners can develop good skills of initiating lovemaking, rather than it being left to one partner – often the man. It is natural for women to feel horny and want a man's body. Men appreciate physical admiration too.

Couples can create arousal by developing skills of communicating one another's turn-ons and avoiding one another's turn-offs. For instance, Hannah's wearing sexy lingerie may be a turn-on for Russ, while Charlie's caressing Lucy's neck and upper back may be a turn-on for her. However, if Hannah wears lingerie that makes her look like a tart, this may be a turn-off for Russ. Also, if Charlie's caresses are too rough and demanding, he will turn Lucy off.

When making sexual advances, use good listening skills, including picking up your partner's vocal and body language as well as what they say. For instance, you need to distinguish between responses that indicate messages such as 'I'm in the mood for love too', 'I'm open to seduction', 'I'm not in the mood for intercourse but willing to help you gain release', or 'I definitely don't want sex now'. When declining your partner's advances, use tact, firmness and honesty. For instance, early in a relationship you might respond to a request for sex with 'I find you attractive, but if we are to make love I want to get to know you better'.

Phase Two: Foreplay

Foreplay can start with intimate caresses on the sofa, lingering deep kisses, helping one another get undressed or showering or bathing together. There is a build-up of sexual tension and excitement as partners pleasure one another with touch on the bed or elsewhere. Apart from lying together, cuddling or hugging your partner with your arms, legs or both, the main ways of touching one another are with your mouth and hands.

Methods of touching with your mouth include kissing one another's lips, kissing with open mouth, kissing and exploring one another's mouth with your tongues, licking, sucking, nibbling, biting, and blowing. Methods of touching with your hands include caressing with your finger tips, stroking, rubbing, scratching, holding, squeezing, patting, smacking, kneading, massaging, and tickling.

Some foreplay activities are simultaneous: for instance, partners rubbing their bodies against one another, concurrently licking and mouthing one another's genitals, or manually masturbating each other. Good foreplay also involves turn-taking in which partners go out of their way to provide pleasure in the way each other likes. In many instances of turn-taking, rather than remaining passive, pleasured partners can still gently caress pleasuring partners.

Vaginal lubrication is the main sign that a woman is sexually excited. Other signs of a woman's excitement include increased size of the clitoris and, for most women, erect nipples. An erect penis is the main sign that a man is physically excited. His penis becomes harder and thicker and points outwards or upwards.

Communication skills

Partners require skills for pacing their foreplay. In foreplay partners can get progressively sexually excited, though not necessarily at the same rate. Also, you may choose to draw out foreplay by allowing it to have its peaks and troughs of excitement. In general, men can become more quickly aroused than women. If more quickly aroused, you require skills of patiently stimulating your mate rather than placing unrealistic performance demands on her or him.

Skilfully let your partner know what you like in bed. Sometimes, you can do this by positive feedback: 'That feels great' or 'Keep doing that, I love it'. On other occasions you may wish to improve or modify an otherwise enjoyable behaviour:

for instance, 'I like it when you play with my testicles, but please do it lower down and more gently'. On still other occasions, you may wish to stop a behaviour: for instance, 'Please stop biting my neck. It hurts.' In addition, you can request sex acts, for instance 'Please lick my cunt', though you may need to be sensitive to language and to your partner's reactions. Also, you can share your sexual fantasies; again, carefully monitor how your partner responds.

Much of the time you disclose yourself as a sexual person through your touch behaviour – how you hug, kiss and use your hands. You can be playful, sensitive and creative in how you touch your partner. In addition, you can use touch skills to guide your partner in how to pleasure you.

Being a considerate and generous lover requires you to be responsive to the flow of feelings and sexual sensations in your partner. By observing, physically feeling and hearing your partner's reactions, you get numerous messages about how he or she experiences various aspects of your lovemaking. Furthermore, if you allow it, your partner may guide you in how to provide more pleasure. Much of this communication may be nonverbal – for instance, your partner may place your hand somewhere and apply the desired amount of pressure or friction.

If you think you are falling into repetitive and less arousing patterns, together you can use skills of toning up your foreplay with experimentation and variety. Create an emotional climate in which each of you feels safe to make suggestions. However, ensure that neither of you feels pressure to do anything that feels disagreeable for you. Those of you who feel a need for ideas to spice up your foreplay can get ideas from books on sex, such as Alex Comfort's *The New Joy of Sex* (1993) or Rosie King's *Good Loving, Great Sex* (1997).

Phase Three: Intercourse

Heterosexual intercourse involves the man penetrating the woman's vagina with his erect penis and thrusting back and forth. There are numerous positions for 'making love' – lying down, sitting, standing up and so on. I now mention five of the more usual positions. Partners can use more than one position during a single lovemaking session.

The first position is man lying on top, with partners facing. This 'missionary position' is probably the most commonly used position in Australasia and Britain. The woman lies on her back with her legs spread apart. She can bend her knees or wrap her legs around her partner. In addition, she can caress him. An advantage of this position is that partners can look at one another and kiss. Disadvantages include the difficulty of manually stimulating the clitoris and the man sometimes being too heavy.

The second position is woman lying on top, with partners facing. Here the woman possesses more control over the timing and depth of her partner's thrusting. However, the man may find it less easy to thrust. Partners can look into each other's eyes and kiss. Since the man does not need to support himself, his hands are free for stroking the woman's breasts, genitals or other parts of her body.

The third position is the woman sitting on top, with partners facing. Here the woman has even more control of the tempo and penetration of the man's thrusting than when lying on top. Partners can see more of each other and play with one another's chests or breasts. In addition, either partner can manually stimulate the clitoris. Mouth to mouth kissing is still possible, if wanted.

The fourth position is lying side by side with partners facing. The side by side position gives partners much opportunity to caress and hug one another. Neither partner carries the other's weight. Disadvantages include insufficient leverage for active penile thrusting and the greater likelihood of the penis coming out of the vagina than in other positions.

The fifth position is rear entry, with the woman kneeling or lying down. With rear entry 'doggy style', the man inserts his penis from behind into the woman's vagina as she kneels. The woman may have her back horizontal or sloping downwards. Some people object to the sheer animality of this position, but others find it exciting. Alternatively, rear entry may take place with the partners lying on their sides, the so called 'spoon position'. In rear entry positions, eye contact and mouth to mouth kissing are difficult. However, usually the man can manually stimulate his partner's clitoris or breasts.

Climax and coming are other words for orgasm. Orgasms may last for a few seconds or go on for a number of minutes, particularly for women. They consist of rhythmic muscular contractions followed by rapid relaxation. Orgasms are usually a time of intense psychological pleasure. However, the intensity of and degree of satisfaction derived from orgasms varies between people and across different occasions for the same person. Though simultaneous orgasms between men and women can occur, as a regular pattern they are more in the realms of fantasy than reality.

For women, orgasm is characterized by simultaneous rhythmic contractions of the uterus, the outer vagina (orgasmic platform), and anal sphincter. Unlike men, if restimulated, women are capable of further orgasms within seconds or minutes of each other. A man's orgasm consists of contractions throughout his penis that cause ejaculation involving the spurting of semen or 'cum' from the tip of his penis. Usually, men take much longer than women to become orgasmic again. However, the 'turn around time' for potent young males may be minutes rather than hours.

Communication skills

Many of the communication skills for the foreplay and intercourse phases are the same. For instance, each of you can disclose what you like and be sensitive to one another's preferences. Also, you can kiss and caress in some intercourse positions. Furthermore, you can introduce variety into having intercourse, both within a single lovemaking cycle and across time.

As in foreplay, you require sensitivity to the pacing of how you share intercourse together. Men can require skills of delaying their ejaculation so that the woman receives more pleasure. Two simple ways of doing this are to thrust more slowly and to pause between bouts of thrusting. Sometimes if the man repetitively comes too quickly, this is a symptom of performance anxiety. As a couple you should consult your doctor or seek sexual counselling for any continuing and serious problems that interfere with your capacity to enjoy intercourse.

Phase Four: Afterwards

'What's for afters?' Intercourse is frequently regarded as the main course in lovemaking, but there may still be significant sexual and emotional pleasure to follow. This phase can separate lovers who are considerate, generous and affectionate from those who are selfish. After intercourse, either or both partners may wish to wash. One partner, usually the woman, may still require more stimulation to be orgasmic and sexually satisfied. In such instances, the man can masturbate her clitoris or hold and caress her as she masturbates herself. When the active part of lovemaking finishes, partners may then choose to wash again.

After having sex, partners in loving relationships stay physically and emotionally connected. For instance, you may talk to one another and perhaps have a glass of wine. In addition, you may snuggle up and possibly gently caress one another. Many couples may then fall asleep with bodies entwined. Especially when young, partners may be taking a rest before another cycle of lovemaking.

Communication skills

After intercourse, if one of you still wants more stimulation, the other partner can revert to using pleasuring skills. When both partners feel sexually satisfied, together you can revert to using your sensual relating skills to ensure that the lovemaking cycle ends in an afterglow of physical and emotional warmth. Also, you can express tenderness and affection with words as well as by touch. In addition, some partners find they enjoy relaxed conversations after sex. Skilled lovers use communication skills to ensure that lovemaking is part of the flow of their ongoing intimate relationship rather than being isolated episodes of carnal affection.

Talking about sex

Partners can communicate about sex both in and out of bed. People vary in what language they find acceptable when talking about sex. Slang terms exist for erogenous parts of both the female and male bodies: for instance, breasts can become 'boobs', 'tits', 'mammaries', 'head lights' and 'fun bags' and a penis can be called a 'cock', 'dick', 'prick', 'tool' or 'bed flute'. No law of nature decrees that some of these terms are right or wrong. Each couple has to develop a language in which they can comfortably discuss sex without the constant fear of giving or receiving offence.

As well as each of you revealing your sexual likes and dislikes, together you will need to discuss and negotiate many issues connected with your sex life: for instance, improving it or dealing with different preferences. When discussing such issues, goodwill, a willingness to understand one another's positions, negotiation and compromise are useful attributes and skills. Sometimes you may need assertion skills to resist sexual pressure. You may need to be firm about ensuring use of condoms, stopping sex talk you find distasteful, and curtailing physical activities you dislike or find painful. In addition, many issues connected with your relationship and lives outside the bedroom may intrude into your sex life. Relating skills that you can use to address such issues include those of managing anger and solving relationship problems, the topics of later chapters in this book.

EMPOWERING YOUR MIND

When faced with two evils I choose the one I haven't tried before.

Mae West

Sex in the head affects sex in bed. How you think about sex strongly influences how well you perform. Masters and Johnson (Masters, Johnson and Kolodny, 1986) illustrated this point by stating that inhibitions and guilt, performance anxiety, erotic boredom, and blind acceptance of sexual misinformation and myths accounted for about 80 per cent of the sexual dissatisfaction in American society. Following are illustrations of the mind skills reviewed in Part Two of the book. Each skill is relevant to empowering your mind so that you can create more happiness and fun in your sex life.

Creating self-talk

You can create coping self-talk to help you to communicate more effectively in specific lovemaking situations. For example, Sophie would like her partner Tom to spend more time stroking her clitoris and to do it more gently. Sophie currently inhibits herself by negative self-talk: for instance, 'I'm only being silly wanting more caressing down there from him', 'Tom is going to get annoyed' and 'I'm too nervous to even think of telling him'. Sophie can replace her negative self-talk with coping self-talk in which she uses clarifying goals, calming, coaching and affirming self-statements. Sophie's goals statement is 'My goal is for Tom to spend more time gently stroking my clitoris'. Her calming self-statements are 'Calm down' and 'Breathe slowly and deeply'. With coaching self-statements Sophie reminds herself how to communicate effectively: for example, 'Use tact and diplomacy. Tell Tom how much pleasure he gives me when he strokes my clitoris and ask him to keep doing it, but more gently.' Affirming self-statements Sophie might use include 'I have a right to sexual fulfilment', 'Tom really wants to please me', and 'I'm capable of making my points when I need to'. Men can also use coping self-talk to help them act effectively with their partners: for instance, they may feel threatened about asking their partner to try a new position, admitting vulnerability or revealing ignorance.

Creating visual images

Sexual fantasies are an important part of being a sexual person. Women and men are more similar than different in their sexual fantasy patterns. The range of content of sexual fantasies is almost limitless. The imagery can differ in vividness and the action can be explicit or vague. The time can be the past, present or future. Common themes in sexual fantasies include your present sex life with your current partner; experimenting with different sexual acts and experiences; seduction and conquest; having sex with different partners; participating in group sex; watching others have sex; idyllic encounters; and sadomasochism.

Sexual fantasies can have many positive functions. Your sexual fantasies can show you what turns you on. You can try out different sexual activities in your mind to see how arousing they are. Also, before you initiate sexual contact, you can arouse your sexual appetite by tuning into existing fantasies or creating new ones. During sex, you can use fantasy to enhance arousal, increase the attractiveness of your partner, and relieve boredom. Also, you can imagine what it would be like to experiment with different activities here-and-now. Such fantasies may lead to more creativity, variety, spontaneity and fun. However, be careful to recognize that having a sexual fantasy does not necessarily mean that you want it to happen. Sometimes it can be sexually stimulating as a fantasy, but a complete turn-off if occurring in reality.

You can use visualizing to help you make love more competently. Lazarus (1984) states that when impotent males and non-orgasmic women imagine themselves engaging in enjoyable and passionate sex, a transfer to real lovemaking soon follows. You can also use visualizing to rehearse and practise engaging in new sexual activities: for example, fellatio (oral stimulation of man's genitals) or cunnilingus (oral stimulation of woman's genitals). Sexual fantasies may also aid masturbation, especially if alone; act as a safety valve for non-socially-sanctioned impulses; and provide what in many instances is a harmless and pleasant way of passing the time.

Creating rules

You and your partner may individually possess unrealistic rules that interfere with your sexual happiness. In addition, you may jointly share unrealistic rules that work against rather than for your sexual relationship. Here are some unrealistic rules in different areas relevant to sex: body image: 'My breasts ought to be big'; sex roles: 'Men must take the initiative'; sexual feelings: 'Women must not show sexual abandonment'; sexual acts: 'We must always have intercourse when we have sex'; and sexual performance, 'Men must be two feet long, hard as steel and able to go all night' (Zilbergeld, 1978).

As shown in Chapter 6, once you have identified unrealistic rules, you can challenge and restate them into more realistic rules that enhance rather than interfere with your lovemaking. For example, questions that challenge the unrealistic rule 'We must always have intercourse when we have sex' include 'Who says we must always have intercourse when we have sex?' and 'What if sometimes we have sex without having intercourse?' A more realistic restatement of the rule might be 'While we enjoy having intercourse most times we make love, we also enjoy other forms of sexual contact like stimulating each other's genitals and masturbation and do not wish to force ourselves to have intercourse every time we have sex'.

Creating perceptions

Some people perceive sex negatively. Woody Allen jokingly says: 'Is sex dirty? Only if it's done right.' The idea that sex is evil or dirty can contribute to sexual problems and dysfunctions. Women, especially, may find it difficult to value their sexuality. The double standard whereby it is OK for males but less OK for females to be open about their sexuality lingers on. In addition, partners may unthinkingly perceive specific sexual acts negatively rather than as part of the range of natural sexual activities.

You may perceive yourself inaccurately. For instance, you may be prone to negative perceptions about your body: 'Parts of my body are not attractive enough' or 'My body is not sexy enough'. Alternatively, you may be narcissistic about your physical attractiveness, perceiving yourself as God's gift to men or women. You may have an inadequate perception of yourself as a sexual person and of your unique sexual wishes and preferences. In addition, you may have wrong ideas about what effective sexual relating entails. For example, you may be sexually selfish and not realize this. On the other hand, you may be quite skilled at lovemaking, but riddled with doubts about your ability to satisfy your partner. Your 'spectating' of how you perform interferes with spontaneity.

At worst, either or both partners can perceive the other as objects for sexual gratification rather than as persons worthy of respect. You may have an incomplete or inaccurate picture of how to pleasure your partner. For example, you may think that what pleasures you is what pleasures her or him. You may inaccurately mind-read what your partner wants. Also, you may think that you can have good sex without needing to talk about it.

Partners can misinterpret one another's sexual behaviour. For example, if your partner masturbates or looks at erotic literature, this does not automatically mean that she or he is no longer sexually interested in you. And if you misinterpret your partner's behaviour, you may feel inferior and find excuses for not having sex.

Ways of counteracting inaccurate sexual perceptions include gathering more sexual information through reading, talking to people, attending courses, and seeking counselling; reality-testing the accuracy of your perceptions by challenging them and searching for evidence that confirms or negates them; and improving how you talk about sex with one another.

Creating explanations

Some explanations of inadequacy in one's sex life may cause and maintain sexual problems. For instance, if you think that 'Sex is natural', you may limit your sexual performance because you insufficiently realize the importance of knowledge and practice as well. Another example is that of creating the explanation 'Our relationship is not the cause'. Partners differ in the degree to which they can compartmentalize sex from the rest of their relationship. A rule of thumb is 'The better the communication outside the bedroom, the better the sex inside it'. Another potentially faulty explanation is 'It's all your fault'. Frequently, blaming a partner just increases the difficulties.

Alternatively, you can assume too much responsibility either for your partner's sexual pleasure or for your own insufficient sexual fulfilment. Good sex is a cooperative activity in which both partners are responsible for successful outcomes. Also, partners can stay stuck in unhappy lovemaking by creating the explanation that 'Improving our sex life is impossible' and then give faulty reasons to back up this explanation, for instance, 'S/he is only interested in her/his own pleasure' or 'S/he never listens'.

Remember that, either on your own or together with your partner, you can identify, challenge and restate any explanation that interferes with your sexual happiness.

Creating expectations

Relaxed sex requires confidence in your performance. Expectations of unsatisfactory performance or of failure are major factors in inhibitions and performance anxieties. Expressing affection, touching and making love become associated with anxiety about failure and not just pleasure. Unfortunately, expectations of sexual incompetence and failure can turn into self-fulfilling prophecies.

Partners can systematically assess the realism of their expectations. Such an assessment entails looking at gains as well as at risks or losses. Often, the best way to assess an expectation is to change how you communicate and then assess the consequences: for example, tell your partner what you prefer sexually and then see how he or she reacts.

Sometimes partners' expectations about poor sexual performance may be due to poor communication skills as much as to poor mind skills. For instance, partners may not know how to make love well. In such instances, you can change your expectations first by becoming better informed and then by developing the relevant lovemaking skills, for example those of pleasuring one another. If sexual problems persist, rather than remain unhappy with your sex life, consider finding out more about the benefits of sexual counselling and then seeking help.

ACTIVITIES

As you see fit, do the activities either on your own, or with your partner, or with some other suitable person, such as a relationship counsellor or trainer.

Activity 14.1   Developing communication skills for enjoying sex together

Part A   Assessment

On your own, assess your good and poor skills in each of the four phases of the lovemaking cycle.

Turning on

- sensual relating
- expressing tenderness and affection
- initiating
- communicating turn-ons to your partner
- listening to your partner's responses to your sexual advances

Foreplay

- pacing
- letting your partner know what you like in bed
- being responsive to your partner's reactions and wishes

- touching with your body
- touching with your mouth
- touching with your hands
- introducing variety

Intercourse

- pacing
- using mutually pleasurable positions
- kissing and caressing
- controlling ejaculation and orgasm
- introducing variety

Afterwards

- further stimulating your partner
- sensual relating
- expressing tenderness and affection

Part B   Change

If appropriate, on your own identify one or more lovemaking skills you wish to improve and develop a plan to change how you communicate. In your plan, specify

(a) your goals, including a time frame,
(b) the steps you intend taking to attain each of your goals, and
(c) how you will monitor your progress.

Part C   Working together

1. You and your partner share and discuss your answers to Part A of this exercise.
2. If appropriate identify one or more lovemaking skills you jointly want to improve and develop a plan to work together to change how you communicate. In your plan, specify

(a) your joint goals, including a time frame,
(b) the steps you as a couple intend taking to attain each of your joint goals, and
(c) how you will together check your progress.

Activity 14.2   Assessing comfort zones for sexual activities

Part A   Assessing comfort zones

On your own, assess how psychologically comfortable you feel about each of the following sexual activities:

Sexual intercourse: man lying on top, face to face; woman lying on top, face to face; woman sitting on top, face to face; lying side to side, face to face; rear entry, woman kneeling or lying down; other positions (specify);

Anal sex: penile-anal intercourse; other methods (specify);
Oral-genital sex: fellatio (oral stimulation of man's genitals); cunnilingus (oral stimulation of woman's genitals);
Masturbation: manually masturbating your partner; manually masturbating yourself, with partner present; manually masturbating yourself, with partner absent.

Part B   Discussing comfort zones

1. Each partner shares your sexual activity comfort zones and, if necessary, discusses your reasons for them.
2. If appropriate, partners agree to modify your comfort zones and activities.

Activity 14.3   Developing skills for talking about sex

Part A   Developing a comfortable language for sex talk

For each of the following parts of the body, items of clothing, sexual responses or sexual activities that are relevant to your sexual relating, you and your partner,

- think of as many ways of naming it/them as you can, and
- agree on the words that you are both comfortable using.

  Parts of the body and items of clothing: penis, clitoris, testicles, vagina, anus, breasts, nipples, underwear (men's), underwear (women's)
  Sexual responses and activities: desire, arousal, undressing, intercourse, orgasm, fellatio, cunnilingus, masturbation, contraception, other protection.

Part B   Discussing improving our sex life

1. Together with your partner, assess how often you discuss how you might improve your sex life.
2. Talk about how well each of you uses verbal, vocal and bodily communication skills when you discuss how to improve your sex life.
3. If appropriate, hold a 'you-me' talk session in which you and your partner use good verbal, vocal and bodily communication skills when discussing how to improve your sex life.

Activity 14.4   Developing mind skills for enjoying sex together

First do the activity on your own. Then, if appropriate, discuss with your partner. Which mind skills are most important in helping you to enjoy sex together? Consult the text if in doubt about any of the mind skills.

Mind skill 1:   Creating self-talk

1. Think of a situation in which you may engage in a phase of the lovemaking cycle less well than you would like.

2. Identify any negative self-talk that contributes to your making love less well.

3. Specify a clarifying-goals statement for the situation and create two calming, two coaching and two affirming statements. Then, if appropriate, develop self-talk that puts together goals, calming, coaching and affirming statements.

4. Put your statements on cue cards or on a cassette and practise them until you know them properly.

5. Use your self-talk in real life and see what happens.

Mind skill 2:   Creating visual images

1. Think of a situation in which you may engage in a phase of the lovemaking cycle less well than you would like.

2. Think of the words and the vocal, bodily and touch communication skills you need that will help you in the situation.

3. Visually rehearse yourself communicating competently in the situation, including coping with any difficulties and set-backs that occur.

4. Accompany your visual rehearsal with appropriate coping self-talk.

5. Practise your visual rehearsal plus coping self-talk skills daily for as long as you find it helpful, then remember to use them in the real-life situation.

Mind skill 3:   Creating rules

1. Detect any unrealistic rules that contribute to your making love and/or enjoying sex less well than you would like.

2. Use disputing and challenging skills to question the most important unrealistic rule that you detected above.

3. Change the unrealistic rule into a more realistic rule.

4. Put your realistic rule on to a reminder card or cassette and rehearse it daily for as long as necessary to learn it properly.

Mind skill 4:   Creating perceptions

Part A: Creating more accurate perceptions of yourself

If you think your lovemaking goes less well than you would like because of inaccurate perceptions of yourself,

1. Identify your inaccurate perceptions of yourself and of how you communicate.
2. Use questioning skills to challenge your inaccurate perceptions.
3. Restate your inaccurate perceptions as more realistic perceptions.
4. Put your more realistic perceptions on to a reminder card or a cassette and rehearse them daily for as long as necessary to learn them properly.

Part B: Creating more accurate perceptions of your partner

If you think your making love less well than you would like is because of inaccurate perceptions of your partner,

1. Identify your inaccurate perceptions of her/him and of how s/he communicates.
2. Use questioning skills to challenge your inaccurate perceptions.

3. Restate your inaccurate perceptions with more realistic perceptions.
4. Put your more realistic perceptions on to a reminder card or a cassette and rehearse them daily for as long as necessary to learn them properly.

Mind skill 5:   Creating explanations

1. If relevant, think about how you learned to make love and/or enjoy sex insufficiently well in the first place.
2. Why do you think you are still making love and/or enjoying sex insufficiently well?
3. Challenge any possibly inaccurate explanations that maintain you in making love and/or enjoying sex insufficiently well now and, if appropriate, either discard them or restate them more accurately.
4. Put your more realistic explanations on to a reminder card or a cassette and rehearse them daily for as long as necessary to learn them properly.

Mind skill 6:   Creating expectations

1. Make up an activity sheet with the following headings, then assess the risks and gains of changing your own communication in one of the phases of the lovemaking cycle.

Gains of changing (pluses)	Risks of changing (minuses)

If the gains outweigh the risks, identify the communication skills you need to perform competently and change your communication.
2. Make up an activity sheet with the following headings, then assess the risks and gains of requesting your partner to change her/his communication in one of the phases of the lovemaking cycle.

Gains of making request (pluses)	Risks of making request (minuses)

If the gains outweigh the risks, identify the communication skills you need to perform competently and make the request.

15

Managing Anger and Communicating Assertively

*Nothing is so strong as gentleness and
nothing is so gentle as real strength.*

Ralph W. Stockman

In this chapter my focus is on individual partner skills of managing anger and asserting yourself, whereas the next chapter focuses on your joint skills of solving relationship problems together. On the one hand, you can destroy happiness in your relationship by not managing your anger well. On the other hand, you can create happiness and avoid unnecessary pain by communicating assertively. American psychologists Robert Alberti and Michael Emmons define assertion as follows: 'Assertive behavior promotes equality in human relationships, enabling us to act in our own best interests, to stand up for ourselves without undue anxiety, to express honest feelings comfortably, to exercise personal rights without denying the rights of others' (1995, p. 6).

In couple relationships, there may be many times when you think it appropriate to stand up for your rights. Such rights include being treated with respect as an intelligent human being; stating your priorities, feelings, opinions and values; saying 'yes', 'no', or 'maybe' and being heard; saying 'I don't know', changing your mind or being able to make mistakes; declining responsibility for your partner's problems; and dealing with your partner without being dependent on them for approval.

Advantages of using assertion skills when faced with negative communication from your partner include the following:

- You increase your partner's awareness not only of their communication, but of your reactions to it. For example, until Ben told Lucy, she did not realize how much joking in public about Ben upset him. Up to now Ben had gone along with the joke and colluded in his misery.
- If your partner accepts the feedback, you have provided them with the opportunity to change.

- If your partner does not entirely accept your feedback, you can discuss your respective viewpoints and try to negotiate a solution.
- Your openness can prevent resentment and secret thoughts that might increasingly poison your relationship.

NONASSERTIVE, AGGRESSIVE AND ASSERTIVE COMMUNICATION

In most situations, you may feel, think and communicate in three main ways: nonassertive, aggressive or assertive (Alberti and Emmons, 1995). Each of these three ways incorporates vocal and bodily communication as well as words. Also, you can react to what your partner says in three ways: nonassertively, aggressively or assertively. In reality, you will react in different situations with various mixtures of nonassertion, aggression and assertion. Nobody is completely assertive.

Nonassertive communication is passive, compliant, submissive and inhibited. You do not like what is happening to you, but you give in and allow it to continue. You buy peace at the expense of denying your rights. Sometimes, realistically, nonassertive communication may be the best option: for instance, for a limited period Ann chooses to put up with her partner Shane's irritability because she realizes that, after a back operation, he is still weak and in pain. On other occasions, though, nonassertive communication may be 'wimping out'.

Aggressive communication is self-enhancing at the expense of your partner. You are unfriendly, quarrelsome and unnecessarily hostile. You behave as though you 'have a chip on your shoulder'. You try to get your way through dominating and overpowering rather than by influencing your partner. Your communication is unnecessarily threatening, even to the point of physical violence. Passive aggression is a variation on aggressive communication. Here you hurt your partner by withdrawing from meeting his or her needs in some way and playing the victim.

Assertive communication reflects confidence and respect for both yourself and your partner. You respond flexibly and appropriately strongly to different situations. You remember that you have responsibilities toward your partner and your relationship as well as rights. When communicating assertively your thinking is disciplined, realistic and goal-oriented; your basic feeling is that of adequacy and you manage to control potentially negative feelings like anger; your verbal, vocal and bodily messages are clear and appropriately firm; and your actions back up what you say.

Assertion, acceptance and anger

A useful distinction exists between feeling angry and communicating aggressively. Anger in relationships can be anxiety-motivated and interact with other feelings like jealousy, which is fear of losing your partner or your place in your partner's affections (de Silva, 1997). But persistent anger is like a psychological toothache. You can become so self-absorbed with your anger and resentment that you can scarcely think of anything else. Then anger can be the mortal enemy of love, especially when you communicate aggressively to your partner.

Angry feelings do not in themselves destroy the fabric of relationships, but managing them poorly may do so. Inasmuch as anger represents a constructive life force to be a person in your own right and to be taken notice of, it has a positive base. In fact, angry feelings can spur you to become more assertive and relate better. For instance, your anger can be a *guide* to a clearer definition of yourself. Both sexes can use anger to become more expert at knowing who they are and what they want. In addition, anger can be a *signal* for yourself and your partner that something is wrong in your relationship and requires attention. This should be a cue to look at your own thoughts, feelings and communications and not just those of your partner. Also, anger can be a *motivator* leading to more honest communication when you are unhappy with aspects of your relationship.

The concepts of acceptance and tolerance touch on anger in many ways. For instance, the degree to which you accept yourself is likely to influence how accepting you are of your partner. Tolerance is the ability to accept variations in the standards you apply to yourself and to your partner. You are less likely to be angry with your partner the more you can tolerate their separateness and difference. In addition, acceptance is related to letting go. For instance, you may become less angry if you relinquish some of your struggle to change your partner. Sometimes either ignoring matters or addressing how you create your own anger is better than asserting yourself all the time.

DEVELOPING YOUR COMMUNICATION

If you are patient in one moment of anger,
you will escape a hundred days of sorrow.

Chinese proverb

Dimensions of assertive communication

Verbal, vocal and bodily communication

When managing anger and being assertive, good vocal and bodily communication is essential in supporting what you say. Where possible, send verbal 'I' messages that accept responsibility for your thoughts, feelings and actions rather than 'You' messages. For instance, 'I would like you to cooperate in this way' (specifying how) is preferable to 'You are uncooperative'. Also, communicate clearly and say what you really mean rather than beat about the bush.

Your voice needs to be easily audible and firm, without being overwhelming. Appropriate bodily communication includes looking your partner directly in the eye when delivering your assertive message; using consistent facial expressions, for instance not smiling when you are serious; sitting or standing with good body posture rather than slouching; and using deliberate and non-threatening hand and arm movements to help express yourself in a constructive fashion.

In this example, Phil wants to stop his former partner, Alison, from keeping coming around to his flat to try to rekindle their relationship. He decides to use the following assertion skills when she next comes to the door.

Verbal communication	Alison, we've *talked enough* already. I *don't want* you to come around again. Please *go now*.
Vocal communication	Firm, reasonably loud, measured pace, emphasis on italicized words.
Bodily communication	Stand erect with chest out, his body facing hers, strong eye contact.

If Alison does not go, Phil can repeat his assertive message; if she still does not go he can slowly but firmly shut the door.

Muscle and timing

When asserting yourself, consider how forceful to be so that your partner 'gets the message'. 'Muscle' refers to the degree of strength of your assertive communication. As a rule, you should use just enough muscle to make your point. Where possible, assume good intentions, be friendly, use tact and diplomacy and be gentle. Your partner's goodwill is precious to maintaining your relationship, so avoid using a cricket bat where a feather would do. It is better for your partner to change willingly rather than under duress. The more muscle you use, the greater the risk of arousing resistances and anger and also leaving a residue of resentment that can surface later.

Timing refers to when you deliver assertion messages. Sometimes you have no choice, for instance if your partner makes an unwanted sexual advance. On occasions, you may require on-the-spot assertion skills to counter remarks you did not expect. Frequently, however, you can choose when and where to be assertive. It may be easier for you to communicate assertively to your partner when your feelings are back under control, your energy level is good, you have sufficient time to do it properly, and you have thought through what to say and how to say it. Also, consider when your partner might be most receptive to really listening to your assertive communication. Though not always possible, try to avoid times when he or she is in a bad mood or concentrating on doing something else.

Become aware of how you avoid being assertive. Frequently, you do better to confront your partner's negative behaviour early on rather than avoid the confrontation. Keeping putting it off can allow your partner to continue, if not worsen, the behaviour. However, on other occasions, you can rightly adopt a wait-and-see approach since the problem may pass without your needing to do anything.

Expressing anger assertively

Assuming you decide it is worth conveying anger to your partner how do you go about it? Though it is not always easy, try to use tact and diplomacy in your verbal messages. You can give specific feedback to your partner about what bothers you; state your feeling as an 'I' message; and let your partner know what you want. Also, beware of put-downs, defensiveness and playing the victim. Below is an example of the difference between expressing anger aggressively and assertively.

Emily to Dave	
Aggressive anger	'You're insulting my dad again. What's wrong with you? Dad's much smarter than you. Shut your bloody gob.'
Assertive anger	'When you call my dad an interfering bastard, I feel very angry. Please stop it.'

When expressing anger assertively, accompany your assertive verbal communication with appropriate vocal and bodily communication. For instance, Emily can speak in a firm voice without shouting, and she can emphasize words like 'very angry' and 'stop'. Also, Emily can make good eye contact and avoid gestures that threaten Dave, such as finger jabbing.

Apologizing and taking corrective action

Partners need relationship repair skills. If you are capable of acknowledging hurtful behaviours when pointed out, and willing to change them, you can not only defuse situations but can also make it easier for your partner to behave likewise. Your honesty and humility can transform ill-will into goodwill.

If you have been unreasonably aggressive, you are likely to have hurt your partner and diminished their self-esteem. When you have cooled down, you may feel genuine remorse and shame. You may wish to put right the suffering and pain you have caused your partner. Making genuine apologies is a vital assertion skill for repairing relationships. A good verbal apology restores balance by acknowledging that you have broken a norm or relationship rule: for example, 'I'm sorry that I was so rude about your dad last night.' You may add an explanation for being so aggressive: for instance, 'I had drunk too much' or 'I've been overworking'. Your partner may perceive a good verbal apology as insincere unless your vocal and bodily communication also show genuine regret. When apologizing, you can physically reconnect with your partner by touching his or her hand, arm or shoulder.

Sometimes, you can make amends by your actions instead of or as well as your words: for instance, by a gift. You can also mend fences by offering some sort of compensation: 'Please let me know if there is anything I can do to make it up to you?'

It is better not to apologize if you do not really mean it. You are likely to do more damage to your relationship rather than repair it if you apologize and then do the same thing again. Corrective actions speak louder than crocodile tears.

Disagreeing, saying 'no', and setting limits

In equal relationships, each partner feels free to disagree. However, you can disagree without being unnecessarily disagreeable. When conversing, one approach to disagreeing is to counter your partner's idea by directly stating your opinion: for example, you counter 'I'd like us to go and play tennis' with 'I'd like us to go to the movies'. You can soften this by reflecting your partner's opinion to show that you have clearly heard them, before stating your own: 'You'd like us to go and play tennis, but I'd like us to go to the movies.' In addition to 'I'd like to ...', words that show you disagree without first signalling disagreement include 'I'd prefer to ...', 'I want to ...', 'I think that ...', and 'I feel ...'.

Another approach to disagreeing is first to state your disagreement and then make an 'I' statement about your position: for instance, 'I disagree. I'd like us to go to the movies.' In addition to 'I disagree', you can start such statements with 'I see things differently', 'I'm not comfortable with that', or 'I'd prefer that we didn't'.

When disagreeing, listen carefully to your partner's reactions. You can avoid being unnecessarily negative if you also show your partner when you agree with all or part of what they say or do.

You may need to learn to say 'no' assertively. Part of this is learning neither to feel afraid nor guilty about saying 'no'. Another part of this is actually saying 'no' backed up by vocal and bodily communication and, if necessary, taking action that shows you mean what you say.

Mary, 42, keeps asking her partner Jack, 47, for money so that she can go to the Casino and gamble. Jack usually starts by saying 'no' and then ends up giving her some money.

In this example, Mary knows that Jack does not mean what he says. Jack's words say 'no', but his actions say 'yes' and he ends up rewarding exactly the kind of behaviour he wants to discourage. It is preferable for Jack to say 'no' firmly and, if necessary, to reinforce his message by calmly taking appropriate action: for instance, never giving Mary gambling money.

In this book, saying 'no' means refusing your partner's or another person's behaviour totally whereas setting limits means placing restrictions on it. In setting limits, you require clarity about your goals.

Sue and Matt, a couple in their late twenties, have a friend called Chloe who lives in a nearby town and keeps phoning them two or three times a week to talk about her problems. Sue and Matt like Chloe and want to help her. However, they also value their privacy and increasingly resent Chloe's intrusions on it. Thinking about their own communication, Sue and Matt realize that they have been rewarding Chloe's dependency on them by taking all her calls and allowing her to talk on at length. Together, Sue and Matt establish a goal of allowing Chloe to phone them once a week at a mutually convenient time. Having established their goal, Sue and Matt decide to let Chloe know next time she calls that they value her friendship, are interested in her and are happy to talk, but would prefer just one good conversation a week. Sue and Matt decide that, if Chloe asks for a reason, they will state that they both lead busy lives and need more space for themselves. If Chloe phones them more than once, they will remind her of their request and ask her to think about it. If Chloe still does not get the message, Sue and Matt can consider saying 'no more phone calls'.

Often, as in the above example, setting limits involves not colluding in another's dependency on you. If your partner has a tendency to off-load responsibility for their problems and decisions to you, some verbal messages that can help you hand back responsibility to him or her are 'What are your choices?', 'What are your goals in the situation?', 'How can you handle the situation better?', or 'What are your options?'

Requesting changes in your partner's behaviour

Partners in relationships build up patterns of behaviour. When you request a change in your partner's behaviour you may have one of three goals: getting them

(1) to do something that they are not already doing;
(2) to do something that they are already doing either more and/or better; and
(3) lessening or stopping an unwanted behaviour.

You may be nonassertive, aggressive or assertive in each of these three areas. Below are some examples.

The first example focuses on *requesting a new behaviour*. Jessica wants Tim to bring her flowers on birthdays and anniversaries.

Nonassertive:	Keep commenting on how other people bring their partners flowers on birthdays and anniversaries.
Aggressive:	'You've got no imagination. Don't you know that a woman likes flowers on birthdays and anniversaries?'
Assertive:	'Tim I've got a request for you. I'd really appreciate it if you gave me flowers on birthdays and anniversaries.'

The second example focuses on *requesting more of an existing behaviour*. George wishes that Jennie would show more interest in his job.

Nonassertive:	Say nothing, but feel bad.
Aggressive:	'You only seem interested in your own job. Why don't you take more interest in mine?'
Assertive:	'I like it when I can talk to you about my job. I genuinely value your opinions and I'd really appreciate your showing more interest in my work.'

The third example focuses on *requesting less of or the stopping of a behaviour*. You study for an exam tomorrow and your partner plays a CD very loud.

Nonassertive:	You thump the table and curse to yourself.
Aggressive:	'Turn that bloody CD player down. Don't you realize that I have work to do.'
Assertive:	'When you're playing a CD so loud, I can't concentrate on revising for my exam tomorrow. Please turn the volume down.'

When requesting a behaviour change, where possible, emphasize the positive by stating what you want rather than what you do not want. In addition, remember your partner is more likely to maintain a changed behaviour if you thank them.

Defensiveness is a common initial reaction to requests for behaviour change. It does not necessarily indicate either that you have asserted yourself poorly or that you may not ultimately be successful. Even if unsuccessful, you can only be responsible for your own communication. The expectation that your partner will always do what you want is unrealistic and can only contribute to your denigrating yourself when he or she does not.

Assuming you decide to persist in the assertion you have a number of options. First, you may pause after the negative response and then calmly yet firmly repeat your behaviour change request. Second, you may reflect your partner's feelings before repeating your request.

Partner A:	When you play a compact disc so loud, I can't concentrate on revising for my exam tomorrow. Please turn the volume down.
Partner B:	Why the hell are you complaining?
Partner A:	I realize you're angry at my request, but I badly need to concentrate on my revision and would be grateful if you could turn the CD player down.
Partner B (still not too pleased): OK.	

A third option is to use more muscle. For instance, you may both use a firmer voice and also strengthen your verbal message by saying 'I'm serious, please turn the CD player down'. A fourth option is to try to negotiate a mutually acceptable solution – for instance, negotiating times when your partner can play the CD player loud and times when you can revise without it. Some skills for jointly solving relationship problems are reviewed in the next chapter.

EMPOWERING YOUR MIND

If a person continues to see only giants, it means he is still looking at the world through the eyes of a child.

Anais Nin

There are many occasions when you can show love and caring for your partner by disciplining your thinking when you feel angry. If you use some central mind skills you can free yourself to manage your anger constructively and to communicate assertively. A one-word amendment to Shakespeare's statement 'Love's best habit is a soothing tongue' involves replacing the word 'tongue' with the word 'mind': 'Love's best habit is a soothing mind'. A soothing mind is the precondition for a soothing tongue.

Creating self-talk

Negative self-talk interferes with your own and your partner's effectiveness in asserting yourselves. Illustrative negative self-talk statements include 'I'm no good', 'I'm a failure', 'I'll only make matters worse', 'Why bother?', 'What's the use?' and 'My partner never takes any notice of me'.

If you tend to be impulsive when angry and 'shoot your mouth', consider creating calming and cooling self-talk. Simple self-instructions like 'calm down', 'cool it', 'count to ten' and 'take it easy' can often give you the time and space to get your feelings more under control.

Let's take the example of cooking a special dinner for your partner who arrives an hour late without contacting you. Your negative self-talk statements might be 'My partner doesn't love me', 'My partner never considers my feelings' and 'After all the trouble I've been to, then my partner does this to me'. You identify your negative self-talk as inaccurate or at least decide to give your partner the benefit of the doubt. You counteract your negative self-talk by creating coping self-talk statements.

- Your clarifying-goals statement is 'My goal is to find out what's happened and, if necessary, to let my partner know I appreciate being contacted, if possible'.
- Your calming statements include 'Relax' and 'Take it easy'.
- Your cooling statements are 'Cool it' and 'Remember, don't let my pride get in the way'.
- Your coaching statements include 'Smile and seem pleased to see him/her' and 'Give him/her the opportunity to explain why he/she is late'.
- Your affirming statements include 'I can handle this' and 'I know my partner cares for me'.

Above I illustrated creating coping self-talk statements for a specific situation requiring you to manage anger and communicate assertively. You can also create self-talk that develops your general ability to be assertive with your partner. For example, you can rehearse and practise the following statements that encourage assertion: 'I have a right to say/do that', 'I have a responsibility to stand up for myself', 'I believe in equality in my relationships', 'My opinions count', and 'I am important'.

Creating visual images

You can create visual images that help you to manage anger better and to communicate assertively with your partner. In Chapter 5 I reviewed some ways in which you could create calming images, for instance imagining lying by the beach, and cooling images for releasing and diminishing your anger.

In addition, you can use visual rehearsal before specific situations needing assertion (Deffenbacher *et al.*, 1996). Start by getting a real picture of the scene in your imagination as if in a photograph and then turn it into a moving picture that contains your assertive communication. You can enhance your motivation by imagining the positive outcomes for yourself and your partner of your assertion. You may also imagine ways of coping with different responses from your partner to your assertion. Before, during and after your mental rehearsals you can create alerting, clarifying goals, calming, cooling, coaching and affirming self-talk, as appropriate. A thorough approach to visual rehearsing increases your chances of using good assertion skills in real life.

Creating rules

Ellis (1977) considers that the main cause of anger is that people are unwilling to relinquish childish demandingness. When growing up, you may have been subject to many pressures to become angry and then not to communicate assertively. Also, you may have lived with parents who managed their anger by aggression or nonassertion. Probably every partner possesses some unrealistic personal rules that generate anger and interfere with assertion. These rules place unnecessary demands on yourself and your partner.

Examples of anger-generating rules include 'A wife/husband must always ...', 'My partner must approve of me all the time', 'My partner must never disagree with me', and 'My partner must not in any way attempt to restrict my freedom'. In addition, some rules can interfere with your ability to communicate assertively: 'I/my partner must be nice'; 'I/my partner must avoid conflict'; 'I/my partner must be liked'; 'I/my partner must not have wishes of my/their own'; and 'I/my partner must never hurt each other'.

Let's take the unrealistic rule about hurting your partner. Once identified, you can dispute and restate it.

Unrealistic rule: 'I must never hurt my partner.'
Realistic rule: 'I prefer not to hurt my partner, but I think it is important to confront significant issues between us, even though sometimes this may cause pain.'

Furthermore, assuming both partners agree, you could make this into a relationship rule: 'While we prefer not to hurt each other, we think it is important to our relationship to confront significant issues between us, even though sometimes this may cause pain.'

Creating perceptions

Perceive yourself accurately

Sometimes you and your partner each see yourself as less powerful, and hence your partner as more powerful, than either of you really are. Furthermore, you may inhibit assertion by seeing yourself negatively: for instance, as 'selfish', 'bossy' and 'domineering'. Adjectives denigrating women's assertion include 'unfeminine', 'bitchy' and 'castrating'. In addition, a partner may keep the other partner docile, by making them feel bad about assertion.

The emphasis in contemporary psychology on partners learning to communicate more assertively brings with it a real danger in couple relationships – you may believe you are being assertive when in fact you are being aggressive. With emotions aroused, standing up for yourself can easily become standing over or treading on your partner.

Perceive your partner accurately

An important skill for partners wishing to avoid this is, wherever possible, perceiving one another through kind rather than unkind eyes. Once a negative framing process starts, partners misinterpret positive or neutral acts as negative and perceive negative acts even more negatively. Such negative perceptions fan and sustain your anger. Furthermore, you may exaggerate the symbolic meaning of your partner's actions. In Chapter 7 I gave the example of Charlie's statement to his wife Fiona 'I've decided we need a new car' possessing the symbolic meaning to Fiona 'Charlie doesn't respect my judgement'. Fiona would now find it difficult to communicate assertively unless she challenged and changed her initial perception.

What skills can you use to perceive more accurately? You question the evidence for your perceptions: for instance, 'Where is the evidence that my partner underestimates me?' As part of this process, you can generate and consider alternative perceptions. Then, you can choose the perception that best fits the available facts.

Creating explanations

In Chapter 8 I discussed how inaccurately blaming others for problems can generate aggressive communication. In addition, there are many explanations of varying degrees of accuracy for being nonassertive. Some explanations focus on yourself: for instance, you are submissive and lacking in confidence because of your nature or upbringing. You may see yourself as the helpless victim of circumstances. You may also think that your partner should know what bothers you without being told. Also, you may have tried unsuccessfully to assert yourself in the past and concluded that it is no use trying again. You may consider your partner's behaviour is so deeply ingrained that it is no use trying to change him or her.

You might like your partner to become more assertive, but think that he or she should be able to do this without your help. Furthermore, if your partner reacts negatively to your attempts at assertion, you may automatically blame him or her for being defensive or bloody-minded rather than search for alternative explanations.

The danger of all these potentially faulty explanations for how you and your partner communicate is that they are dead ends. You need to become aware both of your faulty explanations and of their consequences for you and your relationship. You can then distinguish between fact and inference and form explanations that are more conducive to communicating assertively.

Creating expectations

Many partners underestimate the losses from displays of anger and, consequently, fail to exert sufficient self-discipline. You may underestimate the pain your behaviour causes and how it may create, sustain and escalate problems. You can come on too strong and too frequently. You can fail to give your partner the benefit of the doubt by wrongly expecting that, if you give an inch, he or she will take a mile.

Sometimes assertion in couple relationships seems much more risky than in relationships with less to lose. You may find that you are testing the limits of your partner's commitment to your relationship. You may create expectations of catastrophic consequences resulting from your assertion and greatly overestimate the probability of negative outcomes. Furthermore, you may minimize your ability to cope with any negative consequences you receive from communicating assertively.

However, you can also underestimate the positive consequences of assertion. Minimizing of the possibility of things going right can hold you back. Because you inadequately perceive the possible gains, you are unwilling to take risks.

Awareness of any tendency you may have to either overestimate the negative or underestimate the positive consequences of communicating assertively is the starting point for working on these mind skills deficiencies. Challenge your existing expectations in specific situations by realistically appraising both potential gains and losses. You can also become more confident about being assertive if you acknowledge any strengths you possess in this area. Also, you can acknowledge supportive people, for instance your partner or friends, who can help you to communicate more assertively.

ACTIVITIES

As you see fit, do the activities either on your own, or with your partner, or with some other suitable person, such as a relationship counsellor or trainer.

Activity 15.1   Assessing managing anger

Answer the following questions in the context of your relationship with your partner.

1.To what extent is managing anger a problem for you?
2. How good are you at tuning into your angry feelings?
3. What are the other feelings, for instance hurt or anxiety, that you experience when you are angry?
4. What physical reactions, for instance facial tension, do you experience when angry?
5. How confident a person are you and to what extent does this affect your proneness to anger?
6. In each of the following areas, how do you communicate when you feel angry?

- verbal communication
- vocal communication
- bodily communication
- touch communication
- taking action communication

7. Have you ever been or do you consider you have the potential to be physically violent with your partner when angry? If so, please elaborate.

Activity 15.2   Assessing communicating assertively

Part A: Assessing assertion, nonassertion and aggression

For each of the items below, indicate with the appropriate code which of the following three options best describes how you either do or might respond.

NON	nonassertive communication
AGG	aggressive communication
ASS	assertive communication

You respond Items

1. _____   Your partner tries verbally to bully you to do as they wish.
2. _____   In a cinema your partner keeps talking during a film.
3. _____   Smoke from your partner's cigarette is blowing in your face.
4. _____   Your partner conducts a loud mobile phone conversation in a restaurant.

5. _____ You discuss with your partner a topic about which you feel strongly.
6. _____ Your partner requests a favour that you do not want to give.
7. _____ Your partner is boring you by talking far too much.
8. _____ You think that your partner has given you too little change after a purchase.
9. _____ Your partner wants sex when you do not feel particularly in the mood.
10. _____ Your partner aggressively tells you that you are wrong.
11. _____ Your partner interrupts you when you make an important personal disclosure.
12. _____ Your partner is not doing their fair share of the household chores.

1. Count up the number of times you answered in each category.
2. In general, to what extent do you consider you are assertive, nonassertive, aggressive or a mixture of each and why?
3. In your relationship with your partner, to what extent do you consider you are assertive, nonassertive, aggressive or a mixture of each and why?

Part B Identifying specific problem situations

Fill in the relationship problem list, by identifying specific situations in your relationship with your partner in which you would like to be more assertive.

Relationship problem list

1. _____
2. _____
3. _____
4. _____
5. _____
6. _____

Activity 15.3   Developing assertive communication skills

Part A   Assessment

With regard to your relationship with your partner, assess your good and poor skills in each of the following areas. Remember to focus on vocal and bodily as well as on verbal communication. Where possible, illustrate your assessment in each area with specific examples.

- expressing angry feelings
- apologizing and taking corrective action

- disagreeing
- saying 'no'
- setting limits
- requesting a new behaviour
- requesting more of an existing behaviour
- requesting less of or the stopping of an existing behaviour
- handling defensiveness

Part B   Assertive communication

Either for one of the problem situations you listed in Activity 15.2 or for another problem situation in your relationship with your partner,

1. Clarify and state your goals.
2. Develop a plan to attain your goals by communicating assertively with your partner. As appropriate, take into account verbal, vocal, bodily, touch and taking action communications.
3. Rehearse and practise communicating assertively, including using visual rehearsal.
4. Implement your communicating assertively skills.
5. Evaluate how well you used your communicating assertively skills and the positive and negative consequences of your using them for yourself and your partner.

Activity 15.4   Developing mind skills for communicating assertively

Address the mind skills that you identify as most important to helping you to manage anger and communicate assertively. Consult the text if in doubt about any of the mind skills.

Mind skill 1:   Creating self-talk

1. Think of a situation in your relationship with your partner in which you might manage your anger and communicate assertively less well than you would like.
2. Identify any negative self-talk that contributes to your managing your anger less well and communicating less assertively.
3. Specify a clarifying-goals statement for the situation and create two each of calming, cooling, coaching, and affirming statements. Then, if appropriate, develop self-talk that puts together goals, calming, cooling, coaching, and affirming statements.
4. Put your statements on cue cards or on a cassette and rehearse them daily for as long as you need to learn them properly.
5. Implement your self-talk in real life and assess its consequences.

Mind skill 2:   Creating visual images

1. Think of a situation in your relationship with your partner in which you might manage your anger and communicate assertively less well than you would like.
2. Think of the verbal, vocal, bodily, and taking action communication skills you require that will help you to communicate competently in the situation.

3. Visually rehearse yourself communicating competently in the situation, including coping with any difficulties and set-backs that occur.

4. Accompany your visual rehearsal with appropriate coping self-talk.

5. Practise your visual rehearsal plus coping self-talk skills daily for as long as you find it helpful, then also practise communicating competently in the real-life situation.

Mind skill 3:   Creating rules

1. Detect any unrealistic rules that contribute to your managing your anger and communicating assertively less well than you would like in your relationship with your partner.

2. Use disputing and challenging skills to question the most important unrealistic rule that you detected above.

3. Restate the unrealistic rule you disputed above into a more realistic rule.

4. Put your realistic rule on to a reminder card or cassette and rehearse it daily for as long as necessary to learn it properly.

Mind skill 4:   Creating perceptions

Part A: Creating more accurate perceptions of yourself

If you think that in your relationship with your partner your managing your anger and communicating assertively less well than you would like is partly maintained by inaccurate perceptions of yourself,

1. Identify your inaccurate perceptions of yourself and of how you communicate.
2. Use questioning skills to challenge your inaccurate perceptions.
3. Replace your inaccurate perceptions with more realistic perceptions.
4. Put your more realistic perceptions on to a reminder card or a cassette and rehearse them daily for as long as necessary to learn them properly.

Part B: Creating more accurate perceptions of your partner

If you think that in your relationship with your partner your managing your anger and communicating assertively less well than you would like is partly maintained by inaccurate perceptions of her/him,

1. Identify your inaccurate perceptions of her/him and of how s/he communicates.
2. Use questioning skills to challenge your inaccurate perceptions.
3. Replace your inaccurate perceptions with more realistic perceptions.
4. Put your more realistic perceptions on to a reminder card or a cassette and rehearse them daily for as long as necessary to learn them properly.

Mind skill 5:   Creating explanations

1. If relevant, what do you consider to be the explanations for how you learned to manage your anger and/or communicate assertively insufficiently well in the first place?

2. If relevant, what do you consider the explanations for why, in your relationship with your partner, you still manage your anger and/or communicate assertively insufficiently well?

3. Challenge any possibly inaccurate explanations that keep you managing your anger and/or communicating assertively insufficiently well now in your relationship with your partner. If appropriate, either discard them or restate them more accurately.

4. Put your more realistic explanations on to a reminder card or a cassette and rehearse them daily for as long as necessary to learn them properly.

Mind skill 6:   Creating expectations

1. Make up an activity sheet with the following headings, then assess the risks and gains of changing so that you communicate more assertively in all major areas of your relationship with your partner.

Gains of being more assertive (pluses)	Risks of being more assertive (minuses)

If the gains outweigh the risks, identify the specific skills you need to communicate more assertively and put them in action.

2. Make up an activity sheet with the following headings, then assess the risks and gains of requesting a specific behaviour change from your partner in one area of your relationship.

Gains of making request (pluses)	Risks of making request (minuses)

If the gains outweigh the risks, identify the assertive communication skills you need to perform competently and make the request.

16

Managing Relationship Problems

God, grant me the serenity to accept the things I cannot change,
the courage to change the things I can
and the wisdom to know the difference

Reinhold Niebuhr

This chapter focuses on creating and maintaining happiness in relationships by preventing and managing problems. All partners in relationships crave happiness. Unfortunately, as the high incidence of marital breakdown and distress shows, under the weight of problems many partners fail to maintain the level of happiness created earlier.

Relationship problems can vary in severity, duration and frequency. They can generate more heat than light. In addition, what may seem minor issues from outside may possess symbolic meanings to either or both partners that can create huge rows. Consequently problems are not just matters of difference, but of how these matters are seen and understood.

Difference, change and crisis are three main categories for relationship problems.

- Problems of *difference* reflect dissimilarity in partners' wants, wishes and preferences: for instance, spending money, scheduling daily activities, watching TV, and dealing with in-laws.
- *Change* in individual partners and hence in your relationship can cause problems. Such changes include ageing, developing different interests, the impact of feminism, and either partner becoming better educated and/or joining the workforce. Change and impermanence are part of life. However, harmonious development cannot be guaranteed. As one partner develops, he or she may feel constricted and become out of touch with the other.
- Problems of *crisis* reflect possible turning points in relationships. Such problems include infertility, infidelity, unemployment, and serious health problems. Often crises contain the potential for positive as well as for negative outcomes.

Another way of looking at relationship problems is in terms of skill deficiencies that can ignite, sustain or worsen them. For example, partners possessing good skills of managing problems stand a better chance of avoiding serious and long-standing conflicts than those possessing poor skills. Thus a relationship problem has two dimensions: the problem itself and the skills of managing problems possessed by each partner.

PREVENTING PROBLEMS BY MAINTAINING GOODWILL

Often prevention is better than cure. Skilled partners realize the importance of maintaining goodwill. Goodwill can prevent some problems from arising in the first place and reduce ill will in other areas. In couple relationships, you gain strength by cherishing the very being of your partner as the person most important to you and your best friend. On a daily basis you can reaffirm your love and commitment for one another both by showing you care and by maintaining a good sensual relationship. In addition, you can show your love by how well you listen, share intimacies, enjoy sex, manage anger and assert yourselves.

In a loving relationship, your partner's happiness and well-being is as important as your own, if not more so. Furthermore, partners can celebrate many of one another's differences, which are frequently sources of attraction rather than of tension. In addition, even where genuine conflicts of interest exist, partners can gain strength and happiness by seeing one another becoming more fulfilled. For instance, because of his heavy workload as a busy teacher, part of Jamie wants to spend less time with his in-laws. However, because Jamie sees the joy his wife Helen derives from her relationship with her parents, he too gains fulfilment by often visiting them together. Helen appreciates Jamie's support and kindness. As a result, Helen is more tolerant of some of Jamie's different ways. By kind acts, goodwill is created in a way that builds resilience into the relationship. Then when genuine difficulties arise between partners, you are more likely to address them constructively rather than in a climate of mutual recrimination.

COLLUSIVE, COMPETITIVE AND COOPERATIVE COMMUNICATION

Collusion, competition and cooperation are the three predominant modes of communication partners can use for managing relationship problems. These styles correspond to the threefold distinction between nonassertion, aggression and assertion I described in Chapter 15.

- In the *collusive* communication mode you are unassertive. You collude in avoiding or submerging problems in your relationship. You may wish to keep the peace for fear of the psychological discomfort of confronting problems. You may deceive yourself as to your motivation for colluding and insufficiently acknowledge your anxieties about conflict. In this mode you may be giving way to your partner much of the time. Collusion should not be confused with either rationally accepting important differences or ignoring unimportant negative behaviour.
- In the *competitive* communication mode, you are aggressive. You view the problem as one in which there are scarce resources. Consequently, there has to be

a winner and a loser. The loser is not going to be you. You adopt an 'I win – You lose' approach to conflicts and do all in your power to get your way. Your tactics may include manipulation, not telling the whole truth, not admitting mistakes, and intimidating verbal, vocal and bodily communication. The risks of competitive communication include eliciting aggressive responses, not arriving at the best solution, and your partner feeling violated by you. Though you may win in the short term, you may still pay a high price for your victory.

• In the *cooperative* communication mode, you are assertive. You relate to your partner on the basis of respect. You work as a team both to prevent unnecessary conflicts and also to arrive at mutually satisfactory solutions to real conflicts. You adopt a collaborative mental outlook in which you acknowledge mutual responsibility for problems in the relationship and realize that you may both need to change if these problems are to be managed satisfactorily. You strive to perceive your partner in balanced ways and to act with affection, tact and diplomacy. You do not try to impose your wishes on your partner. You seek solutions that maximize the gains and minimize the costs for one another and for your relationship.

In reality, couples may have complementary communication modes, in which they adopt a predominant mode as a couple, and mixed modes, consisting of different mixes of collusion, cooperation and competition. For example, one partner may collude to avoid open conflict with a competitive mate.

Where only one of you begins solving a problem in a cooperative communication mode, the risk is that you do not maintain it in the face of continued competition or avoidance from your partner. Cooperative partners may require considerable inner strength to counter, and hopefully prevail over, the poor skills of collusive or competitive partners. As relationships mature, both partners can become more skilled at managing relationship problems cooperatively.

DEVELOPING YOUR COMMUNICATION

> *Hatred paralyses life; love releases it.*
> *Hatred confuses life; love harmonizes it.*
> *Hatred darkens life; love illuminates it.*
>
> Martin Luther King

Increasing your exchange of caring communications and solving relationship problems cooperatively are two joint approaches that you can use to improve your relationship. I review each in turn.

Increasing your exchange of caring communications

If necessary, what can you and your partner do to try and improve an unhappy relationship? You can show more care to one another. Partners in distressed relationships give each other more uncaring communication than those in happy relationships. Happy couples keep their relationships rewarding both by maintaining existing caring behaviours and by initiating new ones. However, increasing your exchange of caring communications is definitely not a substitute for developing communication skills for solving relationship problems cooperatively.

Increasing the exchange of caring communication involves first identifying and then increasing caring communications.

Step one: Identifying caring communications

Though it may seem obvious, you may need to become more aware that you and your partner will be more attractive to one another if you are caring rather than uncaring. This basic point can easily get lost in the heat of a conflict. You may also need to remind yourself that how you communicate with your partner influences how your partner communicates with you. If anything, partners tend to respond to negative or uncaring communications more quickly than positive or caring ones. Nevertheless, if you go on making efforts to show you care, chances are good that your communication will soften your partner's attitude.

Both of you may need to become more aware of the care that already exists in your relationship. You can share your perceptions of existing caring communications by each of you making a list of how you show you care. What do you do that pleases? What do you say that pleases? This process can help partners discover not only the kinds of care each currently offers, but also how much or little care you may show. Listing your own gaps in caring may be less threatening than having them pointed out by your partner. These lists of 'How I show I care' can be exchanged and discussed. Refrain from hostile criticism during this discussion.

Now you can move on to making wish lists for additional caring communications. You can choose from two ways to approach this: making your own wish list or anticipating your partner's wish list. In making your own wish list, you address the question 'In what additional ways would I like you to show more care?' This approach helps partners develop skills of requesting care.

To anticipate what your partner would request, you address the question 'How else would you like me to show I care in ways that would improve our relationship?' This approach, of anticipating your partner's wish list, helps you assume responsibility for providing care.

In either approach, include some small caring communications that are not necessarily in your areas of major conflict, to allow you and your partner to take some easy first steps. In addition, try to make some of these communications the sort that can be performed almost daily — for example, 'Ask me how my day has been when I get home from work'. When both of you have had enough time to make your wish lists, exchange and discuss them.

Step two: Increasing caring communications

To increase caring communications, each of you can develop willingness lists for caring communications. Your goal here is to make an agreement in which you both state that you will perform some additional caring communications for the other for a specified time period, say the next two weeks. Each of you should feel free to choose which additional caring communications you put on your willingness list. If necessary, clarify each other's requests and offers.

A choice in making agreements or contracts is whether they should be on a something-for-something basis – 'If you do this, I'll do that' – or based on good faith – 'My actions are independent of yours'. Good faith agreements are preferable in personal relationships since they make each of you responsible for your own communication. You can always review your partner's communication of care at the end of the agreement. The number of items on your willingness lists can be unequal, but try to avoid large imbalances.

Following is a simple good faith contract made between Scott and Maggie, both of whom wanted to improve their stormy relationship. During the next week

---

Scott agrees to:
1. have a happy talk period for at least ten minutes each evening when both are at home;
2. go out to dinner together at a restaurant they both like;
3. give Maggie a cuddle at least once a day;
4. phone home when leaving the office late;
5. empty the garbage daily;
6. return Maggie's library books.

Maggie agrees to:
1. have a happy talk period for at least ten minutes each evening when both are at home;
2. go out to dinner together at a restaurant they both like;
3. give Scott one body massage;
4. have sex together at least once;
5. keep books and magazines off the living room sofa;
6. mow the lawn.

Each partner should have a written copy of the agreement. The agreement can be signed and countersigned if you think it will help you to keep it. Partners can post the agreement in places where you are likely to be frequently reminded of its terms – for instance, on a bedroom mirror or on the fridge. Changing your pattern of communication from uncaring to caring may be difficult. If necessary, make a plan for how you are going to stick to your agreement. If you wish to perform further caring actions outside your willingness list, feel free to do so.

A skill of implementing your agreement is to acknowledge and show gratitude for one another's attempts to be caring. For instance, you can say, in a sincere voice, 'Thank-you', 'That's great', 'I like that', or 'I appreciate your saying/doing that'. Also, you can give smiles and loving looks. Possibly in the past you both may have received fewer caring communications from one another because you inadequately showed your gratitude.

When your contract expires, hold a joint review session in which each of you goes through everything you tried. Questions to ask in such sessions include 'Was it noticed?', 'Was it appreciated?', 'What was it like for the giver?', 'What was it like for the receiver?' and 'Could you keep doing it in future?' Where appropriate, you can fine-tune your agreement or make it a stepping stone to another.

Solving relationship problems cooperatively

To jaw-jaw is always better than to war-war.
Winston Churchill

There are five steps involved in solving relationship problems cooperatively:

1. confronting the problem;
2. understanding one another's perspectives;
3. defining the problem;
4. solving the problem; and
5. acting and evaluating.

Some conflicts can be handled more informally. However, on other occasions, you will need to be systematic.

Step one: Confronting the problem

> Lucy and Debbie had been living together for two months and thought each other special. However, both were aware of tensions in their relationship over how much time Debbie spent with her parents. They avoided talking directly about this problem for fear of hurting and then losing each other.

> Lauren was getting increasingly furious because Jordan was not doing his share of cleaning the flat. Lauren kept her resentment to herself until one evening she blew her stack and said a whole lot of things she later regretted.

Some of you, like Lucy and Debbie, may find it easier to avoid than to confront relationship problems. Others, like Lauren, may collect trading stamps and one day cash them in by going for the jugular. There are many skills of confronting relationship problems in ways that are likely to initiate rational rather than destructive processes.

When you become aware of a problem, you may still choose whether or not to confront it openly. Considerations here include what will be gained and whether the problem is important enough to either or both of you to bring it out into the open. Assuming that you decide to bring the conflict out into the open, the following skills may help. Even if you have had a flare-up, you can use your skills of managing anger to calm yourself down. Although you want your partner to take notice of you, you want to avoid being unnecessarily threatening. Shouting and screaming are likely to alienate your partner and risk consolidating unwanted behaviours.

Choose a proper time to raise the issue that there is a problem between you. Also agree on a suitable place to discuss your problems that is quiet, comfortable and free from interruptions and distractions. Possibly kitchens and lounges are better locations than bedrooms for raising and solving problems.

Confronting relationship problems can involve assertion. Use 'I' messages and civilly state the existence of the problem. You can neutrally state the problem as a difference – 'You want to see more of your mother and I want us to spend more time together' – rather than personalizing it – 'There you are, off to your wonderful mother again'. If your partner still does not agree that the problem exists, you can persist until your partner recognizes that this is a problem for them as well as for you. For instance, you can keep looking at your partner directly and use repetition and emphasis to make your point.

Some differences may be resolved quickly and amicably once they are out in the open and discussed. If this is not the case, try to enlist your partner in cooperating to solve the problem. In essence you say: 'We have a problem in our relationship. Let's see if we can cooperate to solve it together for our mutual benefit.' Both of you then need to set aside sufficient time and energy for dealing with it.

Step two: Understanding one another's perspectives

> Ryan and Lisa are unhappy in their marriage. When they argue neither of them really listens to the other. Instead they shout, finger point and make comments like 'You *never* think of anyone but yourself' and 'You have *always* been selfish.'

Partners can agree that, at the start of discussing a problem, each takes turns in having uninterrupted 'air time' to state your perspective. During your air time the only talking that your partner should do is to reflect and clarify your perspective. Each of you is more likely to listen once safe in the knowledge that you will have your turn. If your partner interrupts, you have a number of choices including pausing; saying something like 'Please let me finish, you have had/will have your turn'; and putting out your arm with your palm facing them – a standard body message requesting silence.

Some skills of understanding your partner's perspective when it's your turn to talk include

- focusing on stating your own perspective rather than on analysing your partner;
- sharing your feelings in an open, yet tactful, way;
- using reason to support your points;
- where appropriate, translating complaints, such as 'You're not affectionate enough', into specific requests.

Often it is better to use 'soft' rather than 'hard' disclosures. Hard disclosures, for instance making angry remarks, do not reveal vulnerability. Soft disclosures, for instance sharing feelings of hurt, fear and uncertainty, reveal you as vulnerable to your partner. Christensen and his colleagues (1995) provide the example of Michael, who will not be accepting of Donna's viewpoint if he sees her as just angry at him for not giving her enough attention. However, Michael may be more accepting if Donna discloses her pain at his withdrawal and her loneliness when he is absent. Similarly, Donna may be more accepting of Michael's viewpoint if he discloses his fear of being overwhelmed by her.

When partners become very angry, they can both view themselves as victims of one another's behaviour. However, if you can communicate some insight into how you may have contributed to the problem, you may help your partner to become less self-protective and aggressive. An example of a conciliatory statement might be: 'It's true that I have been irritable lately'. Also, if your intentions toward your partner are positive, clarify them. For instance, Liam truthfully says to Joe: 'I really do want to spend more time with you, but I'm worried sick about making enough money to pay our bills'.

When it's your turn to listen to your partner's perspective, use good skills of listening and showing understanding. Pay particular attention to tuning in to your partner's feelings: this, above all, may help them to feel understood by you. When something your partner says is unclear, tactfully request clarification – for instance, 'I think I hear you saying ..., but I'm not altogether certain?' Where appropriate, show your support and agreement. At the end of your partner's initial statement of perspective, you can summarize to check you have understood it properly. Checking and summarizing helps prevent your making unwarranted assumptions and inferences.

When listening to your partner's perspective, try to turn a deaf ear to any less than flattering remarks about you. See negative remarks as symptoms of hurt and anger and strive for the inner strength to resist 'tuning out' or retaliating. However, look after yourself. If the abuse persists, you can change your tactics by challenging it or by leaving the situation.

In light of any significant new information, update your perspective of your partner and the problem. Acknowledge where you have misunderstood your partner's communication and intentions. Also, be willing to say you are sorry.

Step three: Defining the problem

> Having raised three children, Amy wanted to return to the workforce. Her husband Rod was unhappy about Amy going back to work because he was already under pressure with his job and did not want any extra work at home. Once they became calmer, they both agreed to define the problem as how to get the housework done. Rod admitted he had changed his position from not wanting Amy to have a job once they agreed to define the problem in a way that allowed the preferences of both of them to be met.

In the previous step, each of you may have offered your own definition of the problem between you. Conflicts can become extremely destructive when partners compete to define the problem on their own terms. Both of you risk repetitively stating your positions and getting increasingly frustrated and resentful. Your task in this step is to arrive at a mutually acceptable definition of your problem. In step three, the talking and listening roles that partners adopt are less clear than in step two. Consequently, the risk of destructive arguing is greater.

When you are defining problems, avoid unfair fight tactics and competitive put-downs that show a lack of respect for your partner. Unfair tactics include mindreading and ascribing negative motives; attacking psychologically vulnerable spots; using guilt-engendering tactics, such as playing the victim or crying; and emotionally withdrawing.

Identify and acknowledge any common ground. An important way you can both create common ground and defuse emotions is to acknowledge your own mistakes and hurtful communication. Also, try to deal with the real rather than the surface agendas. For instance, if Paul suspects his partner Julie is having an affair, picking on her in a whole range of other issues is not the best way of trying to define and solve the problem.

The end product of this step is a simple statement of the problem. Avoid personalizing the problem unnecessarily. Where possible, move from defining the problem in 'you-me' terms to defining the problem as an 'it'. As with Rod and Amy, you and your partner may find it easier to address a relationship problem with some detachment if you define it neutrally as a shared problem.

Step four: Solving the problem

Craig and Janet both hated doing the washing up. They also disliked their kitchen sink being full of dirty dishes. After reviewing other solutions, they agreed that they would buy a dishwashing machine. Their agreement included details of how they would share the dishwashing until the machine arrived, how they would go about purchasing the dishwasher, and how they would share the dishwashing once the machine was installed.

Having defined the problem, possibly as an 'it', you can now cooperate to search for mutually acceptable solutions. Searching for alternative solutions is best done in two distinct stages: first, generating solutions and, second, assessing them rationally.

Generating solutions is a creative process. The objective is to generate a range of options, among which there may be some effective ones. Sometimes it helps to brainstorm. The object of brainstorming is to discover ideas. The rules for a brainstorming period include avoiding criticism and evaluation of ideas and coming up with the greatest quantity possible. Whether you brainstorm or not, offer solutions constructively and tactfully: for instance, 'One solution might be to …' as contrasted with 'We should …' – the latter wording can set up a further conflict.

Assess solutions on the basis of what is best for both of you. If you have brainstormed, agree on which solutions seem feasible and assess the possible consequences of each of them. Both partners need to state reactions to possible solutions as preferences rather than demands. Provide logical reasons for your preferences. Also, be prepared to acknowledge if some of your reasons are more emotional than logical – such reasons may still be important. If necessary, ask your partner for their preferences among proposed solutions and the reasons for them.

If you ask couples what makes for a stable relationship, many will answer 'give-and-take'. Some relationship problems, as with the example of Rod and Amy above, lend themselves to 'win-win' solutions for both partners. However, many relationship problems are not so straightforward. Sometimes, the best you can achieve is a 'no-lose' solution, based on give-and-take, where neither party feels violated. When assessing solutions, you may be faced with choices as to whether or not to modify your position. In such circumstances, making realistic trade-offs and compromises can be a useful skill. For instance, regarding household chores, you can either take turns or divide the tasks. Acknowledge and show appreciation for any concessions made by your partner. Also, if necessary, remind her or him of any concessions that you make.

State your agreements clearly. Unclear agreements are more likely to be broken than clear ones, if only through misunderstanding. Often it is desirable to put agreements in writing. Writing out your agreements helps you to verify that they are clearly understood and to avoid future conflicts over the terms of the agreement. Written agreements can also be posted in places where they serve as reminders to implement them. Some agreements involve planning how to implement them. For instance, Craig and Janet's agreement specified who was responsible for purchasing the dishwasher and how this task was to be performed.

Step five: Acting and evaluating

Relationship problems are not solved unless agreements are kept. It is critical to back up your agreements by your actions. Never agree to do anything unless you have sufficient commitment to keep your word. If, for whatever reason, you cannot live within an agreement, renegotiate rather than break it. Also, be careful to avoid overreacting to seeming non-compliance to an agreement by your partner. Assuming your partner still wants the agreement, your goal is to achieve willing adherence rather than to alienate.

When evaluating agreements, couples can modify and change them where necessary. Some solutions may turn out to be deficient when you come to apply them. Frequently, only minor modifications to initial agreements are needed. However, on other occasions, either or both of you may discover that the 'best' solution has major weaknesses. Possibly you have another reasonable solution available from your earlier search for alternatives. Otherwise you need to generate and evaluate further solutions.

EMPOWERING YOUR MIND

How strange to see with how much passion
People view things only in their own fashion.

Molière

Some partners look for trouble and destroy their happiness by turning their relationship into a vale of tears. Others manage mainly to avoid creating unnecessary problems, solve those that can be solved in a mutually satisfactory fashion, and accept that their relationship may contain elements of unsatisfactoriness, but overall it is well worth staying in it. Most couples fall somewhat short of their potential for creating happiness and avoiding pain. Using your mind skills can empower you to manage your relationship problems better.

Creating self-talk

When faced with problems in your relationship, the risk is that you talk yourself into feeling powerless and collusive or competitive rather than into feeling compassionate and cooperative. Instead of each of you focusing on one another's shortcomings, you can join together and create self-talk focusing on thinking and communicating constructively. For example, a cooperative goals statement for increasing the exchange of caring communications might be 'Our joint goal is to cooperate to find ways we can become better at showing more love and affection to one another'. A cooperative goals statement for solving problems together might be 'Our joint goal is to solve this problem in a loving and mutually acceptable way'.

Each of you may need to use calming and cooling statements to keep your anxiety and anger under control. Furthermore, you can coach yourselves through the steps of increasing the exchange of caring communications or of solving problems cooperatively. For instance, in the step of understanding one another's perspective, you might say to yourself: 'Remember – don't interrupt. Instead, use my skills of listening calmly and clearly showing my partner that I understand his/her perspective. I will have my turn to talk.' Also, both of you can create affirming self-talk to remind yourself of good problem-solving skills you have successfully used in the past, the strengths of your relationship, and the underlying love that you and your partner feel for one another.

Creating visual images

Be careful not to create unnecessarily negative images about one another and about the processes and outcomes of solving your relationship problems. You can accompany your affirming self-talk with visual images about the strengths of your relationship and the lovable qualities of one another. Also you can create clear images of the negative outcomes of hurtful communication and the potentially positive outcomes of trying to communicate lovingly, however difficult that may be in times of conflict.

When cooperating to increase the exchange of caring communications, you can each use your imagination to identify what you might do and say to make one another happier in your relationship. Furthermore, you can mentally rehearse communicating competently in the additional ways that you agreed to show care. Also, you can imagine yourself using good skills of showing gratitude for the care your partner shows you.

You can mentally rehearse the steps in the process of cooperatively solving relationship problems in which your skills require improving. In addition, you can use time projection to imagine your relationships at some stage in the future, say three months later, when you have used good problem-solving skills and are much happier together. Furthermore, even if you do not get all of your way in a conflict, you can imagine yourself getting on with life with your partner in a mature way rather than nursing resentment.

Creating rules

In Chapter 15, I mentioned some skills by which partners can become more accepting and less demanding of one another. Partners can also learn to become more accepting and less demanding about problems. Some problems are not easily amenable to compromise and accommodation. Unrealistic rules about the continuing presence of problems in relationships include 'We must have the perfect relationship', 'All problems in our relationship must be solvable', and 'We must never have conflict in our relationship'.

In addition, partners can challenge and restate unrealistic rules about the processes of dealing with relationship problems: for example, 'We must compete with one another' or 'We must collude with one another'. It is much better to create a rule that 'We would prefer not to have major conflicts, but problems will inevitably arise in any close relationship and we can use our skills to manage such problems cooperatively'. If problems persist, partners may need to challenge rules, such as 'We must never seek the help of outsiders', that may block them from obtaining relationship counselling or sex therapy. In addition, some partners may need to challenge and change rules such as 'I must never admit I was wrong and apologize' or 'I must never forgive and move on'.

Creating perceptions

You may need to alter the way you perceive problems in relationships from being nuisances to being challenges. Relationship problems can be opportunities to show your self-restraint and love. Furthermore, together you may develop greater trust and intimacy if you can learn to work together in difficult as well as good times. Also, on the principle that two heads are better than one, together you may arrive at creative solutions to your problems that are better than your individual solutions.

Perceiving yourself inaccurately

When in conflict, take care not to lose sight of the fact that, in many respects, your partner is a precious part of you rather than alien to you. A risk is that, when you feel threatened, you retreat into a self-protective rather than a compassionate way of viewing both yourself and your partner. You may insufficiently perceive the harshness of your judgements and communication. You may perceive yourself as a problem solver when, in reality, you are a problem sustainer. When feeling threatened, you may lose sight of and fail to use some of the cooperative problem-solving skills you possess. Perceiving yourself as relatively powerless, you may make matters worse rather than better. Instead, attempt to realistically acknowledge your strengths and skills in managing problems. In addition, try to perceive accurately and work on those of your skills requiring improvement.

You may also need to guard against your partner's attempts to manipulate your definition of yourself so that you are in the wrong and he or she is in the right. In couple relationships, this can become the tyranny of the weak in which the more vulnerable partner controls the more adequate partner by playing on guilt feelings and wishes for a peaceful life. You may need to confront a manipulative partner with your reactions to how they communicate and invite discussion of what is going on between you.

Perceiving your partner accurately

You may be too kind or too harsh about perceiving negative aspects of your partner and of how they communicate when problems arise. On the one hand you may 'demonize' them and see every problem-solving attempt they make in an unnecessarily negative light. When your partner engages in hard and angry disclosures rather than softer disclosures revealing their vulnerability, you may have to work extra hard to perceive and respond lovingly to their underlying fragility, pain and neediness. On the other hand, you may be insufficiently aware of your partner's manipulations and power plays. If so, both mentally and in how you communicate, you may need to become more assertive.

When problems arise, be careful not to lose sight of positive aspects of your partner and of your relationship together. Without forgetting the pain you feel, you can still acknowledge your partner's attractive features and the happy times you have shared. Often, if couples can identify and acknowledge the strengths in their relationship, their perspective on problems alters and the process of change begins (Christensen *et al.*, 1995).

Creating explanations

An important skill for explaining problems is to view them in terms of the communication patterns between partners. Both of you could genuinely be trying to solve a problem, but your attempts to improve the situation might worsen it. For instance, in the demand-withdraw communication pattern, as one partner demands more closeness, the other partner withdraws. Another communication pattern is that of blamer-placater: as one partner blames, the other attempts to placate. Still another communication pattern is that of overfunctioner-underfunctioner, in which one partner keeps 'picking up the slack' for the other partner and hence rewarding underfunctioning (McKay *et al.*, 1994).

It is easy for partners to locate the cause of their problems externally rather than accept the explanation that together they maintain mutually reinforcing unproductive patterns of communication. Sometimes, if you can step back and review the processes of your communication, you can see how you engage in repetitive patterns that help you stay stuck rather than move forward.

How can you alter this situation? First, you can identify what your genuine differences are. Then you can define the problem as both of your attempts to deal with these differences rather than the differences themselves. Next you can cooperatively search for alternative solutions to how each of you can communicate better about your differences, including recognizing how your own communication influences one another's communication. Then, together you may be in a stronger position to reach a compromise or accommodation about your original differences.

Creating expectations

Be careful about being too quick to create pessimistic expectations about the processes and outcomes of jointly addressing your relationship problems. Instead of expecting non-cooperation, frustration and sabotage, give love a chance by creating positive expectations about the gains of increasing your exchange of caring communications or solving relationship problems cooperatively. If you both are genuinely attempting to develop better mind and communication skills, you have good reason to possess more positive expectations about the processes and outcomes of dealing with your relationship problems in future.

In addition, if each of you has developed skills of becoming more accepting and tolerant of your differences and of the presence of continuing problems in your relationship, you will be less inclined to expect disastrous consequences if you do not get everything you want. Furthermore, remember to expect positive consequences from keeping agreements and negative consequences from breaking (rather than renegotiating) agreements. The more love and concern you as a couple can show when addressing relationship problems, the more grounds you have for expecting that your relationship will continue to flourish and deepen.

ACTIVITIES

As you see fit, do the activities either on your own, or with your partner, or with some other suitable person, such as a relationship counsellor or trainer.

Activity 16.1   Identifying relationship problems

Part A   Identifying relationship problems on your own

Answer the following questions (a) by circling the number that best represents your assessment; and (b) by identifying areas (questions 1–3) and reasons (question 4).

1. Do problems of *difference* characterize our relationship?

Not at all   1   2   3   4   5   6   7   8   9   Very much

Please specify main problem areas.

2. Do problems of *change* characterize our relationship?

Not at all   1   2   3   4   5   6   7   8   9   Very much

Please specify main problem areas.

3. Do problems of *crisis* characterize our relationship?

Not at all   1   2   3   4   5   6   7   8   9   Very much

Please specify main problem areas.

4. Using the scale below rate how satisfied am I with our overall relationship?

Not at all   1   2   3   4   5   6   7   8   9   Very much

Please state main reasons for your assessment.

Part B   Sharing and discussing with your partner

1. You and your partner share and discuss your ratings of relationship problems in each of the following categories:

- difference problems;
- change problems;
- crisis problems.

2. Are there any mutually reinforcing self-defeating patterns in your relationship conflicts, for example, demand-withdraw or blamer-placater? If so, please elaborate.
3. What do you think of the overall level of satisfaction in your relationship?
4. Currently are there any important problems in your relationship that you might want to solve together?

Activity 16.2   Assessing problem-solving modes

Part A   Identifying problem-solving modes on your own

1. Assess the degree to which *you as an individual* solve relationship problems by being:

- collusive
- competitive
- cooperative.

2. Assess the degree to which *your partner as an individual* solves relationship problems by being

- collusive
- competitive
- cooperative.

3. Assess the degree to which *you and your partner as a couple* solve relationship problems by being

- collusive
- competitive
- cooperative.

Part B   Sharing and discussing with your partner

1. Share and discuss your answers to each of the questions in Part A of this activity.

2. Specify what you have learned that you can use to improve your skills of solving relationship problems

(a)   as individuals
(b)   as a couple.

Activity 16.3   Increasing your exchange of caring communications

Part A   Assessing and making wish lists

Work through the procedures described in the text for acknowledging existing caring communications and make wish lists for additional caring communications (pp. 222-3).

Part B   Making an 'If... then ...' statement

Together make an 'If ... then ...' statement.

If we agree upon the following willingness lists for performing caring communications (partners write out two copies of their willingness lists, keeping one and exchanging the other) and implement our agreement,
then these consequences (specify) are likely to follow:

a.
b.
c.
d.

Part C   Implementing and reviewing

Implement your agreement. Review how you implemented your willingness lists. If necessary, fine-tune your agreement and/or use it as a stepping stone to a further agreement. Assess the positive and negative consequences for yourself, your partner and your relationship of increasing the exchange of caring communications. What, if anything, have you learned that may help increase the satisfaction and stability of your relationship in future?

Activity 16.4   Solving relationship problems cooperatively

Part A   Assessing your own and your partner's skills in solving relationship problems cooperatively

1. Assess *your own* good and poor communication skills for each of the following steps in cooperative problem-solving:

Step 1   Confronting the problem
Step 2   Understanding one another's perspectives

Step 3   Defining the problem
Step 4   Solving the problem
Step 5   Acting and evaluating

2. Assess *your partner's* good and poor communication skills for each of the steps.

Part B   Sharing and discussing with my partner

1. You and your partner share and discuss your answers to Part A of this activity.
2. What communication skills, if any, do you need to develop, both as individuals and as a couple, to improve how you solve relationship problems cooperatively?

Part C   Using the steps in cooperative problem-solving

1. Choose a problem that you identified when completing Activity 16.1 or another problem in your relationship that both of you wish to solve (Step 1, Confronting the problem).
2. What have been your attempted solutions to the problem to date? What have been the positive and negative consequences of your attempted solutions? So far, what have been your good and poor skills in trying to solve the problem?
3. Pick a suitable time and place for one or more problem-solving sessions.
4. During your problem-solving session(s) systematically proceed through the following steps:

Step 2   Understanding one another's perspectives
Step 3   Defining the problem
Step 4   Solving the problem

5. Review how well you, individually and as a couple, used the communication skills required for each step.
6. If appropriate, carry out Step 5, acting and evaluating, in relation to the solution you agreed on in your session(s).

Activity 16.5   Developing mind skills for solving relationship problems cooperatively

Partners can choose from two approaches to doing this mind skills activity: either together from the start or separately then together. Address the mind skills that you identify as most important to help you solve relationship problems cooperatively. Consult the text if in doubt about any of the mind skills.

Mind skill 1:   Creating self-talk

1. Think of an existing or anticipated problem that you and your partner might attempt to solve less cooperatively than you would like.
2. Identify any negative self-talk that contributes to your being collusive or competitive in solving the problem.
3. Specify a cooperative clarifying-goals statement for solving the problem and create two

each of calming, cooling, coaching, and affirming statements. Then, if appropriate, develop self-talk that puts together goals, calming, cooling, coaching, and affirming statements.
4. Put your statements on cue cards or on a cassette and rehearse them daily until you know them properly.
5. Use your self-talk in real life and assess the consequences.

Mind skill 2:   Creating visual images

1. Think of an existing or anticipated problem that you and your partner might attempt to solve less cooperatively than you would like.
2. Think of the communication skills (verbal, vocal, bodily, touch and taking action) you will need to communicate competently in the situation.
3. Visually rehearse yourself communicating competently in the situation, including coping with any difficulties and set-backs that occur.
4. Accompany your visual rehearsal with appropriate coping self-talk.
5. Practise your visual rehearsal plus coping self-talk skills daily for as long as you find it helpful, then practise communicating competently about the real-life problem.

Mind skill 3:   Creating rules

1. Detect any unrealistic rules that contribute to you and your partner solving relationship problems less cooperatively than you would like.
2. Use disputing and challenging skills to question the most important unrealistic rule.
3. Change the unrealistic rule into a more realistic rule.
4. Put your realistic rule on to a reminder card or cassette and read or hear your new rule as many times as is necessary to get it into your mind more permanently.

Mind skill 4:   Creating perceptions

Part A: Creating more accurate perceptions of yourself

If you think that, in your relationship with your partner, your solving relationship problems less cooperatively than you would like is partly due to inaccurate perceptions of yourself,

1. Identify your inaccurate perceptions of yourself and of how you communicate.
2. Use questioning skills to challenge your inaccurate perceptions.
3. Replace your inaccurate perceptions with more realistic perceptions.
4. Put your more realistic perceptions on to a reminder card or a cassette and read or hear your new perceptions as many times as you need to get them into your mind more permanently.

Part B: Creating more accurate perceptions of your partner

If you think that solving relationship problems less cooperatively than you would like is partly maintained by inaccurate perceptions of your partner,

1. Identify your inaccurate perceptions of her/him and of how s/he communicates.
2. Use questioning skills to challenge your inaccurate perceptions.
3. Replace your inaccurate perceptions with more realistic perceptions.

4. Put your more realistic perceptions on to a reminder card or a cassette and read or listen to them as many times as necessary to get them into your mind more permanently.

Mind skill 5: Creating explanations

1. If relevant, why do you think you learned to solve relationship problems less well than you would like in the first place?
2. Why do you think you still solve relationship problems less well than you would like?
3. Do you detect any pattern of mutually reinforcing communication that contributes to you and your partner maintaining one or more significant problems in your relationship?
4. Challenge any possibly inaccurate explanations that maintain you and your partner in solving relationship problems less well than you would like and, if appropriate, either discard them or restate them more accurately.
5. Put your more realistic explanations on to a reminder card or a cassette and read or listen to them until you have got them into your mind.

Mind skill 6: Creating expectations

1. Make up an activity sheet with the following headings, then assess the risks and gains of changing so that you and your partner communicate to solve problems more cooperatively throughout your relationship.

Gains of changing (pluses)	Risks of changing (minuses)

If the gains outweigh the risks, identify the specific skills you need to solve relationship problems more cooperatively and put them in action.
2. Make up an activity sheet with the following headings, then assess the gains for you and your partner of keeping your agreements and the risks of breaking them.

Gains of keeping agreements (pluses)	Risks of breaking agreements (minuses)

If the gains far outweigh the risks, please bear this in mind in future.

Postscript

Cultivating Happy Relationships

To keep a lamp burning we have to keep putting oil in it.

Mother Teresa

Relationships, like gardens, require constant cultivation. Many relationships founder because partners fail to nurture them adequately. Instead of keeping tilling the soil, removing the weeds, and applying fertilizers, you allow the beauty, love and happiness in your relationship garden to deteriorate.

In this book I have outlined the mind skills and the communication skills you can develop and use not only to create, but to keep recreating and sustaining your happiness as a couple. Together with courage, persistence, humour and good skills you can continue to enjoy your beautiful relationship garden. I sincerely wish you both the strength and skills to keep creating, cultivating and sharing much happiness and warmth. Then as partners in the true sense of the word you will enrich and deepen your mutual love.

Bibliography

Alberti, R. E. and Emmons, M. L. (1995) *Your Perfect Right: A Guide to Assertive Living* (7th edn). San Luis Obispo, CA: Impact.

Alden, L. E. and Wallace, S. T. (1995) Social phobia and social appraisal in successful and unsuccessful social interactions. *Behaviour Research and Therapy*, **33**, 497–505.

Alford, B. A. and Beck, A. T. (1997) *The Integrative Power of Cognitive Therapy*. New York: Guilford.

American Psychiatric Association (1994) *Diagnostic and Statistical Manual of Mental Disorders* (4th edn). Washington, DC: APA.

Argyle, M. (1987) *The Psychology of Happiness*. London: Routledge.

Argyle, M. (1991) *Cooperation: The Basis of Sociability*. London: Routledge.

Argyle, M. (1992) *The Social Psychology of Everyday Life*. London: Routledge.

Argyle, M. (1994) *The Psychology of Interpersonal Behaviour* (5th edn). London: Penguin.

Argyle, M. and Henderson, M. (1985) *The Anatomy of Relationships and the Rules and Skills to Manage Them Successfully*. Harmondsworth: Penguin.

Bandura, A. (1995) Exercise of personal and collective efficacy in changing societies. In A. Bandura (ed.) *Self-Efficacy in Changing Societies* (pp. 1–45). Cambridge: Cambridge University Press.

Beall, A. E. and Sternberg, R. J. (1995) The social construction of love. *Journal of Social and Personal Relationships*, **12**, 417–38.

Beck, A. T. (1976) *Cognitive Therapy and the Emotional Disorders*. New York: New American Library.

Beck, A. T. (1988) *Love is Never Enough: How Couples Can Overcome Misunderstandings, Resolve Conflicts, and Solve Relationship Problems through Cognitive Therapy*. New York: Harper and Row.

Beck, A. T. and Emery, G. (1985) *Anxiety Disorders and Phobias: A Cognitive Perspective*. New York: Basic Books.

Beck, A. T. and Weishaar, M. E. (1995) Cognitive therapy. In R. J. Corsini and D. Wedding (eds) *Current Psychotherapies* (5th edn, pp. 229–61). Itasca, IL: Peacock.

Berg, J. H. and Derlega, V. J. (1987) Themes in the study of self-disclosure. In V. J. Derlega and J. H. Berg (eds) *Self-Disclosure: Theory, Research and Therapy* (pp. 1–8). New York: Plenum.

Berne, E. (1964) *Games People Play: The Psychology of Human Relationships*. New York: Grove Press.

Bowlby, J. (1979) *The Making and Breaking of Affectional Bonds.* London: Tavistock.

Bruch, M. A. and Pearl, L. (1995) Attributional style and symptoms of shyness in a heterosexual interaction. *Cognitive Therapy and Research,* **19**, 91–107.

Cautela, J. (1967) Covert sensitization. *Psychological Reports,* **20**, 459–68.

Chodron, T. (1990) *Taming the Monkey Mind.* Lutterworth: Tynron Press.

Christensen, A., Jacobson, N. S. and Babcock. J. C. (1995) Integrative behavioral couple therapy. In N. S. Jacobson and A. S. Gurman (eds) *Clinical Handbook of Couple Therapy* (pp. 31–64). New York: Guilford Press.

Comfort, A. (1993) *The New Joy of Sex.* London: Mitchell Beazley.

Cozby, P. (1973) Self-disclosure: a literature review. *Psychological Bulletin,* **79**, 73–91.

De Angelis, B. (1997) *The Real Rules: How to Find the Right Man for the Real You.* London: Thorsons.

Deffenbacher, J. L., Lynch, R. S., Oetting, E. R. and Kemper, C. C. (1996) Anger reduction in early adolescents. *Journal of Counseling Psychology,* **43**, 149–57.

de Silva, P. (1997) Jealousy in couple relationships: Nature, assessment and therapy. *Behaviour Research and Therapy,* **35**, 973–85.

Dowrick, S. (1991) *Intimacy and Solitude.* Melbourne: Mandarin.

Dowrick, S. (1993) *The Intimacy and Solitude Self-Therapy Book.* Melbourne: Mandarin.

Duck, S. (1998) *Human Relationships* (3rd edn). London: Sage.

Eakins, B. W. and Eakins, R. G. (1978) *Sex Differences in Human Communication.* Boston: Houghton Mifflin.

Egan, G. (1977) *You and Me: The Skills of Communicating and Relating to Others.* Monterey, CA: Brooks/Cole.

Egan, G. (1998) *The Skilled Helper: A Problem Management Approach to Helping* (6th edn). Pacific Grove, CA: Brooks/Cole.

Ekman, P., Friesen, W. V. and Ellsworth, P. (1972) *Emotions in the Human Face.* New York: Pergamon.

Ellis, A. (1977) *Anger: How to Live With and Without It.* Melbourne: Sun MacMillan Australia.

Ellis, A. (1985) *Rational Humorous Songs.* New York: Institute for Rational-Emotive Therapy.

Ellis, A. (1988) *How to Stubbornly Refuse to Make Yourself Miserable about Anything, Yes Anything!* Sydney: Pan Macmillan.

Ellis, A. (1995) Rational emotive behavior therapy. In R. J. Corsini and D. Wedding (eds) *Current Psychotherapies* (5th edn, pp. 162–96). Itasca, IL: Peacock.

Ellis, A. (1996) *Better, Deeper and More Enduring Brief Therapy: The Rational Emotive Behaviour Therapy Approach.* New York: Brunner Mazel.

Epstein, N., Pretzer, J. L. and Fleming, B. (1987) Role of cognitive appraisal in self-reports of marital communication. *Behavior Therapy,* **18**, 51–69.

Fincham, F. D. (1997) Understanding marriage: from fish scales to milliseconds. *The Psychologist,* **10**, 543–7.

Frankl, V. E. (1988) *The Will to Meaning: Foundations and Applications of Logotherapy.* New York: Meridian.

Frankl, V. E. (1997) *Viktor Frankl Recollections: An Autobiography.* London: Insight Books.

Freud, S. (1949) *An Outline of Psychoanalysis.* New York: W. W. Norton.

Gardner, H. (1993) *Frames of Mind: The Theory of Multiple Intelligences* (2nd edn). London: Fontana.

Glasser, W. (1984) *Control Theory: A New Explanation of How We Control Our Lives.* New York: Harper and Row.

Goleman, D. (1995) *Emotional Intelligence: Why It Can Matter More than IQ.* London: Bloomsbury.

Gordon, T. (1970) *Parent Effectiveness Training: The Tested New Way to Raise Responsible Children.* New York: Wyden.

Gouldner, A. (1960) The norm of reciprocity: a preliminary statement. *American Sociological Review,* **25**, 161–78.

Hall, E. T. (1966) *The Hidden Dimension.* New York: Doubleday.

Hazan, C. and Shaver, P. R. (1987) Romantic love conceptualised as an attachment process. *Journal of Personality and Social Psychology,* **52**, 511–24.

Henley, N. M. (1977) *Body Politics: Power, Sex and Nonverbal Communication.* Englewood Cliffs, NJ: Prentice Hall.

Jacobson, E. (1976) *You Must Relax.* Boston: Unwin Paperbacks.

Jung, C. G. (1939) *The Integration of Personality.* New York: Farrar and Rinehart.

Kassorla, I. (1984) *Go For It!: How to Win at Love, Work and Play.* New York: Dell.

Kehoe, J. (1996) *Mind Power: Into the 21st Century* (10th anniversary edition). West Vancouver, BC: Zoetic Inc.

Kelly, G. A. (1955) *A Theory of Personality: The Psychology of Personal Constructs.* New York: W. W. Norton.

Kendall, P. C. and Hollon, S. D. (1989) Anxious self-talk: development of the anxious self-statements questionnaire (ASSQ). *Cognitive Therapy and Research,* **13**, 81–93.

King, M. L. (1963) *Strength to Love.* New York: Harper and Row.

King, R. (1997) *Good Loving, Great Sex: Finding the Balance When Your Sex Drives Differ.* Sydney: Random House.

Lange, A., Richard, R., Kiestra, J. and van Oostendorp, E. (1997) Cognitive treatment through positive self-verbalization: a multiple case study. *Behavioural and Cognitive Psychotherapy,* **25**, 161–71.

Lazarus, A. A. (1984) *In the Mind's Eye: The Power of Imagery for Personal Enrichment.* New York: Guilford Press.

Lewinsohn, P. M., Munoz, R. F., Youngren, M. A. and Zeiss, A. M. (1986) *Control Your Depression* (rev. edn). New York: Prentice Hall.

Litvinoff, S. (1992) *The Relate Guide to Sex in Loving Relationships.* London: Vermilion.

Lu, L. and Shih, J. B. (1997) Sources of happiness: a qualitative approach. *The Journal of Social Psychology,* **137**, 181–7.

MacLeod, A. K. and Cropley, M. L. (1995) Depressive future-thinking: the role of valence and specificity. *Cognitive Therapy and Research,* **19**, 35–50.

Market Research Section (1997) *Sunday Life! Relationships and Intimacy Survey.* Melbourne: The Age/Sun Herald.

Maslow, A. H. (1968) *Towards a Psychology of Being* (2nd edn). Princeton: Van Nostrand.

Maslow, A. H. (1970) *Motivation and Personality* (2nd edn). New York: Harper and Row.

Masters, W. H. and Johnson, V. E. (1970) *The Pleasure Bond.* New York: Bantam.

Masters, W. H., Johnson, V. E. and Kolodny, R. C. (1986) *Masters and Johnson on Sex and Human Loving*. London: Pan Macmillan.

May, R. and Yalom, I. D. (1995) Existential psychotherapy. In R. J. Corsini and D. Wedding (eds) *Current Psychotherapies* (5th edn, pp. 262–92). Itasca. IL: Peacock.

McKay, M. and Fanning, P. (1992) *Self-Esteem: A Proven Program of Cognitive Techniques for Assessing, Improving and Maintaining Your Self-Esteem*. Oakland, CA: New Harbinger.

McKay, M., Fanning, P. and Paleg, K. (1994) *Couple Skills: Making Your Relationship Work*. Oakland, CA: New Harbinger Publications.

McMillan, M. (1997) The experiencing of empathy: what is involved in achieving the 'as if' condition? *Counselling*, **8**, 205–9.

Meichenbaum, D. H. (1977) *Cognitive-Behavior Modification: An Integrative Approach*. New York: Plenum.

Meichenbaum, D. H. (1983) *Coping with Stress*. London: Century.

Nelson-Jones, R. (1995) Lifeskills counselling. In *Theory and Practice of Counselling* (2nd edn, pp. 349–84). London: Cassell. Also in *Counselling and Personality: Theory and Practice* (pp. 412–51). Sydney: Allen and Unwin.

Nelson-Jones, R. (1996a) *Relating Skills: A Practical Guide to Effective Personal Relationships*. London: Cassell. Published in Australia as *Human Relating Skills: A Practical Guide to Effective Personal Relationships* (3rd edn). Sydney: Holt, Rinehart and Winston.

Nelson-Jones, R. (1996b) The STCs of lifeskills counselling. *Counselling*, **7**, 46–9.

Nelson-Jones, R. (1997) *Practical Counselling and Helping Skills: Text and Exercises for the Lifeskills Counselling Model* (4th edn). London: Cassell. Distributed in Australia, New Zealand and South-East Asia by Astam Books, Sydney.

Pietromonaco, P. R. and Rook, K. A. (1987) Decision style in depression: the contribution of perceived risks versus benefits. *Journal of Personality and Social Psychology*, **52**, 399–408.

Powell, J. (1969) *Why Am I Afraid to Tell You Who I Am?* London: Fontana.

Raskin, N. J. and Rogers, C. R. (1995) Person-centred therapy. In R. J. Corsini and D. Wedding (eds) *Current Psychotherapies* (5th edn, pp. 128–61). Itasca, IL: Peacock.

Rogers, C. R. (1951) *Client-centered Therapy*. Boston: Houghton Mifflin.

Rogers, C. R. (1961) *On Becoming a Person: A Therapist's View of Psychotherapy*. Boston: Houghton Mifflin.

Rogers, C. R. (1973) *Becoming Partners: Marriage and Its Alternatives*. London: Constable.

Rogers, C. R. (1980) *A Way of Being*. Boston: Houghton Mifflin.

Salovey, P. and Mayer, J. D. (1990) Emotional intelligence. *Imagination, Cognition, and Personality*, **9**, 185–211.

Satir, V. (1972) *Peoplemaking*. Palo Alto, CA: Science and Behavior Books.

Seligman, M. E. P. (1991) *Learned Optimism*. Milsons Point, NSW: Random House Australia.

Sichel, J. and Ellis, A. (1984) *RET Self-Help Form*. New York: Institute for Rational-Emotive Therapy.

Simonton, O. C., Matthews-Simonton, S. and Creighton, J. L. (1978) *Getting Well Again*. New York: Bantam Books.

Spencer, C. (1997) Funeral address for Princess Diana. *The Sunday Times*, 7 September, p. 8.

Steele, A. A. and McLennan, J. (1995) Suicidal and counter-suicidal thinking. *Australian Psychologist*, **30**, 2, 149–52.

Steiner, C. M. (1974) *Scripts People Live*. New York: Bantam Books.

Stopa, L. and Clark, D. (1993) Cognitive processes in social phobia. *Behaviour Research and Therapy*, **31**, 255–67.

Sumedho, A. (1995) *The Mind and the Way: Buddhist Reflections on Life*. London: Rider.

Teasdale, J. D. and Dent, J. (1987) Cognitive vulnerability to depression: an investigation of two hypotheses. *British Journal of Clinical Psychology*, **26**, 113–26.

Thitavanno, P. (1995) *Mental Development*. Bangkok: Mahamakut Rajavidyalaya Press.

Uehara, E. S. (1995) Reciprocity reconsidered: Gouldner's 'moral norm of reciprocity' and social support. *Journal of Social and Personal Relationships*, **12**, 483–502.

Woods, E. (1997) *Training a Tiger: A Father's Guide to Raising a Winner in Both Golf and Life*. New York: Harper/Perennial.

Woody, R. (1996) Effects of focus of attention on anxiety levels and social performance of individuals with social phobia. *Journal of Abnormal Psychology*, **105**, 61–9.

Zilbergeld, B. (1978) *Male Sexuality*. New York: Bantam.

List of Activities

Name Index

Subject Index